AF882262

ESSAYS ON

VEDIC AND INDO-EUROPEAN CULTURE

MLBD SERIES IN LINGUISTICS

General Editor
DHANESH JAIN

VOLUME XII

ESSAYS ON VEDIC AND INDO-EUROPEAN CULTURE

by

BORIS OGUIBÉNINE

MOTILAL BANARSIDASS PUBLISHERS
PRIVATE LIMITED • NEW DELHI

First Edition: Delhi, 1998

© MOTILAL BANARSIDASS PUBLISHERS PRIVATE LIMITED
All Rights Reserved

ISBN: 81-208-1499-1

Also available at:

MOTILAL BANARSIDASS

41 U.A. Bungalow Road, Jawahar Nagar, Delhi 110 007
8 Mahalaxmi Chamber, Warden Road, Mumbai 400 026
120 Royapettah High Road, Mylapore, Madras 600 004
Sanas Plaza, Subhash Nagar, Pune 411 002
16 St. Mark's Road, Bangalore 560 001
8 Camac Street, Calcutta 700 017
Ashok Rajpath, Patna 800 004
Chowk, Varanasi 221 001

Published with the assistance of Embassy
of France in India

PRINTED IN INDIA

BY JAINENDRA PRAKASH JAIN AT SHRI JAINENDRA PRESS,
A-45 NARAINA, PHASE I, NEW DELHI 110 028
AND PUBLISHED BY NARENDRA PRAKASH JAIN FOR
MOTILAL BANARSIDASS PUBLISHERS PRIVATE LIMITED,
BUNGALOW ROAD, DELHI 110 007

DEDICATED

To the Memory of
A Great Man, the
Late Sh. Roman Jakobson

To the Memory of
A Friend,
Enrico Campanile

Preface

Most of the essays in this volume are texts that were originally oral exposés made on various occasions. They have been revised and improved, then published or prepared for publication.

Chapter 1 is the text of a paper presented at a seminar organised by Mr. J.P. Vernant at the Collège de France (15 January, 1978). It later appeared in the *Journal Asiatique*, No. 266, 1978, pp. 257-290 (*"Complément à l'image du guerrier Indo-européen. A propos d'une hypothèse"*).

Some of the essays which together form Ch. 2 (2.1, 2.2, 2.3) are lectures delivered by me for the Religious Sciences Department of the *Ecole Pratique des Hautes Etudes* (1980-1981). This is the first time they are being published. I am grateful to my audience at the E.P.H.E. for their questions and suggestions which enabled me to improve the texts.

The essay which constitutes Ch. 2.4 is a slightly revised version of my paper read out at the Indo-European Studies Week organised by the *Institut d'Etudes Indo-Européennes* of the Jean Moulin Lyon III University in July 1982. It first appeared in print in the review *Etudes Indo-Européennes* published by Mr. Jean Haudry (No. 5, 1983, pp. 1-17, *"Le symbolisme de la razzia d'après les hymnes védiques"*).

Ch. 3 is a hitherto unpublished collection of my considerations on recent studies of the relation between Indo-European concepts of war and religion.

Ch. 4 was read out in July 1982 at a symposium organised by Mr. Eugène Vance of the University of Montreal at the *"Centre International de Sémiotique et de Linguistique"* of the

University of Urbino. It was later published in the *Journal Asiatique* (No. 271, 1983, pp. 263-275).

Ch. 6 was briefly presented at the Institute Kern of the University of Leiden on 13th May, 1983, and published in the *Indo-Iranian Journal* (Vol. 27, No. 2, 1984, pp. 85-101).

The last chapter is the text of an article which appeared in the *Bulletin de la Société de Linguistique de Paris* (1984), but the section relating to Roman facts has been added now.

I thank the editors of the above-mentioned periodicals for their permission to reprint the articles which have been revised and corrected. I have also added fresh observations and footnotes regarding recent publications.

Three of the essays published in this book (Chapters 4, 5 and 7) were presented by me at conferences held at the Department of Linguistics of the University of Pisa.

I am particularly grateful to the Department of Linguistics of the University of Pisa for having invited me to lecture. This gave me the opportunity to visit this centre renowned for its studies on Indo-European culture and linguistics, and to meet my Italian colleagues who work there.

I gratefully think of late Mr. Enrico Campanile who included this volume of essays in the collection published by him.

Boris Oguibénine
University of Strasbourg

Contents

Acknowledgement

This book appeared first in French as *Essais sur la culture védique et indo-européenne* (Pisa: Giardini, 1985). It has been fairly well-received by the scholars as shown by several reviews in various journals (by R. Della Casa in *Salesianum*, 48, 1986, pp. 399-400, by C. Calame in *Museum Helveticum*, 43, 1986, p. 264, by R. Schmitt in *Kratylos*, 31, 1986 (1987), pp. 188-190 and by F. Crevatin in *Indo-Iranian Journal*, 31, 1988, pp. 142-144. For objectiveness' sake, mention must be made of a short notice by Chlodwig Werba in *Die Sprache*, 1986 (Indogermanische Chronik 31b, pp. 320-321) which has been the only discordant voice and, to say the least, a strange one, since its author has been short of any properly scientific criticism.

I would be happy if the English translation could arouse the interest of my Indian colleagues who might have had no access to the book published in Italy.

I owe a special debt of gratitude to Mr. Pierre Barroux, Counsellor for Cultural, Scientific and Technical Cooperation, French Embassy, and to Mr. Rajesh Sharma, Publications Adviser of the Embassy. Both had most readily welcomed the idea of the English translation. I also thank Mr. N.P. Jain of Motilal Banarsidass for his willingness to publish it, as well as Mrs. Hema Parthasarathy for taking up the task of the translation.

Boris Oguibénine
University of Strasbourg
April-May 1997

Introductory Notes

Correlating Vedic culture and Indo-European culture is not as far-fetched as it may seem; it merely reflects a methodological approach that is gaining acceptance these days.

E. Campanile has recently authored a text which elucidates the problems faced in the reconstruction of Indo-European culture and ideology.[1] Readers will see that we share the same views and that essentially, we have a similar approach to the subject. Nevertheless, I think it is necessary to make a few clarifications about my personal work, for it will offer a better understanding of the conclusions set out in this volume.

Each field of Indo-European imposes a particular point of view or perspective. No field, least of all Sanskrit, can be expected to realise an exact and complete reproduction of the Indo-European culture which is but the result of reconstructions and not a reproductible entity. Since each field has a limited scope, there can be only a partial understanding of the common heritage. It is thus evident that a reconstruction of the Indo-European culture from the perspective of, say, the Anatolian languages cannot be the same as the one using Indo-European dialects such as the Indo-Iranian or the Balto-Slavic as its reference point. In comparing the two we can only have (and therein lies the essence of comparative studies) the correspondences based on lexical similarities or on the resemblance between the religious, social and cultural structures. This is perhaps because the field in which one is engaged is rich in genres that place emphasis on the material rather than the spiritual aspects of culture; this preference could be dictated not by the genre of the text but by the culture itself which leans more towards one aspect than the other. Or perhaps the textual, mythological or literary tradition as we know it has some lacunae. Other than the losses caused by unfavourable conditions and time, it is likely that we are faced with structural lacunae or gaps; cultures are not comprehensive and do not overlap, be it in the presentation of facts or in the number of facts.

Languages and cultures (i.e. discourses on cultures) whose interrelations pose an eternal problem for comparatists seeking to go beyond the confrontation of languages alone, have two common parameters: systems of communication in which the values or the structure of values attached to the facts take on a greater importance than the facts themselves; languages and cultures are by themselves complete for they are sufficiently explicit and effective for those native to them[2] but they are incomplete or even deficient as compared with other cultures, Indo-European or otherwise.

Their inadequacies as well as their excesses are related to the information they convey and more particularly to the nature of information which they consider important.

For instance, in the hymns of the Ṛgveda, the main information pertains to gods and their actions, to cosmogony; men and their relation to the Divine are dealt with according to this very relation. In Homeric poems which can be compared to the poetry of hymns in some respects,[3] the heroes of the past and the present take to a great extent the place of the old Indo-European gods; the Homeric bards, though they talk of Indo-European and typically Greek gods, sing of the glorious exploits of heroic men rather than of the miraculous deeds of the gods.[4]

This differential nature of information becomes more apparent when one considers the problem that the comparatists have to contend with. The problem is one of paradox of cultures—they can be understood and correctly interpreted only when studied in relation to one another. The models that the subjects of a culture create for their own purposes—and they remain the same during the course of communication within their culture—are latent and escape analysis if a particular culture is not compared with another.[5]

It is only then that one can establish more correctly the purpose of cultural reconstruction. Whether or not one shares the views of G. Dumézil on the importance of the tripartite ideological structure of the Indo-Europeans, one appreciates his approach when he opposes the fossils of the trifunctional Indo-European religion which is still existent in Rome to the traces of the Indo-European functional philosophy found in the religion of Zarathushtra.[6]

This perspective offers a better understanding of the complex problem discussed by E. Campanile in the works mentioned earlier. What is the object of cultural reconstruction? Is it the material culture of the Indo-Europeans or is it their intellectual, spiritual and religious culture?

It is a fact, and E. Campanile has established the same through concrete analyses, that reconstruction of the material culture of the Indo-Europeans cannot be attempted within the scope of an objective scientific research; it is impossible to establish a direct relationship between reconstructed lexemes and a culture whose material and even archaeological characteristics are sought to be understood through these very reconstructions. In other words, a lexical sign denoting a material object such as the cart or the yoke remains a sign of the Indo-European lexical system even though it is tempting to insist on the existence of these objects in a reconstructed culture[7] and on their diacritical functions in that culture.

It is possible to reformulate this problem of access to the material culture of Indo-Europeans by clearly defining that aspect of the problem which has always presented itself to philologists and linguists.

Though it may seem obvious, it should not be forgotten that the lexical terms used in reconstructions are necessarily part of a discourse and that the discourse is itself a complex linguistic sign, for the degree of its complexity is greater than that of a word. This observation is valid even if the discourse is only partial or preserved only in ruins or in an otherwise damaged state, particularly as the original information is lost in the process.

It is infinitely more enriching and fruitful for comparative study of ancient civilisations to regard discourses—the only clear object of analysis—as complex signs; we know that values attached to lexical signs are subject to modifications precisely because the *signifié* of an isolated sign is relativised by the *signifié* of the discourse. These modifications cannot be ignored and it is not sufficient to explain them as simple contextual changes in the structure of the lexical sign, particularly if one seeks to attain a reality beyond the sign itself and if one holds that the reconstructed reality is that of a totality of diverse but related structures.

The comparatist is undeniably concerned only with the results of the communicative process i.e. the discourses or the texts: as far as possible the reconstitution of the chief parameters of this process must be done through reconstruction. It is often forgotten that the texts were created not only to meet the needs of intracultural communication (between the subjects of one culture) but also for intercultural communication (between subjects of different cultures).

It is by restoring to their natural setting these texts bequeathed to us by the Indo-Europeans that we can have a better understanding of the meaning as well as the significance of lexical, phraseological and textual correspondences between the various texts. Benveniste in his time had proclaimed a principle that had been tested by him in the field of Indo-Iranian studies: "... this linguistic notion (Indo-Iranian) should be extended to cover other types of correspondences that are found not just in the forms of the various elements but in their relationship, their syntactic structure, the stylistic figures of which they are constituents or even in their particular manner of denotation".[8] Having indicated the presence of 16 surviving elements evidenced by the correspondences between the Vedic and the Avestan texts he concluded that "...the presence of a relatively large number of surviving elements in the Gāthās makes one believe that a "Vedic" style of worship and liturgy prevailed in the milieu where Zarathushtra preached".[9]

Here it would be pertinent to consider a new element that does not contradict the spirit of Benveniste's observations.

The "Vedic" style mentioned here is very much a tangible reality for it concerns the linguistic and religious community of the Indo-Iranians. But the analyst has access only to descriptions of the intellectual life in branches separated from the community. He will have to admit that if elements of Vedic ideology (for it is ideology that induces the use of formulaic expressions) for having been introduced or continuously kept in a discourse, should have remained comprehensible, contain an accessible communicative content and should represent situations and concepts that can be interpreted by Iranians as well as Indians. Obvious though it may be, this fundamental aspect of the formation and survival of a linguistic and cultural community has apparently never been the object of serious research.

Thus what the philologist and the linguist attempt to reconstruct does not present itself as a world of objects and concepts (material objects, conceptual elements, representations etc.) but as signs of objects and concepts in a discourse or in a set of discourses.

When one succeeds in putting together the interpretative contents of a simple or a hyper-complex sign, i.e. the contents intelligible within as well as outside a culture, one is able to isolate the parts of a discourse referring to a common prototype—words, syntactic sequences such as etymological figures, formulaic expressions or relatively long texts. One is then able to form an idea of the linguistic and cultural community in terms that are best suited to the object of linguistic analyses, i.e. in terms of language and signifying structures that are intelligible because they are mutually translatable.[10]

But a problem arises when one considers the fact that discourses belonging to a distinct area of Indo-European culture transmit only specific and clearly determined information. For instance, Vedic religious texts show marked preference for *signifiants* which largely pertain to fables, speculation, the miraculous, the cosmic, the Absolute according to dharma, morality and mystery; in contrast, Roman thought has been historical, national, empirical, political and juridical in nature.[11]

Distinct discourses of Indo-European origin thus occasion partial reconstructions of Indo-European *signifiés*, reconstructions that vary according to the preferences of a particular Indo-European culture. Material objects, concepts that can be grasped through poetic language, the myths and rites that we know through texts in Indo-European languages can be comparable or even identical though they belong to different species. The common *signifié* will however be represented only fragmentally and this is due not only to the differences in approach of individual cultures to the common *signifié*—this obvious fact needs no mention. In fact, the interesting feature of the formation of signs belonging to a particular culture is the disparity and the variety in the conceptual effort of various Indo-European fields when dealing with elements of their common heritage.

This can be seen by examining some specific interpretations of three elements of the material culture to which the Indo-European character is generally, but not freely attributed. (See 3 further on.)

1. I.E. * *iugóm* which means "yoke", the essential part of the harness used by Indo-Europeans. Nothing else can be said about this piece of equipment which was common to

all types of harness, irrespective of the yoked animals-horses, oxen, mules, asses etc. On the other hand it is clear that the ancient intellectual culture of Vedic India created a concept of the yoke and speculated on the act of bringing the animals under the yoke. Hence it is impossible to ignore the importance of the object (nor its function) insofar as it helped create and evolve a thought process by which the object itself was replaced with a concept of the object.

Later on in this book there is a discussion on the transformations of the *signifiant* * *iugóm* and an exposé on the values given to it in various Indo-European religious and poetic traditions. In certain traditions, these transformations and values were brought about by the consciousness of the relationship between the yoke and the act of bringing under the yoke. This is true of Greek, Avestan and Vedic traditions, as already mentioned, and also of the Hittite tradition, (but apparently not so of Old Persian or Balto-Slavic tradition little known in this respect).

Two of the Indo-European religious traditions have opposing views on the yoke. They are the Roman and the Vedic (the former has been briefly mentioned further on in pp. 241-243, while only certain features of the latter have been analysed). These largely divergent views converge only on some points. Nevertheless the Roman augurs had a rule concerning the yoke which implies, according to G. Dumézil, "a whole theory on the mystic values of the yoke"[12] which Vedic authors have at least remembered.

That the Indo-Europeans knew the use of the yoke is a very meagre and superficial piece of information (although we will never really know what this object looked like). On the other hand, what they thought of it will lead to some interesting conclusions.

2. The Vedic *śīra* denotes the plough, probably the plough-cum-seeder, an implement that was used in ancient times in China, Syria and Mesopotamia. It consists of a plough fitted with a bin for the seeds.[13] This implement is

a possible proof of prehistoric links between India and Mesopotamia.[14] Bloch's assumptions are based on possible analogies (in India there was a plough-cum-seeder at the time when his work was published). The linguistic analysis is only secondary (*sīra* is probably derived from **sē* "to sow", cf. Pokorny, *Idg. etym. Wb.*, pp. 889-890; see also Mayrhofer's discussion in *Kurzgefasstes etym. Wb. des Altind.*, III, p. 476 which points out the difficulties of this etymology without refuting Bloch's conclusions. If Bloch's explanation of the meaning of the word *sīra* is accepted, it can be shown that the poetic metaphors created by Vedic authors on the subject of the plough are extremely edifying for the reconstruction of the nature of the object denoted by *sīra*. To my remarks on ṚV 10.101.3 and 4b (pp. 210-211 of this book), I must add that the continuation of the two verses confirm Bloch's hypothesis,yet Bloch himself was not aware of this.

Indeed, the poet exhorts the officiants of the sacrifice to harness the ploughs and "to fix up, to strain" the yokes (*sīrā yuj-, yugā́ ví-tan-*), to accomplish two actions that have a deep religious significance. He then uses such expressions and narrative techniques which lead one to believe that the land was ploughed and the furrows simultaneously filled with seeds, and this is compatible with Bloch's description of the plough-cum-seeder. Consider ṚV 10.101.3ab:

yunákta sīrā ví yugā́ tanudhvaṃ
kṛté yónau vapatehá bī́jam.

"Harness the ploughs, fix up the yokes, in these prepared furrows, sow the seeds," followed by 3cd:

girā́ ca śruṣṭíḥ sábharā ásan
no nédīya ít sṛṇyàḥ pakvám éyāt.

"If the generous hearing (given to our word) carries the same weight as the word (itself), the ripe fruit will come nearer the sickles," and also 10.101.4ab:

sīrā yuñjanti kaváyo / yugā́ ví tanvate pṛ́thak.

"The Seers harness the ploughs, they fix up the yokes separately," followed by 4c:

dhī́rā devéṣu sumnayā́

"They that know in order (to gain) the favour of the gods."[15]

In these two verses the poet speaks of what is achieved after the ploughs and yokes have been put to work. Only, he is not referring to agricultural activity, but to his own which is comparable to ploughing and sowing. In this hymn, there is a subtle link between the two activities. The combined imagery serves to underline their common object. Let us see how this happens.

The series of exhortations in verse 10.101.3 (*yunákta* "harness!", *tanudhvam* "fix up for yourselves", *vapata* "sow!") serve to place these actions on the same time plane, they are either simultaneous or separated by a negligible interval of time. This is borne out by the fact that the officiating poets who are the protagonists of the hymn, first use exhortations (see 10.101.1-2, 4), then make known their own objectives and not the objectives of the act of ploughing. This they do by clearly showing the relationship between the deeds and their consequences. This explains the reference to the hearing which brings out the importance of the poets' discourse (literally, the weight, *sábharas* means "which counter-balances"[16]), and to the favour of the gods bestowed on the wise. The deeds are so closely associated with their outcome that it is probable that the poets thought of bringing together as near as possible the actions of ploughing and sowing and their ultimate consequence—reaping the fruit, both in terms of agricultural benefits, and the benefits gained from the sacrifice by the officiants. In Vedic hymns this is quite frequent, especially when referring to ploughing. ṚV 1.23.15: *utó sá máhyam indubhiḥ ṣáḍ yuktā́ṅ anuséṣidhat/góbhir yávaṃ ná carkṛṣat* "May the (land) as if be ploughed using oxen (to yield) barley, by pushing towards me six harnesses with the drops of soma!" Here, the expected reward and success of the officiant of soma[17] are the direct and immediate results of a task represented as ploughing.

In 10.101.3-4, the poet's intentions are unmistakable, he gives a succint description in which the deeds and their effects are linked and merged; he is more preoccupied with the effects than with differentiating the tasks which bring them about.

Sīra is not the only word which denotes the plough-cum-seeder, *vṛ́ka* is another (ṚV 1.117.21 *vṛ́keṇa vap-*"sow with the v." and ṚV 8.22.6 *vṛ́keṇa karṣ-*"plough with the v.").[18]

Thus the complex functions of the *sīra* can be established by means of a dual analysis. Bloch's approach was to show that implements had analogies in the ancient world (not only Indo-European), and also to study the etymology. This is complemented and corroborated by an analysis of the discourse of the hymns. The reconstruction of the appearance and the function of an object belonging to material culture (the referent) thus gains credibility thanks to the discovery of the *poetic signifiant*. It must be reiterated that the latter technique produces more reliable results. The *signifiant* of a discourse is of prime importance, it is more authentic than philological and historical speculations, especially when these do not take into account the references provided by the discourse (after rigorous analyses, no doubt). Discourse is the basis of all investigations aimed at reconstruction.

3. I shall give a brief account of a controversy in which the reconstruction of the *signifié* was and still is a never-ending subject of dispute. Following some suggestions that certain people consider out-moded, I had proposed that the etymological association between Ved. *dhénā* and Av. *daēnā* was more positive than was generally believed. These two words are connected to the cult of the Indo-Iranian goddess *Ušas, known to Vedic Indians as Uṣas and to Avesta Iranians as Ušå. Basic to this cult is the direct

connection between cows on the one hand and poetic vision and expression on the other.[19] Two essays in this volume ("The *signifiant* and the *signifié* in Vedic sacrifice" and "The quest for booty and meaning in Vedic sacrifice") deal with a theory doubtless of Indo-Iranian origin, but which is also most certainly a unique reinterpretation of an Indo-European intellectual technique. This theory unfolds a strategy for the perception of a signified object by means of the *signifiant* in a poetic discourse. By this theory, the referent "cow" becomes a sign of poetic vision and the identity of the sign and the animal assumes importance. The cow, in the most concrete sense of the word, and poetry then become one for the Indo-Iranians.

What has been said earlier about the yoke in Indo-European society is applicable to this too. The notion of the cow like that of the yoke must belong to an Indo-Iranian "theory" (which apparently has some striking analogies in other Indo-European societies, which can be construed as common surviving elements). While seeking to understand what was the significance of a material object in a civilisation, we are necessarily obliged to look to the intellectual perceptions of this object. Thus the reproach that Indo-European intellectual practice has been given too much consideration is unjustified. Nor is it valid for the overall study of Indo-European culture.

The animal in question was most certainly a great economic asset to Indo-Iranians (and doubtless to other Indo-Europeans, but not an exclusive one as it was associated with other species of animals). It would, however, be wrong on our part to misinterpret the evidence that is available, such as texts from the Ṛgveda and the ancient Avesta. These texts do not merely list all the objects and their uses at the various times of the composition of the texts which covered several centuries. They elucidate the *interpretation* of the objects and their uses. References, if any, to cows, their breeding and milking are fraught with symbolic meanings (or *signifiant*, if the word "symbolic" is to be avoided). A treatise on cattle-breeding, if it had existed along with these texts, and if it were available to us, would probably have referred to cattle in a quite different manner.[20]

Religion and poetry have given further dimensions to the Ṛgveda and the Avesta which are to the represented world what the semantic structure of a language is to extra-linguistic reality. Language refers to this reality just as speech refers to the represented world, and the denoted elements cannot be understood other than by the analysis of the inherent correlations in the substance of the respective semantic structures.

I therefore feel that it is necessary to stress on the primordial nature of the *signifiants* which a comparatist studies, at least in the Indo-Iranian context. These *signifiants* have both poetic and religious import, even though in varying degrees, and they cannot be neglected. What comes between the *signifiant* of a text of this kind and the denoted object is the conscious will of the author to transform the *signifiant* into a value in itself, and to depict the object so that it corresponds to the intent of the text.

I feel that this is how the problem of reconstruction of the elements of Indo-European culture presents itself. Finding a direct connection between words and objects is not an advisable method for, according to E. Campanile, this presupposes the synchronic existence of the word and the object. His suggested method "completely sets aside material culture and concentrates on intellectual culture. Moreover, the latter does not call for any transition from linguistic references to extra-linguistic references, given that extra-linguistic references (religious, juridical, mythological etc.) are actually based on the contents of the discourse".[21]

It is perhaps worthwhile to add some observations to the preceding ones. Details regarding the expression of the texts which the comparatist uses are called for.

Let us consider the signs for denoted objects, either a

material object, or a notion of intellectual culture (which shows the efforts made by subjects of a culture to understand each other and to give shape to these efforts). They may be signs for objects or signs for signs, and they naturally lend themselves to metaphors. Indeed, metaphors are frequently used in texts which represent ancient Indo-European culture.

These metaphors are the discourse units of varied extension (a word, a phrase) which convey, in the manner of concise formulae, the presentation of the observed phenomena *in relation to each other*. Could anything be more interesting to a comparatist? When such a correlation is being made, it is easy to understand the working of the mind behind it, the intentions which motivated it.

These correlations between various phenomena seen from their respective standpoints give rise to two types of problems:

Firstly, even if a metaphor appears in an undeniably Indo-European text, it could be extraneous to the text. Can it then be of Indo-European origin? A few years ago, E. Campanile put forward an effective criterion—the more a metaphor is isolated, that is, it has no analogies in the same group of texts, the less it can be explained. Nevertheless, it can be explained by means of similar expressions taken from another culture. If these expressions came from an Indo-European culture, the expression being studied is of old Indo-European origin. But if the analogies are found only in non-Indo-European cultures, it is obviously more difficult to come to a decision. One can conclude that the expression was either borrowed or created in the manner of *Elementarver-wandtschaft*.[22]

This method of identifying origins has the advantage of taking into account the translatability of the messages conveyed by the metaphor. The translation is possible only if the codes or the whole representations are related to each other as well as the corresponding forms. A case in point is a Homeric metaphor discussed by Campanile [*èn*] *nuktòs amolgōi* "in the middle of the milk of the night" ("in the nocturnal twilight"), Od 4.841, Hym.Hom.XVIII.7. It is foreign to Greek culture and can be explained only by referring to a Vedic metaphoric phrase.[23]

In effect, it is in the Ṛgveda that is found the image of the couple Night and Dawn: 1.186.4 *samānė áhan... víṣurūpe páyasi*" (I create the song) the same day (to the time which is common to them), (in the middle of this) milk which has many forms," (or: "various forms", cf. ṚV 1.123.7).[24] All things considered, this interpretation of this Greco-Vedic parallel is derived from the etymology of Greek *amolgós* (<**sa-mḷg'*?), but on the whole Campanile's explanation is justified. Twilight at dawn was visibly imagined in Greece and in Vedic India as the time when night met daybreak. This is an ancient Indo-European metaphor, an expression of the Indo-European perception of the brief period of twilight. In the essay "The Vedic warrior and the *skhétlios* of Homer," I have analysed a case of corresponding similarities between Vedic mythology and a Homeric concept: the image of a warrior as represented in Vedic mythology has a counterpart in an epithet that describes a person having warrior-like traits in the Odyssey.

The other problem is the differentiating of metaphors which although found in texts of Indo-European origin, could possibly come from a source other than Indo-European or could be universal. Such a metaphor is the man/woman couple, often represented by bull/cow. This is one more instance of *Elementarverwandtschaft*. Campanile's criterion is also applicable in cases where the non-availability of Indo-European correspondences for an unexplained metaphor necessitates the search for non-Indo-European corres-pondences. There is, however, a complication. There is a large number of metaphors common to the Indo-European and another large linguistic family, the Chamito-Semitic. These metaphors are connotated in the so-called basic lexicon: cf. Semitic *g-w-l, g-l-l, g-w,* I.E. *kw/gw* which combines the sememes [circularity, round object, abdomen, intestine or other parts of the body], cf. Arabic *ġauf* "cavity, abdomen", Lat. *caput* "head" or Sem.*ṭ-ġ-r*, I.E. *dh-(w)-r* combining [irrupt, door, *semen (effundere)*, penis etc.][25], cf. Skr. *dvāra* "door", Ar. *ṭurṭubu* "penis" etc. The "nostratic" theory or the cultural history common to the two families then comes to mind. Metaphors are indeed "a strategic instrument for the analysis of cultures" (Rapallo).

There is a theme common to some of the essays which constitute this book. It is the Vedic theme of connections or mystical links which authors of the Ṛgveda hymns took pleasure in exploring. They felt that one of the tasks of Vedic poets was to establish and disclose these links. L. Renou has written a masterly essay on the theme of connections,[26] and I am also convinced that this theme is fundamental to the reflections of Vedic authors on sacrifice. To put these reflections in the Indo-European context, I have dwelt upon aspects of sacrifice as seen in the Ṛgveda hymns which belong to that fraction of Indo-European religion dealing with the rules of warfare and poetry. (See "Aspects of sacrifice in the Ṛgveda," "The quest for booty and meaning in Vedic sacrifice" and also "Notes on war and religion in Indo-European civilisation").

I have given a great deal of importance to the theme of connections for it is a guiding principle in the explanation of various phenomena which are doubtless of Indo-European origin.

This theme is consistent with an old form of Indo-European poetry, the *Aufreihlied*, a song in which the linking of the narrative constituents is both the dominating feature as well as the object of the narration. The events are connected by taking one of them, the principal one, as model for the rest which follow in the exposition.[27] According to F.R. Schröder, instances of this are found in various Indo-European traditions, ṚV 1.51.3-6; 10.49.2-6;

Yašt 19.41-43, verses that sing the praises of Thórr of the Icelandic Vetrlii and a fragment of Virgil's Aeneid (8.287-303). In these texts and in others composed in the same way, variations of a rule have been put into practice.

For example, the linking is done by using a single predicate (a verb) for several arguments (nouns), as in Aen. 8.293-295: *tu...Hylaeumque Pholumque, manu, tu Cresia mactas prodigia et uastum Nemeae sub rupe leonem* "Thou didst fell with thy hand...Hyleus and Pholus, thou (didst fell) the Cretan monster and the terrible rock lion of Nemea"; cf. ṚV 8.43.14 *tvám̐ hy àgne agnínā vípro víprena sán satā́ sákhā sákhyā samidhyáse* "For thou, O Agni, it is by Agni (thou who art) the poet inspired by the inspired poet (thou who art) the real (god), by the real (officiant), (thou who art) a friend, thou art lighted by the friend."

Or else, the same predicate is repeated, and is followed by various arguments, as in ṚV 2.37.6 *jóṣy agne samídham jósy ā́hutiṃ jóṣi bráhma jányaṃ joṣi suṣṭutím* "rejoice in the fire, lit up, O Agni, rejoice in the oblation, rejoice in the speech emanating from men (who are intimately associated with thee), rejoice in worthy praise!"

These two methods are combined as in Yašt 19.41-43 *yō janaṭ gandarəvəm yim zairi. pāšnəm... yō janaṭ hunauuō yaṭ paθanaiia nauua hunauuasča niuuikahe hunauuasča dāštaiiānōiš. . . yō janaṭ arəzō-šamanəm. . . yō janaṭ snāuuiδkəm* "Keresaspa who hath slain the yellow-heeled Gandharva, who hath slain the sons, (more) precisely, the nine (sons) of Paθana and the sons of Nivika and the sons of Dāštayāni...who hath slain Arezō-šamana...who hath slain Snāvidka." Here, the predicate (the verb *gan* "to slay" is repeated several times to make a syntagm with arguments (objects in the accusative case), but each argument is different and their number is greater than the frequency of the single predicate.

The connections or identifications hitherto noted in Vedic hymns but more amply shown in the Brāhmaṇa and in Buddhist texts, are based on the same linking technique—

two or more arguments are connected by means of the predicate of existence (the verb "to be") or its semantic variants (for example, verbs of producing or becoming).

I am tempted to interpret in this way the definitions of the identity of the gods in the Ṛgveda hymns. These definitions often take the form of successive nominal sentences, for example ṚV 3.20.2: *ágne trī́ te vā́jinā,* 4 *agnír netā́ bhága iva kṣitinā́ṃ daívīnāṃ,* "Threefold (are) thy victory-forms, O Agni, Agni (is) the leader of the divine populations, like Bhaga". In these elementary statements identifying Agni as well as the connected phenomena, the nouns are linked, whereas the predicate "to be", which is common to them is suppressed. The technique of comparison is used to explain the connection. This succession is in a significant context—there is indeed a *bándhu* "link, (parental), connection" with the god Agni, a truth recognised as general[28] by the authors of the hymns.

One definition of identity which uses the term *nidāna,* a synonym of *bándhu* is given in the Aitareya Brāhmaṇa (II. 11.5=VII.1): *yajamāno vā eṣa nidānena yatpaśuranena* "The sacrificer is indeed, by virtue of this connection, the animal victim." Equating the sacrificer to the victim is done not only by the juxtaposition of the words denoting them, but also by the semantics of the sentence carrying the word *nidāna,* literally "link" (from the verbe *dā-* "to link"). In Sāyaṇa's commentary, the verb denoting existence is found in its two variants (*as-* "to be", and *bhū* "to become"). In the sentence explained above, a simple link serves to connect the two arguments that are being defined, each one of which combines with a zero predicate.

This is quite different in the following sentence from the commentary: *yaḥ paśurastyeṣa nidānena śūkṣmadṛṣṭinirūpanena yajamāna eva bhavati* "He is that victim by the link (intimate with the victim), he becomes the sacrificer by the analysis (by means of) a penetrating look."[29]

Although the poetic technique in the Indo-European

songs using linking is the same as these formulae for identification, there is, however, a difference which is the number of predicates and arguments linked, a number that can be increased or decreased according to the intention of the narrator. Renou felt it was possible to trace the source of another term meaning "connection", "link", that is, the word *nimitta*, which is Brahmanic rather than Buddhist according to Oldenberg. Its meaning was "cause" towards the end of the Vedic period as used by Sanskrit grammarians, and "sign" after the Vedic period. The word indicates (according to Renou) first of all the "connection" between a signifying thing and a signified thing. He adds that the Indo-European radical **mei-*"join, attach"[30] is preceded, in Sanskrit, by the preverb *ni*-which can be found in a number of words denoting "link": *nibandhana, nidāna, niyut, niyam-* etc.[31]

Generally speaking, when I think of Vedic culture and its relationship to Indo-European culture, I am reminded of a comment formulated by C. Watkins after he had stressed on the possibility of enriching our knowledge of Indo-European culture by studying Homeric poems, and, inversely, understanding Homer's works by applying Indo-European studies to them. This comment has the advantage of reminding the comparatist that the object of his analysis is first and foremost a linguistic phenomenon: "Like the Saussurian notion of the twofold character of language, each of the two aspects is dependent on the other; each is meaningful and each *signifies*, only by virtue of its opposition to the other. The twofold, duplex, dual structure whether it be Indo-European and Homer, or linguistics and philology, or langue and parole, or code and message, is a unitary whole. It is the task of the linguist to work out the modalities of the interrelations of this duplex structure." He then goes on to quote Roman Jakobson: "In language and in use of language, duplicity plays a cardinal role." These words of Jakobson are equivalent to a programme.[32]

REFERENCES

1. *La ricostruzione culturale* in *Studi di cultura celtica e indoeuropea,* Pisa, 1981, pp. 11-23. See also his remarks in *Ricostruzione linguistica e ricostruzione culturale,* a cura di F. Crevatin, Trieste, 1983.
2. For the totalitarian nature of the poetic culture of the Indo-Europeans see E. Campanile, *Ricerche di cultura poetica indoeuropea,* Pisa, 1977, pp. 78-96.
3. This is the topic of my essay 'Les stratégies de l'aède homérique et le sacrifice du poète officiant védique' that will be published some day.
4. See G. Dumézil's enlightening account on the various ways in which Indo-European people conceive, imagine and construct what he calls their "ideological fields". This gives rise to contrasting pairs: Vedic Indians and Romans (*La religion romaine archaïque,* Paris, 1974, pp. 129-130, cf. *L'Héritage indo-européen a Rome,* Paris, 1949, pp. 170-172), Romans and Iranians (*Naissance d'archanges,* Paris, 1945, pp. 181-188), Romans and Celts (*Horace et les Curiaces,* Paris, 1942, pp. 65-68).
5. For a deeper reflection on the necessity of comparing living cultures that are otherwise in danger of being stifled, see E.T. Hall, *Beyond Culture,* New York, 1976.
6. *Naissance d'archanges,* pp. 183-187.
7. For further details, refer to E. Campanile, *La ricostruzione culturale,* pp. 12-14.
8. E. Benveniste, *Phraséologie poétique de l'indo-iranien* in *Mélanges d'indianisme à la mémoire de L. Renou,* Paris, 1968, p. 73.
9. E. Benveniste, *ibid.,* p. 79.
10. See my essay *Sprachwissenschaft und die Erforschung mythologischer Texte (Die Aufgaben der Semiotik im Bereich der Etymologie)* in *Studi italiani di linguistica teorica ed applicata,* VIII, 1979, pp. 121-135.
11. This contrast in perspectives has been established by G. Dumézil, *L'Héritage indo-européen à Rome,* pp. 170-172. It is not of consequence that his version of contrasts between India and Rome has been re-established by Dumézil after about 10 years (see *Religion romaine archaïque,* 1974, pp. 129-130). One realises that the list of features of these two civilisations may invite some comment. I would like to emphasise the importance Dumézil attaches to the differential nature of individual Indo-European cultures.
12. G. Dumézil, *La religion romaine archaïque,* p. 103, and especially his essay, *Le* iuges auspicium *et les incongruités du taureau attelé de Mudgala* in *Nouvelle Clio,* 5, 1953, pp. 252-266, summarised and commented in G. Dumézil, *Mariages indo-européens* followed by *Quinze questions romaines,* Paris, 1979, pp. 280-293 (see also pp. 241-243 of this book).

13. J. Bloch, *La charrue védique* in *Bull. of the School of Oriental Studies,* 8, 1936, pp. 411-418.
14. J. Bloch, *ibid.*, p. 418.
15. ṚV 10.101.3 and 4 are quoted according to the translations of L. Renou, *Hymnes spéculatifs du Véda*, Paris, 1956, p. 109.
16. L. Renou, *Études védiques et pāṇinéennes,* X, Paris, 1962, p. 87.
17. According to L. Renou, *Études védiques et pāṇinéennes,* XVI, Paris, 1967, p. 79.
18. J. Bloch, *ibid.*, p. 415.
19. There exists a small literature on this question ever since the debate was re-opened more than 20 years ago: B. Oguibénine, *Baltic Evidence and the Indo-Iranian Prayer*, in JIES, 2, 1, 1974, pp. 23-45; H.P. Schmidt, *Is Vedic "dhénā" related to Avestan "daēnā"?* in *Acta Iranica*, 5, 1975, pp. 165-179; the reply to this essay: B. Oguibénine, *Védique* dhénā, *avestique* daēnā: *examen des critiques de H.P. Schmidt* in *Lautgeschichte und Etymologie*, Wiesbaden, 1980, pp. 293-316; H.P. Schmidt, *Zarathustra's Religion and his Pastoral Imagery*, Leiden, 1975. I know of two reactions: one is the refusal to accept that the element of Indo-Iranian material culture, "cow", was soon seized by the religious poetic discourse to become a metaphor (very special and more real than the economic reality that some try to reconstruct to measure the importance of the Indo-Iranian cow): B. Lincoln, *Priests, Warriors and Cattle. A study in the Ecology of Religions*, University of California Press, 1981, p. 102, n. 32. On his part, Ph. Gignoux in *Abstracta Iranica* 4, 1981, p. 16 "is reluctant to accept that the *daēnā* of the Avesta may designate the cow metaphorically".
20. For a more detailed discussion, read the essay *Védique* dhēnā *et avestique* daēnā: *examen des critiques de H.P. Schmidt*, p. 308.
21. I quote according to E. Campanile's reply to the questionnaire given in the volume *Ricostruzione linguistica e ricostruzione culturale*, a cura di F. Crevatin, Trieste, 1983, p. iv.
22. E. Campanile, *Indo-European Metaphors and Non-Indo-European Metaphors*, in JIES, 2, 3, 1974, pp. 247-248.
23. E. Campanile, *ibid.*
24. Following K.L. Janert, *Sinn und Bedeutung des Wortes "dhāsi"*, Wiesbaden, 1956, pp. 29-30.
25. According to U. Rapallo, *Metafore indoeuropee e camito-semitiche* in *Atti del Sodalizio Glottologico Milanese*, Vol. XXI, 1979-1980 (1981), pp. 76-77. In fact, it is more than just usual metaphors, it is combinations of sememes which show themselves common to about thirty radicals of the two families, but the commonness is often not quite evident.
26. L. Renou, *"Connexion" en védique, "cause" en bouddhique* in L. Renou, *L' Inde fondamentale*, Paris, 1978, pp. 149-153.

27. "Beside the hymns....which magnify a single divine action into the greatest, there are others which narrate and glorify in a concise and allusive manner a whole series of actions of one god and links them one after another, the *Aufreihlieder*, as we would call them." (F.R. Schröder, *Eine indogermanische Liedform* in R. Schmitt ed. *Indogermanische Dichtersprache*, Darmstadt, 1968, pp. 177-186, cf. R. Schmitt, *Dichtung und Dichtersprache in indogermanischer Zeit* Wiesbaden, 1967, pp. 52-55 and pp. 138-141.
28. On the nominal clause expressing "general truths", E. Benveniste, *La phrase nominale* in *Problèmes de linguistique générale*, Paris, 1966, p. 162.
29. Cf. L. Renou, *"Connexion,"* p. 151, and H. Oldenberg, *Die Weltanschauung der Brahmanatexte*, Göttingen, 1919, p. 117.
30. J. Pokorny, *Indogermanisches etymologisches Wörterbuch*, Bern, 1959, p. 710. It is however true that the existence of the Indo-European root **mei*-with this meaning is not, as Renou points out, definitely acceptable. Cf. the doubts of M. Mayrhofer, *Kurzgefasstes etymologisches Wörterbuch des Altindischen*, III, Heidelberg, 1976, p. 634 and the categorical rejection of T. Burrow, *Sanskrit* mā- *'to approach, meet, join'*; (trans) *'to bring to'* in *Bull. of the School of Oriental and African Studies*, Vol. XLIV, Pt. 1, 1981, p. 94.
31. L. Renou, *"Connexion"*, p. 153.
32. C. Watkins, *"Let Us Praise Famous Grains"* in *Proceedings of the American Philosophical Society*, no. 1, 1978, p. 9.

CHAPTER 1

The Vedic Warrior and Homer's *skhétlios*

Franklin E. Horowitz in his article published in *Studia Linguistica*, XXIX, 1975, pp. 99 ff.,[1] has propounded a comparison which seems unusual. Although it is not totally acceptable, it is of use if approached in a different manner.

The author has used a method which has gained acceptance and which is certainly most promising: two levels of language, or rather two types of language, the language of linguistic signs, and the language of mythological or ideological structures are very clearly distinguished. He has thus used a historical linguistic relationship to establish another relationship which creates a synthetic image of the Indo-European warrior. The word "synthetic" is used deliberately, for the relationship between linguistic forms gives the most accessible articulation in the two fields of the Indo-European world which the author has exploited to form a composition made up of the elements contained in Indo-European ideology. It is worthwhile to emphasise this aspect which is in fact quite common in comparative linguistics. Of late, the tendency is to consider facts of mythology and ancient culture as a specific kind of language with its own structure. This may appear to be a simple exercise encouraged by the spectacular growth of structuralism in human sciences, but it is in fact of prime importance. This has already been mentioned on several occasions. Suffice to say that the types of mythological characters, the types of agents peculiar to a specific human culture, the types of relationship between figures as well as the types of events in which the latter are used are all so many elements of a *code* established by a society, or its poets or anonymous authors of myths and legends, and have a status similar to that of facts of language.

This is exactly how Horowitz deals with the matter. Referring to the works of Dumézil and Wikander, he states that one can justly believe that there exists the type of Indo-European warrior whose main characteristics are as follows: "one who is so self-willed as to show no regard for reasonable constraints, whether these be imposed by moral or religious obligations, the claims of fellow-feeling or compassion, the superior power of others, or the limitations of one's body", or further, "one who overcomes all resistance, who is restrained by no will of his own".

A type, a generalised image, accepted in Indo-European societies, must have a name; that is, there must be a word which could be reconstructed as **(s)khetlio* according to Horowitz's analysis. I must, however, specify that this word does not come from Horowitz, it only indicates what could arise from combining Greek **skhetlón* with Sk. *kṣatríya*, without, I hope, any kind of disfiguration.

In order to verify this suggestion which as far as I know has never been made before, it was natural to follow the same combined path, that is, to look for a linguistic form (though I doubt it exists as proposed by Horowitz), and connect it to the contents of texts used by comparatists. Since a direct relationship between the Sanskrit word and the Greek word was naturally impossible, a morphological analysis was necessary to find out if these two words resulted from analogous developments in their respective languages.

Herein lies the difficulty in accepting Horowitz's conclusions and even his methods. In a bid to find the equation which would lead to the establishment of the formula arising from the comparison (though for some reason he has not mentioned it), the replica of a representation common to the Greeks of the Iliad and to the Indians, the author would appear to have introduced into the known factors of Indo-European morphology a seemingly quasi-morphological procedure, and it is this which has to be studied carefully. Another point in the reasoning of Horowitz is that when he applies his morphological procedure to the Indo-European root **seg'h-*, it becomes the required common element which by its form as well as its linguistic content, calling for extensions of meaning in the field of mythology, explains the existence of Skr. *kṣatrám* (hence, *kṣatríya*) and Greek **skhetlón*. These two words would designate "the condition or function of one who performs the action, or possesses the quality of **seg'h-*".

The Skr. *kṣatrám* would be to the Skr. *sáhas* "vigour, strength", and "warrior strength" in particular, what the Skr. *hotrám* "activity of the officiant *hotṛ́-* (Wackernagel-Debrunner, *Altindische Grammatik*, II/2, p. 705:" Abstrakta [der] Nomina auf *tṛ-*, die den Inhaber eines Amts oder einer Lebensstellung bezeichnen; in v. *hotrá-* geht die Bedeutung "Geschäft d. Hotar" neben "Opfer" her", but the name of an instrument according to Minard, *Trois énigmes sur les cent chemins*, 1956, 21c) is to Skr. *havás* "invocation".[2] Horowitz's argument implies the conclusion that the Greek **skhétlios* is derived from the hypothetic **skhetlón*, as the Skr. *kṣatríya* is derived from the Skr. *kṣatrá*. No details are given, however, about the derivation of the two Greek words, or about the Greek, or more generally, Indo-European procedure which would enable this formation. One cannot arrive at Horowitz's conclusion that Skr. *kṣatríya* corresponds to Greek *skhétlios* "in every phonetic feature but the position of the accent and the initial consonant cluster" (p. 104). Is it not wrong and against the principles of linguistic analysis to compare forms by considering their phonetic elements without considering their morphological functions? Even if you set aside the difficulties presented by the accents in the two nouns and their initial phonetic cluster, it can be seen that the phonetic elements which seem identical at first sight are really far from being so. To give the comparison its rightful value, it is enough to consider the functions of those elements that can be isolated in these two words.

The identification of the two words is the starting point, but I feel that it would be wiser to compare Skr. *kṣatrám* and Greek **skhetlón* (without, however, anticipating success), which is done without sufficient proof (see below). If the common origin is to be traced, the first thing which seems contestable is the identification of the Sanskrit suffix *-íya* and its juxtaposition to a fictitious Greek element (*-io-* ?). By comparing them Horowitz implies that he thinks it is possible to compare them (in particular, see his reference to Gr. *ágrios* related to Skr. *ajryà* and also *ajriyà* "which is found on the plain"); he therefore attributes the secondary suffix *-*yo-* to Gr. *skhéthlios*. This is not correct. *Skhétlios* does not contain any suffix which could originate from this Indo-European suffix; according to several experts (Schwyzer, *Griech, Gr.*, I, p. 533, Frisk, *Griech. et. Wb.*, Lief. 18, p. 838, conveniently summarised by Chantraine, *Dictionnaire étymologique de la langue grecque*, t. IV-1, 1977, p. 1081), this Greek word comes from **skhéthlios* (derived from a **skhéthlos*), after the dissimilation of the second aspirate and the suffix is *-thlós* which is also found in Gr. *esthlós* "good, upright, honest" (but Benveniste, *Origines de la formation des noms en indo-européen*, p. 191 gives *esth-* as the base, cf. another treatment p. 203 where he himself mentions the Greek suffix *-thlo-* derived from I.E. **dhl*). Therefore, *skhétlios* "bold, ruthless, cruel" as used by Homer is not comparable by its suffix to Skr. *kṣatríya* in the Indo-European perspective. In fact the comparison is even less possible if the true origin of the Sanskrit suffix *-íya-* is considered (and not *-iy-*, as Horowitz says p. 104): this suffix which dates back to ancient times, tended to replace the suffix *-ya-* in order to re-establish the disyllabic nature of the latter (Wackernegel-Debrunner, *Altindische Grammatik*, II/2, p. 358); the two suffixes have also co-existed in certain texts; this could arise from their written form (*ibid.*, p. 359, see also Renou, *Grammaire sanscrite*, pp. 249-250).

It is nevertheless true that Gr. *skhétlios* is derived from the Greek root *skhe-* which represents an aoristic base of the Greek verb *ékhô-* " to have" which indeed seems to be a derivative of the I.E. **seg'h-* just like the Sanskrit *sah-*, see Pokorny, *Idg. etym. Wb.*, p. 888, Chantraine, *Dictionnaire étymologique*, p. 392-394. It is interesting that Pokorny postulates a verbal base of the old Indo-European root having zero vocalism from which the Greek word in question comes, though it is not known how this happens; this is indirectly similar to what Horowitz has to say, but I think it is more correct to say that there has been an intermediate stage in the evolution, notably the one in which the Greek root *skhe-* has arisen (and this has, precisely, zero vocalism). This explanation has the advantage of elucidating at the same time the formation of the second aorist of the Greek verb *ékhô*, the form in which the zero vocalism of the root **seg'h-*, **sg'he-* is displayed (for the latter form, see Kurylowicz, *L'apophonie en indo-européen*, p. 72).

Hence it cannot be accepted that the Gr. *skhétlios* is formed from the unproved **skhetlón* in the same way that the Skr. *kṣatríya* was derived from the Skr. *kṣatrá-*. All the more reason why the interpretation of the origin of the word as given by Horowitz is untenable: in fact, how can we understand that Gr. **skhetlon* is "an abstract noun based on a PIE agentive formation with a suffix-*tel* added to **skhe-*, same stem as in Gr. *skhésis*"? Indo-European has agent nouns with suffixes **-tor-* and *-ter* which have been inherited in Greek as *-tōr-* and *-tēr-*; on the contrary, there is no known Greek suffix *-*tel* which corresponds to the Indo-

European suffixes given above.

In order to explain the formation of the Skr. *kṣatrá*, Av. *xšathra-*, is it possible to refer to the verbal base **sk'he-* which is declared to be Indo-European, whereas we have just seen that this base was productive only in Greek? If the opinion currently accepted in etymological works that the two Indo-Iranian words mentioned are formed on Skr. *kṣayáti*, Av. *xšayeiti* "to be master, to dominate" (see Benveniste, *Vocabulaire des institutions indo-européennes*, I, p. 18, but also Pokorny, *Idg. etym. Wb.*, p. 626) is to be questioned, more proofs would be required which could confirm the suggestion of metathesis ("or some other still-to-be determined process") by which **seg'h-*, **sk'he-* would result in the Indo-Iranian consonant groups *kṣ/xš*. Not that the metathesis is impossible, but it is easier, if not exclusively possible, to prove on the basis of the transformations of phonetic sequences in texts if these use them. Otherwise, a simple affirmation which also goes from the level of Indo-European to that of really attested languages is not sufficient to accept that there has been a quasi-morphological process which would result in the derivation of the Indo-Iranian words in question from the Indo-European root **seg'h-*. Since the Sanskrit verb *sah-* is clearly derived from this root, and since its meanings can be compared to those of the Greek *ékhô*, it is correct that **seg'h* is a formula by which their common Indo-European origin can be acknowledged, but neither Skr. *kṣatrá*, Av. *xšathra*, nor even more Gr. *skhétlios* even in its primitive form can be explained on the basis of this root.

It seems fairly obvious that the comparison of Gr. *skhétlios* and Skr. *kṣatríya* cannot be maintained. They are different in more important features than just by accent and initial consonant groups. But since linguistic expression alone is not sufficient for successfully establishing a synthetic and composite image of the Indo-European warrior, it must be recognised that Horowitz's suggested method can be effective. For a great deal has been learnt about the warrior as he appeared to Romans, Scandinavians and Indo-Iranians (and in this respect, the works of G. Dumézil and S. Wikander are fundamental), but few efforts have been made to determine Homeric parallels which would complete the image of the Indo-European warrior. These parallels are not devoid of interest, even though they are made in contexts which do not give close indications of warrior ideology.

By virtue of its place in discourses made by characters and its consequent functional value, the Greek word *skhétlios* is indeed used in the description of the warrior who is not always quite like the Indo-European warrior in the sense that many elements identified by G. Dumézil to define his features are missing. But I feel it is more important that, if the analogies between the characters of Homer's epics and the warrior are accepted, even if these analogies are seen in episodes which do not relate to war in the strictest sense of the word, it is possible to uncover some complex relations which the concept of war must have maintained in Indo-European ideology, and in particular in the ideology of the Ṛgveda.

The language used to describe war conflicts can be found in the accounts of conflicts and confrontations which are not really war-like in the true sense of the word, but which are akin to it *through this very language,* because it is generalised and thus lends itself to transformations within the limits of a mythological system or an epic work. The extension of the usage of this language is flexible, as the usage translates those needs of the description which imply the passages and transformations together producing the cases that Horowitz has tried to study. The examples that he has taken from the Iliad have the advantage of being oriented towards the research of this extension: although the effect of this extension on linguistic expression is not produced in the Indo-European itself, linguistic expression is an outcome of it. Moreover, another case of the widespread use of the I.E. root **seg'h* is known. It is used in the formation of the names of the heroes whose warrior nature is perhaps not their sole attribute (if one maintains the hypothesis that the derivatives of this root are noticeably marked by the warrior function, for example *sáhas* in the Rgveda hymns), such as Hector (*héktōr* "who is steadfast" according to Chantraine, *Dictionnaire étymologique*, p. 330 who sees in it the same Greek root *ékhô* "to have", but also and especially originally the meanings "to possess, hold, retain" see Chantraine, p. 392), and also Sahadeva of the Mahābhārata. It would appear that there has been a restructuring within the tradition followed by Homer which has credibly retained a part of the Indo-European heritage. Accordingly, Hector, a figure within the scope of Dumézil's third function, forms a duo with Paris, identical to the Nakula-Sahadeva duo[4].

Thus despite the peculiarities in the semantic developments of the root **seg'h-* in Greek, Greek *skhétlios* could continue to have the meaning that Vedic *sáhas* has when it is used in the scope of the warrior function. Horowitz lays explicit stress on this word despite G. Dumézil's opinion that the Skr. *sáhas* has a magico-religious function (see G. Dumézil, *Jupiter Mars Quirinus*, IV, pp. 101 ff.). Considering that the respective functions digress into other spheres, it is not impossible that **seg'h-*, between the Indian and the Greek, should denote two kinds of force, the force of power, and the force which is shown so that victory can make this power real. This is indeed what happens from one Indo-European language to another. If in Sanskrit *sáhas* means "superiority over others" its meaning evolves to give "victory" in Germanic, that is, victory in war (G. Dumézil in the same volume says, "even in military matters, *sáhas* is not reduced to mere force, this vulgar kind of power; it comprises "dominium" which can be expected of a concept related to Greek *ékhô*, p. 107). In the Veda, even the notions *sáhas, ójas,* "physical force" [which Dumézil considers as belonging to the manifestations of the warrior function, in the vocabulary of god Indra (p. 106)], and the notion, sometimes personified, denoted by the term *manyú,* somewhat complex[5] of which one of the meanings is "warrior fury", form a whole that cannot be dissociated from a precise moment in the sautrāmaṇī rite celebrated in honour of Indra.[6] This last detail is significant for a number of reasons; yet it is suggestive to evoke its reference to the myth in which Indra is reconstituted by an alcoholic drink to which are added the ingredients representing *ójas, manyú and sáhas.*[7]

All in all, with the help of the definition, which is more of an interpretation, albeit incomplete but which serves to establish one characteristic at least of the nature of the warrior as described by Dumézil, Horowitz rightly quotes some passages from the Iliad. He discerns what others have called "excessiveness", and which the Greeks have denoted by the word *húbris.* It also means "arrogance, insolence", and also "fierceness, excessive ardour, impetuosity", and as an action noun "outrage, bad treatment, violence", and much later, "damage, destruction". If there existed a Greek agent noun derived from this word, it would be easy to imagine that, by virtue of its meaning, it would be grouped with *skhétlios* (a distinctly malevolent agent, often characterised by his excesses, "going to the extreme", according to the definition given by Chantraine, *Dictionnaire étymologique,* p. 1081). This word is apparently most often used in a definitely reprobative and negative sense, according to research oriented towards the study of contrasts and identities which mark this word in the vocabulary of expressions figuring in the beginning of discourses in Homer's works (and *skhétios* is one of these expressions).

The excessiveness is reproached in a dual manner, for the word itself is a reproach by its content but, contrary to other words of interpellation (in the vocative of evaluation), it is frequently followed by at least one sentence which details the denounced behaviour. Sometimes, an expression of warning, advice or forbidding follows this kind of apostrophe.[8] This means that *skhétlios* is used to qualify a behaviour which is criticised because of the actions which constitute this behaviour, and these actions are seen as functions of the agent. Going back to what Benveniste had to say regarding the distinction of Indo-European agent nouns in **tōr-* and in **tēr-*, it can be said that if the norms for Greek derivation had allowed it, then in the place of *skhétlios,* there would have been an agent noun in **tēr-* which "characterises the being as allotted a function, and in a way, enclosed within this function".[8] From this point of view, any character could become *skhétlios,* on condition that he took on functions that were ascribed to him. This fact is not without importance when it comes to finding the meaning of the word in its various uses which combine together to form a coherent whole

This word also appears in the Odyssey (nine times as compared to thrice in the Iliad as a vocative of evaluation, according to E. Brunius-Nilsson, p. 46), but Horowitz does not take this into account. This is probably because the Iliad is more likely to provide information about Greek warriors for they and their character lend themselves to the search for an equivalent to the Sanskrit *kṣatríya,* because of their badly adjusted or displaced behaviour. In fact, the Odyssey is always given less importance when Homeric warriors are studied. To quote a recent example, it has been said that Ulysses is not a true warrior, and the story he narrates to his swineherd Eumaeus is probably a pure invention of this unsociable braggart who is more akin to Thersites of the Iliad.[10] Ulysses of the Odyssey is no longer the glorious lancer of the Iliad, but rather an archer coming from the depths of the Achaean world, and this judgement is apparently very deprecatory when it comes to describe a Homeric warrior.[11]

Yet I feel that it is possible to consider certain passages of the Odyssey which highlight other aspects of the warrior which have been less featured in the Iliad. These aspects are doubtless less obvious, for the Odyssey does not revolve around military confrontations, but what is evident is the language of mythology peculiar to discourses on warriors, their nature and their characteristic behaviour, which is used in the Odyssey in certain specific cases. These cases prove to be of value, because they deal with conflicts and adversaries who can be considered in the perspective of war only because of the vigorous use of the language of war mythology, an intervention that is decisive, as it determines both the nature of the conflict which can therefore be seen otherwise, and their presentation by means of linguistic signs. It is precisely here that we see the type (for there obviously is one) of *skhétlios* which can easily be defined as equivalent to *kṣatriya* although the correspondence between the series of images and the terms which designate them is not established. This is unfortunate for comparative studies that are aimed at finding as many lexical correspondences as possible which could be corroborated by the correlations of institutional modalities (in the sense given to the latter after E. Benveniste). But referring to such cases is nonetheless important, for they definitely show the perceptible permutations which have taken place in the series of images and words, both of which obey laws of structure.

It is natural that the Greek *skhétlios* of the Odyssey, becomes so following excesses committed in various fields which represent numerous aspects of ideology, but each one of them tends to converge towards the notion that G. Dumézil has characterised as the expression of exuberance,[12] which is easily disguised as violence which is burdened with military connotations, however indirect they may be. These excesses are indulged in by an individual or a group whose nature has interesting Indo-European parallels. (See also and specially S. Wikander, *Der arische Männerbund*, Lund, 1938.) Some of them are not connected to the warrior type of adversary, but the extensions of vocabulary should be explained in each individual case.

The following are some examples of *skhétlios*. They seem to be the least contestable, and call for comparative reflections:

1. When Zeus wants to prevent the sailors from returning, he is *skhétlios*, since he provokes an *éris* (Od. 3. 161 *hós r'érin ôrse kakèn*, "he causes a noisome quarrel to arise", cf. V. Berard's translation "his wrath once again unleashes the scourge of a second quarrel", in which the reference to Zeus' wrath is indicated in the word *skhétlios*). There is a point that is not obvious at first sight: *órnūmi érin*, a phrase which is present in the quoted line, is in fact a revelatory etymological figure. The verb and the noun which together give the meaning "to provoke a quarrel" come from the same Indo-European root **er-*, **or-* "set in motion, arouse, incite, provoke" (in Greek, most of these meanings have been retained) which goes with the extension in **-i-* for the noun. The primary meaning of this noun in Greek is "quarrel with weapon in hand, struggle, combat, rivalry"[12]. It cannot be denied that this phrase is related to the vocabulary of war hostilities. What is more, it is very probable that it comes from the Indo-European past, as shown by many passages of the Ṛgveda in which this phrase is found through the various meanings that it has acquired. Thus, in the Ṛgveda 4.42.5 **He/or-er-nu-*[13] seems to be used in a discourse of Indra, the god of war: . . .*mā́ṃ vṛtā́ḥ samáraṇe havante kṛṇómy ājím maghávāhám índra íyarmi reṇúm abhíbhūtyojāḥ* "It is to me, when they are encircled in combat, that they appeal; I create the combat (I make the combat), I, Indra the generous One, I raise dust, I who possess superior strength." The Vedic expression *ar- reṇúm* is a clear parallel to this other expression in the same line, *kṛ- ājím* "create the combat" or, according to the context,

"provoke a contest (around a trophy)", but even outside this string of phrases, to say that the god Indra raises the dust is far from fortuitous, it is a way of referring to his activity as a warrior who incites men to combat or incites himself to fight in the battle. [I quote from ṚV 4.17.13 *íyarti reṇúm. . . vibhañjanúr* "he raises dust, he who breaks (the enemy's resistance)", *sá yudhmáḥ sátvā khajakṛ́t samádvā . . . bṛhádrenuś cyávano mā́nuṣīṇām . . . . kṛṣṭīnā́m* "he, the combatant, the warrior who makes the combat, who likes the combat, who raises high the dust, who shakes up the human peoples (=incites them to combat)", ṚV 6.18.2, cf. ṚV 3.43.7.] Other references are not any the less revelatory in the sense that they can easily be associated with the typical warrior roles taken on by Indra in his state of excitation which is a measure of the realisation of his warrior nature, cf. ṚV 8.1.7 *álarṣi yudhma khajakṛt puraṃdara* "thou arousest thyself, warrior who creates the combat, breaker of citadels", and ṚV 1.56.4 *yó dhṛṣṇúnā śávasā bā́dhate táma íyarti reṇúm bṛhád arhariṣváṇiḥ* "he who pushes back the darkness with his bold strength, he raises high the dust with a cry of triumph" (according to L. Renou, *Etudes véd. et pāṇ.* t. XVII, p. 22), especially remarkable for the repetition of the same phrase *ar- reṇúm* in the same warrior context. This phrase therefore had a very precise meaning and it was on a par with others expressing the same meaning "to provoke a combat, a contest between rivals", in which the Vedic verb *ar-* in its various forms was invariably present on the left or right side of the phrase. One would almost expect the creation of the expression **ar- samáraṇam (samaryám, sámṛtim)* which is no doubt hypothetic, and which would join the two elements inherited from the Indo-European, the same as in the attested expression *ar- reṇúm,* but in which the second element means "combat, war encounter, military conflict". It can be assumed that the poetic language of the Ṛgveda did not favour such direct expressions and preferred periphrase such as *ar- reṇúm,* see ṚV 4.17.12 *yó. . . śúṣmam muhukaír* *íyarti* "(Indra) who sets off his (combative) fury with war cries", ṚV 2.17.3 *ádhākṛnoḥ prathamáṃ vīryàm mahád yád asyā́gre bráhmaṇā śúṣmam aírayaḥ* "then thou didst the first great virile-deed (consisting of this) that at first thou didst stir up the fury thanks to the *brahman* of this (singer)" and ṚV 4.38.7 in which the contest of steeds which was like a combat and the dust which is raised refer to the same symbolism which associates combat and dust: *vājī́ sáhurir. . . kirate reṇúm* "(steed), winner-of-prizes, dominant. . . . pushes out the dust. . ." (according to L. Renou, *Et. véd. et pāṇ.*, t. XV p. 163).[14]

2. Contrary to what one would believe about Ulysses of the Odyssey, he is indeed *skhétlios*. As in the preceding example, this trait is attributed to him by virtue of his character which shows itself precisely at that instant (12.116). Circe makes matters clear as soon as she speaks of the difficulty in facing Scylla whom Ulysses wishes to attack: his warrior ardour would be in vain, Scylla is unassailable (*oudè makhētón* 12.119); but before describing this monster, she says to Ulysses: *skhétlie kaì d'aû toi poleméia érga mémēle kaì pónos* "(warrior) untiring (or obstinate), thou didst only deal with that which is war and fighting". Also, Athena's reproach to him seems to refer to his warrior status which he shows although he tries to hide his identity from the goddess. (Od.13.293-295): *skhétlie poikilomēta dólōn ât' ouk ár'émelles, oud' en sêi per eôn gaíei, lḗksein apatáōn múthon te klopiōn [phíloi] hoí toi paidóthen eisín* "Wild and artful being! Is it possible that on thy return to thy country, thou canst help but (invent) unbelievable patchwork stories like those thou didst cherish in thy childhood!" No doubt this speech from Athena mainly refers to the tricks used by Ulysses to avoid being recognised but it is tempting to interpret it with respect to the fate that is awaiting him on his return to Ithaca which the goddess reveals to him: he will have to suffer many ills and even fight human beings. (Od. 13. 310 *bías hupodégmenos andrôn* "receiving as an enemy the

violence of men". Considering that Gk. *anḗr* continuing Indo-European **ner-* has a military connotation, this phrase can be believed to refer to the confrontation with warriors, see G. Dumézil, *L'homme: ner- et uiro-* in *Idées romaines*, pp. 226-241). Athena also encourages Ulysses on other occasions: When the latter is pondering on the means of attacking Penelope's suitors (Od. 20. 45 ff. *skhétlie kaì mén tís te khereíoni peítheth'hetaírōi hós per thnētós t'esti kaì ou tòsa mēdea oîden* "Valorous (warrior?), is it not true that being mortal, one trusts even weaker companions without even having such great plans?"); then when Ulysses begins to fight against the suitors and asks Athena who is disguised as Mentor to intervene, she chides him for wanting in courage and ardour (Od. 22.226).

This last passage has been commented by Benveniste (*Vocabulaire des institutions indo-européennes*, II, pp. 72-74) who sees a sort of inner strength in this *alkḗ* which Athena tries to arouse in Ulysses and which is the ability to "face perils without ever retreating, not to give in when attacked", that is, the ability to resist the enemies as a warrior does. Perhaps it is not quite correct to translate *skhétlios* as "valorous (warrior)" in Od. 20.45, but the force of Athena's incitation seems to lie in the beginning of her discourse by which she promises to help him in all his future travails. It has already been pointed out that this goddess is associated with war in a very precise way—she protects the one she patronises and thus enables him to win the battle, rather than help directly.[15] This is the explanation of the two cases in which Athena orders Ulysses to exercise an attribute that is in him, but she has to kindle it so that he takes on the role called for by the circumstances.

3. When Circe or Athena address Ulysses, they try to make him understand that it is either desirable for him to manifest an excess of the attribute that they consider lacking in him, or that it is good or bad for him to manifest this attribute. In any case, the advice is to show excessive-

ness, but what is at the core is either a change in the present behaviour which ensures the excessiveness in relation to what the protagonist represents, or the continuation, desirable or undesirable, of the excessiveness which is acquired by his deeds. While it is true that the connections between the excesses and the field of the warrior deeds are not always the same, the deeds which reveal an abuse invariably seem to have a connection with the warrior field so that they acquire a different colour. The resulting nuance is a point of reference by which a character or characters are identified in relation to the warrior function.

Achilles, appearing as a ghost, reprimands Ulysses for having descended into Hades, which he thinks surpasses his own feats (Od. 11.474: *skhétlie típt' éti meîzon enì phresì mẽseai érgon* "How dost thou propose in thy mind to accomplish greater feats"?).[16] These feats belong obviously to the past, whereas the two heroes are together in combat. Circe is not any the less terrifed when she learns that Ulysses and his companions have penetrated Hades as living beings, thus becoming *disthanées* "those who die twice"; similarly, it is the same term that she attributes to them (Od. 12.21-22: *skhétlie hoi zõontes hupẽlthete dôm' Aídao disthanées hóte t'álloi hápax thnẽiskous' ánthrōpoi* "s., ye the living, ye have penetrated into the abode of Hades, ye shall therefore die twice whereas men die only once"). This latter usage of the term seems to be derived from the one in Od. 11.474, quoted earlier. However, it must be admitted that the two passages only show indirectly the attribute of Ulysses the warrior. Even if this value of the term can be maintained, other usages bring it out more clearly.

We have just seen that the attribute of *skhétlios* is also that of a group; as it happens, they are companions of Ulysses the warrior. They will once again be so in an indirect way, in a situation narrated by Ulysses: on leaving Aeolus' place, Ulysses and his crew are once again brought back towards him. Ulysses' men, jealous of the gift he received from Aeolus take advantage of Ulysses' being asleep and untie the bags containing winds and these winds blow the vessels back to Aeolus' island. According to Ulysses himself (Od. 10.68-69) this antagonism between him and his crew can be imputed to the latter: *áasán m'hetaroí te kakoí prós toîsi té húpnos skhétlios* "my wicked companions have troubled my spirit as well as the unfortunate sleep". But the dialogue between Aeolus and Ulysses and Ulysses' story itself show some interesting contradictions regarding the unexpected return to Aeolia: Od. 10.31, the sleep which Ulysses can no longer resist as he is overcome by fatigue, is *glukùs húpnos* "gentle slumber"; if the chorus questions him about the causes, it will be said (Od. 10.64 *tís toi kakòs ékhrae daímōn*) "What wicked divinity attacked you?", and he himself will reply, by accusing his companions and the sleep, the one being qualified as malevolent and the other as wicked. This says a lot about the conflict between Ulysses and his crew, all the more because, on two more occasions, this adversity will serve as a pretext to call Ulysses *skhétlios* before his companions.

4. In both cases, Ulysses is deliberately alone and facing the group (cf. Ulysses' reply to Eurylochus, spokesman of the group Od. 12.297 *ê mála dô me biázete moûnon eónta* "it is because I am alone that you use force against me", in which is found the notion of *bíē* "violent force"); either the group or its representative declares itself against Ulysses. The first time is when the latter provokes Polyphemus beyond measure (Od. 9.494 *skhétlie típt' ethéleis erethizémen ágrion ándra* "s., why dost thou seek to exasperate this wild man?"; note the relation of the verb *erethízō* "to provoke a combat, to exalt, to set in motion" to the verb *órnumi* which was mentioned earlier: Ulysses seems to incite Polyphemus to a confrontation which his other companions would like to avoid, for it would signify their defeat); the second time is when Ulysses is the only one who wants to avoid the Island of the Sun because of Tiresias' portent (Od. 12.279-

280: *skhétlios eis Oduseû perí toi mênos oudé ti guîa kámneis* "thou art s. Ulysses, thy spirit is superior and thy limbs are not tired out"). No doubt there is another possible interpretation of this passage, which would only consider the motive which urges Ulysses to continue on his way despite the extreme tiredness of his crew (Od. 12.280 ff.), but the information brought by Eurylochus, the sailor who treats Ulysses as *skhétlios* makes one believe that the discord between Ulysses and the others is the result of his strength which is superior to that of his group of sailors (moreover, *ménos* can be related to Vedic *manyú-* in a comparative perspective which no doubt has limited scope here, although the Greek word takes on a warrior value, and comes to mean "fury" and "ardour, impetuosity" of the combatants.[17])

Even more important is the fact that in either case, Ulysses is qualified as *skhétlios*, by this very crew which he himself treated in the same way. Once more, it can be seen that this attribute is mobile, it is attached to one person (exceptionally to sleep when it is personified, for it then becomes an agent) or a group of persons only by virtue of particular events and, which is even more significant, that in these conditions of rivalry which takes on the form of a confrontation, it is conferred as much on one as on the other.

5. One of the most striking cases is the one in which the various stages of Ulysses' adventure with the Cyclopes are traced by this epithet attributed to his antagonist of the moment, Polyphemus. Od. 9.351 Polyphemus is *skhétlios* as he shows an uncontrollable rage (*sú dè maínei oukét' anektôs*): he devours several companions of Ulysses who in vain offers him his wine; similarly, Od. 9.478-479 (an interpolated passage, according to V. Bérard), Polyphemus is treated as *skhétlios* since he brazenly devours those to whom he owes hospitality (it is not without importance that his misdeeds are *kakà érga* "outrageous and abusive deeds".[18]

It is thus not surprising that in the same song 9 of the Odyssey, the deeds of Polyphemus are sometimes *kakà érga* and sometimes *skhétlia érga* (9. 295). (One may also wonder why Ulysses, when he remembers this day, says he possesses *ménos áskhetos* "irresistible spirit" in which is found the same verb *ékhô*). For *skhétlia érga* are eloquent and suggestive when referring to the evil deeds of Penelope's suitors. Their *kakà érga*, abominable crimes that anger the gods, alternate with their *skhétlia érga* in the discourses of the characters of the Odyssey. They are obviously two kinds of misdeeds. Moreover, it is seen in the swineherd's narration that (Od. 14.80 ff.) *skhétlia érga* are in opposition to *aísima érga* "measured deeds" (see Bailly, *Dictionnaire grec-français*, p. 50) and that the *kakà érga* of the suitors are quite naturally associated and even identified as their *húbris* "excessive audacity (and reproved by the gods)", Od. 23. 63-64: *tis athanáthōn kteîne mnēstêras agauoús húbrin agassámenos thumalgéa kaì kakà érga* "an (immortal) god came to kill the noble suitors, angered by their excessive audacity and their grievous crimes". Consequently the *skhétlia érga* will be punished by Ulysses himself, but the passage Od. 22.413 would perhaps be better understood if it were translated as "it is the destiny of the gods that has mitigated them and their violent crimes" (*toûsde dè moîr' edámasse theôn kaì skhétlia érga*), and not, as suggested by V. Bérard, "it is the destiny of the gods that kills them and their crimes" since the notion of *moîra* implies the idea of a lot or a share given out in just measure, and since the verb *damázo* signifies not only "kill" or "to cause to perish", but also "overcome, submit to the yoke", that is, "impose the necessary measure" (cf. also E. Benveniste's reflections on the notion of measure in Indo-European, *Vocabulaire des institutions*, II, pp. 123-132, see note 16 above). It is very probable that the frenzied band of Penelope's suitors can be considered advantageously in the comparative perspective of the Indo-European

"Männerbund". Indeed, the suitors show more than once the characteristics which make them comparable to the society of Indo-European warriors—in addition to the excesses which have just been referred to, they are guilty of various kinds of violations, in particular those related to sexual mores and social rules. It cannot be forgotten that this group of young noblemen of Ithaca will meet Ulysses in a frightful combat, Ulysses who is a *skhétlios* like they are, and this seems to support the inevitable conclusion that the parties who confront each other are given the attribute expressed by the word *skhétlios*.

6. Before presenting more general conclusions, I must mention that, as is often the case when evaluating meanings of a word that summarises a situation or a configuration of events, there always exists a residue, a series of usages, however reduced they may be, that can at least be considered as apart from the more frequent usages. Od. 5.118 is the least truncated of these: Calypso treats the gods as *skhétlioí* at the time when Hermes comes to announce Zeus' wish to release Ulysses. There certainly is antagonism among the gods, brought out when Calypso remembers the two cases of the gods' jealousy when goddesses keep a mortal lover. Both the situations begin with rivalry and end in massacres, in which the weapons are either Artemis' sweet arrow or Zeus' livid thunder (*argḗs keraunós* which does bring to mind Indra's *árjuna vájra*, ṚV 3.44.5, although in this case the pressed soma is compared to the resplendent *vájra*). It must be remembered that Zeus, whom Calypso accuses of being jealous, is the one who provokes combat, consequently when all these facts are considered, the jealousy of a god is a clear prefiguration of a war confrontation. But it must be admitted that the two other usages of the term are less clear, although one of them, Od. 4.729, can be compared to imagery created around the suitors. Their nature calls for excesses and they are impelled to mislead Penelope's serving-maids, hence

the latter will be called *skhétliai* but only on another occasion. And Penelope herself is described as *skhétlia* even though the circumstances are those of a cunning stratagem by Ulysses who makes it known after the death of the suitors that the queen has transgressed the limits of decency and that she had decided not to wait for her husband to return (Od. 23. 150).

Thus, it is easy to realise that *skhétlios* has a value of a term, an element of vocabulary which is remarkable in that it denotes a situation of adversity. But, as I have tried to demonstrate, this term has a singular quality which can be called the ability to shift the discourse to which it belongs to a specific situation, and to evoke this in such a way that it is immediately transformed into a circumstance which is either of a war conflict or one which is very close to it or paves the way for it. Whatever be the circumstance, it follows the manifestation of an excessiveness or outrage. The term in question often shows only one aspect of the outcome. Whatever be the aspect, what is important is that it is indicated without any other traits of the character who will be defined *in the given circumstances.*

Moreover, since it has been said that the value of the role or the attribute of *skhétlios* was especially due to its evaluative impact, this fact seems to imply *a relationship* caused by and following a conflict between possible adversaries. It has already been seen that if the blamed and accused party is declared in some way guilty of the conflict, this is done by the opponent in his discourse, with certain rare exceptions wherein a third party indicates this name as belonging to both parties simultaneously (for example, Eumaeus in what he narrates to Ulysses).

Since this term refers to a functional relationship, it is not surprising that the adversaries become equal when viewed in the perspective indicated by this relationship.

Considering this question from the comparative aspect,

it would be worthwhile to find out how the above analysis can help in understanding the mythical and religious matter provided by ancient India.

In his *Heur et malheur du guerrier*, G. Dumézil explains that a person's becoming a warrior is a very important event which finds a special place in Indo-European mythology and legends. To express this notion briefly: one *becomes* a warrior and acquires this attribute after a series of various kinds of feats and deeds which are either for the initiation of the young warrior, or for his promotion in his military career.

But in the Indo-European world, the warrior is often portrayed by virtue of his special role of defender of what Indo-Iranian calls *kṣatrá* (Avestan *xšathra*). It is not certain that these terms, attested as they have been in the oldest Indo-European, as well as, with modification, in Iranian languages less archaic than those of the Ṛgveda and the Avesta, refer exclusively to the notion of the grace of the king, the supreme chief of warriors, or of the *Herrschaftsmacht* conferred on him by other gods or other groups of noblemen authorised by the gods (this is the main idea of B. Schlerath, *Das Königtum im Rig- und Atharvaveda*, 1960, pp. 126-127). Although it is conceded that in ṚV 1.157.2, *kṣatrá-* means the land sprinkled with honey and melted butter, and over which the king has absolute dominion, B. Schlerath tends to consider this an exceptional case. The notion of the empire, the protected and governed territory, is generally believed to be associated with the Iranian term, solely so, at a period of time only particular to Iranians (see also Benveniste, *Vocabulaire des institutions*, II, p. 17 ff.). Now, in the Ṛgveda as well as the Atharvaveda, the Indian term has a meaning in which one can easily see this same spatial component which Benveniste attributed solely to the late Iranian period.

Without furnishing detailed proof, I will only point out that, at least in the Vedic usage, *kṣatrá-* is clearly identical to another term which designates both sovereignty and the kingdom, i.e., *rāṣṭrá-*. This can be seen in a poetic and rhythmic phrase in which the two terms have a revelatory closeness, AV 10.3.12 *rāṣṭrám ca kṣatrám* followed by another pair of notions *paśū́n ójaś ca (me dadhat)* "May it confer on me power and cattle", so much so that the composition of the verse reveals its main idea: the wooden amulet is supposed to guarantee two pairs of wealth whose names are so distributed in the syntax as to form a significant balance of notions.[21] It can be accepted that the phrase of the AV quoted above (*rāṣṭrám ca kṣatrám ca dhā-*) is comparable to a whole series of expressions mentioned by Schlerath (*Das Königtum. . . .*, pp. 129-130), which include the two Indo-Iranian terms, Ved. *kṣatrá-* and Av. *xšathra-* in the accusative governed by a verb. Schlerath acknowledges the Indo-Iranian nature of these expressions (p. 129) but on p. 131 he maintains that for the Iranian term "Herrschaft" has been slipped in for "Reich". However, Benveniste mentions that in the linguistic history of Iranian, from the Avestan term *xšathra-* to the Old Persian *hšaça* which is an extension of the same, the basic ambiguity has existed since ancient times—the two expressions stand for "both the power and the area over which this power is exercised, royalty and the realm".[22] In fact, the charisma of royalty, the "Herrschaftsmacht" of Schlerath, and the physical spatial aspect of *kṣatrá-/xšathra* do not exclude each other but, on the contrary, presuppose each other reciprocally. It can be believed that Old Persian *hšaçapāvan* "who defends the realm", based on Skr. *kṣatrapa* having the same meaning (in which can be seen a compound based on a hypothetical turn similar to the ones quoted by Schlerath, that is, **kṣatrám pā-*),[23] reproduces the old model known in Vedic mythology, but the way followed cannot be traced.

For not only does this non-attested expression which means "to protect, to defend k."[24] correspond to actually attested expressions in Indo-Iranian (*kṣatrám̥ dhar-* "maintain k.", *kṣatrám vardh-* "to invigorate k.", *kṣatrám dhā-* "to provide with k.", [25] *kṣatrám̥ van-* "confer k., put k. at the disposal of", *kṣatrám āp-*, *kṣatrám aś-*, *kṣatrám̥ naś-* "to attain k.", *kṣatrám̥ bhar-* "to carry or bear k.", and also a more obscure case *kṣatrám ukṣ/vakṣ*[26] "sprinkle water on, make k. grow", but it also represents a clear parallel of the Ṛgveda texts that deal with an important trait of the Vedic divinities. Summarised as "to embrace all that exists",[27] this trait is expressed by a series of Vedic verbs of which a few are: *vyac-*, *pari bhū-* and *cakṣ-* meaning in the Ṛgveda the actions of "embracing, encircling, surrounding etc.", with a specification for the last verb which holds one's attention:the preverbs *abhi-*, *ava-*, *sam-* modify its meaning and this verb comes to mean "embrace with the look" [(cf. Renou, *Ét. véd. et pāṇ.*, V, and ṚV 7.60.3, see also ṚV 9.97.33, 10.85, 18, 10.139. 2 of which the last two among others speak of the god Sūrya, the sun who embraces with his look all beings, or, with this apparent restriction, all men (*nṛcákṣas*)]. This theme of the look is all the more important as the sun is also said to watch over the firmament (*pāti nā́kam*, ṚV 4.13.5), as an unknown god is said to defend the boundaries of the Universe (ṚV 5.47.3 *pāty ántau*), which is akin to the concept of the king, defender of his people and territory. These last two include each other and the Vedic kings as well as the sovereign gods are protectors and defenders of the communities and the space occupied by them. The functions they exercise are such that they resemble those of a pastor of human beings (despite what Schlerath has to say about this).[28] In this perspective, Vedic expressions such as *jánasya gopā́* or *bhúvanasya gopā́* (see again the reflections of Schlerath who sees no relationship between the king and the keeper of cows) can also be compared to Skr. *kṣatrapa-*. The object to be protected would thus be both a human entity, merging with the territory it occupies[29] and, following a comprehensible abstraction (but is it as ancient, as Schlerath believes, stressing as he does on the royal charisma?), the very principle that ensures the power over the object which thus becomes multiple. But this multiplication seems to be situated only at the end of a long route which would be easier to explain on the basis of a primitive and territorial meaning, which cannot be separated from the meaning which is closely associated with it, the one which refers to a human community (which in the Vedic view was identified with the mass of cattle). Thus when the Vedic *kṣatrá-* has to be translated either by "temporal power" or "principle of the warrior function"[30], one can remember that these notions are the result of a semantic development whose starting point was situated around spatial notions. If these did not originate from Vedic ritual, they perhaps had a known counterpart in them.

In fact, three royal rituals assign an important value to the Vedic king's affirmation of his supremacy and his power considered triply in relation to: the royal family (the social group of his origin, explains Dumézil), the other social classes, finally, kings of foreign lands. What links these three rituals (here, I continue to refer to the reflections of Dumézil who found a common denominator) is that each of them, either in their preparation or in their execution, includes a set of gestures by which the king or a king-aspirant ensures pre-eminence for himself, and the essential element in them is moving across a space. Whether this is imaginary and fictitious (as in the *rājasūya* ritual, in which the king goes forth on his chariot into the midst of the cows belonging to his blood relations, thereby dispossessing them as a rival), or real but symbolic (as in the *vājapeya* in which the king wins a chariot race and in the *aśvamedha* in which the royal steed runs through foreign lands), this space is traversed by the king who seeks to drive out his existing or possible enemies outside its boundaries. It matters very little that in the *rājasūya* as well as in the *vājapeya*, the chariot or chariots start off from the same point to which they come back after the course is over. Although it is associated with the renovation of the universe,[31] the king's course like the horse's in the *aśvamedha*, is required to demarcate the spatial zone over which the royal power will extend and into which those who try to threaten the king and his "charysma" in one way or the other are prevented from entering.

The concept of the *kṣatrá-* endowed with royal and warrior features, for the two cannot be dissociated, implies a fundamental notion: the status of king, chief of the *kṣatriya* has to be regularly affirmed and re-affirmed. These various kinds of manifestations of the royal character are the outcome of acts of rivalry which are close, if not identical to those which are usually subsumed under "warrior acts". In fact, the former can be considered as more general and comprehensive than the latter. Of course, in rituals the models established by acts of war are followed with conviction all the more because the ritual itself is an imitation of a confrontation between two parties, each of whom pursues a goal and tries to obtain what the other has and refuses to yield. The details of Vedic rituals, as seen by Dumézil, have the advantage of revealing the fundamental element of the quest of the Vedic king, the spatial component of his aspirations very clearly expressed by the very practice of the rituals, for the movements of the person or persons are not only factors of strategy, but are also significant by themselves.

It is well-known how much importance is given to signs of spatial orientation in socio-cultural human systems, and this is yet another example supporting this commonly accepted but insufficiently researched observation of expressly significant human behaviour. These signs seem to crown a number of others so that when considering the benefits to which the Vedic king aspired, it will be easy to speak of the social value and importance of space. Consequently it is impossible to imagine how the temporal power of the king or his "charysma" could be established without this extension of the principal features of the warrior king's rituals. It is significant that the more abstract aspects of the king (that is, more abstract in relation to the underlying spatial oppositions) fail him at the moment when he is about to make a foray into the herd of cows belonging to his rival kin, and that it is in order to regain the attribute that is known as *indriyáṃ vīryàm* "vigour, Indrian energy" in the Śatapatha Brāhmaṇa as well as in other sources (Dumézil in *Fêtes romaines*, p. 122 explains these terms as "the force of the nature of Indra") that this foray is made. The same text says (ŚB 5.4.3.10-11, see Dumézil, *ibid.*, pp. 122-123) "as for the reason why he goes forth in the midst of the cows belonging to his *sva*, (it is) that everything which goes out of a man, whether it is his glory *(yáśaḥ)* or anything else, passes into his *sva*, as if preferentially. This energy, this vigour, he therefore takes them back for himself from his *sva*. That is why he stops in the midst of the cows belonging to his *sva*". Can it be accepted that the movement of the king from one place to the other is only a manifest expression of the act of recovering the values that he fears he will lose (and that he pretends to lose, since there is a great importance given to simulation in rituals)? This act is only an expression, but it is significant by what it indicates in itself, that is, the perseverance of the king who is anxious to safeguard the essential values that he is sure to possess once he demarcates and enlarges his own personal space. Here, I have only alluded to details of the *rājasūya*, but the same importance given to space can be shown in the two other royal Vedic rituals.

Thus, the creation or the promotion of the king in Vedic India seems to correspond by its very nature to the identical concern of the Indo-European warrior.

The major tendencies in his becoming so seem to comprise a moving forward signifying the keeping up or conquest of values, judging by the characteristic traits of the one who is presented as the functional rival in Greek epics. These tendencies also correspond to the deliberate excessiveness in which the Vedic king indulges even more obstinately, for that alone ensures the affirmation of his own essence. This leads to the Homeric hero who appears in situations of conflict modelled on those of war and to Vedic kings. The two can be compared easily by virtue of their natural tendency and also the tasks they are forced to take on because of their anxiety to affirm their own nature. No doubt there are also differences, which the comparatist cannot ignore, whether they are due to the method or the modalities of the presentation of the two notions, and this is an important circumstance. One of them, as has already been seen, appears through a discourse, speech in its proper sense, which only shows the hero according to the possibilities presented by the epic situations. The other notion, on the contrary, is found in the very core of the rituals so devised as to show its significance. And the discourse of the ritual, just as that of its scenario, is hardly equivocal, as opposed to the epic in which a considerable number of situations are put together, and only a few of them can be reduced to a possible ritual scenario, and even so, they are left in suspense and incomplete.

Consequent to this comparison, certain reflections make themselves clear regarding the principle of comparative study, which is like a path that leads from one field to another, and on the way, the recognised elements of comparison are confronted. But the same path can be retraced with light shed on it by corrections brought about by new facets in any one field which can be found in another. I would like to mention in this way the principles of comparison found in the works of Dumézil. From numerous passages, I choose one which I think particularly significant: "comparison appears only in filigree. The various methods and earlier results of comparison bring about the problem which thus acquires a meaning in the whole of which it is a part".[34] Comparatism, at least in the Indo-European field, goes beyond the juxtaposition of linguistic forms which correspond to a content, when the search for concepts begins. Among the Indo-Europeans, there must have been a common heritage of concepts and ideas which goes beyond correspondence of forms. It would perhaps be unnecessary to repeat this principle,[35] if the case studied in the preceding pages did not show this special relationship of two *different* linguistic forms to an *identical* concept. Reducing them to a common original form is strictly excluded, but comparatism must not stop at the irreductability of the form, for there exists a more complex universe beyond isolated forms. It is here that one should look for correspondences which could offer possibilities for further research on correspondences, not of isolated forms, but of more important elements (sentences, groups of sentences, etc.). From these elements one should move backwards into concepts which have been pointers to the beginning of research in correspondences which would perfect the conceptual presentation of the Indo-European world.

But this is a vast problem which has presented itself frequently in recent times.[36] It has also been emphasised that in the search for common mythological types (what I have here referred to as facts of mythological discourses), the functional identity considered outside the language forms can be useful only if one seeks to establish typological convergences which can certainly go beyond the context of the Indo-European world, thus transcending the genetic relationships of Indo-European mythology. The case just studied here has every chance of belonging to this kind of parallel, but the few instances of resemblance between lexical formulae seem to support the hypothesis that the type of Indo-European warrior probably existed on two planes simultaneously, one suggesting the common traits that were attributed to him, and the other being reflected in the usage of the language without having a common name.

REFERENCES

1. Franklin E. Horowitz, *Greek, skhétlios, Sanskrit* kṣatríyaḥ *and the Indo-European Image of the warrior.*
2. In fact the relationship of the Sanskrit verbal and nominal theme *háva-* to the root *hū-, hvā-* "to invoke, to call" is not quite obvious, since another root *hu-* "to pour, to offer" can also be taken into account if one maintains that *hotṛ́-* is the *ho-* form derived from *hu-* and not from *hū-* and if one follows the reasoning of J. Manessy (*Les substantifs en* -as *dans la Ṛk-Saṃhitā,* Paris, 1961, pp. 169-170), according to which *havás* "invocation" should be dissociated from the family of words to which Sk. *havís* "oblation" belongs. See the detailed discussion in A. Minard, *Trois énigmes sur les cent chemins,* I, Paris, 1949, 346a and in the second volume of the above-mentioned work, 265b.
3. J. Puhvel, *The Warrior at Stake* in *Homage to Georges Dumézil* (JIES Monograph, No. 3, 1982), p. 32 however seems to endorse Horowitz' findings; in any case, he refers to his essay without adding any criticism.
4. These suggestions are from C. Scott Littleton, *Some Possible Indo-European Themes in the "Iliad"* in J. Puhvel (ed.), *Myth and Law among the Indo-Europeans,* University of Califòrnia Press, 1970, p. 236. The author closely follows S. Wikander, *Nakula and Sahadeva,* in *Orientalia Suecana,* 6, 1957 and tries to situate the two Greek heroes in the conceptual plan of G. Dumézil. Even if his explanation of what he calls "the metathesis", in fact, the exchange between the mythological matter and the names which depict it, is not perfectly convincing, it is useful as an example of the usage of linguistic elements which have changed their sphere of connotation. For the two pairs to be accepted as identical, it would be preferable to have more precise references than the ones in Iliad, 6. 506-512 in which Paris is compared to a stallion whereas Nakula disguises himself as a groom when it is necessary.
5. After G. Dumézil, this term is studied in the work of Ch. Malamoud, *Manyúḥ svayambhûḥ* in *Mélanges d'Indianisme à la mémoire de L. Renou,* Paris, 1968, see especially p. 497, note 7.
6. For this rite, P.E. Dumont, *L'Aśvamedha,* Paris, 1962, p. 208, and,

in the Indo-European perspective, G. Dumézil, *Tarpeia*, 1947, pp. 133-138; *Rituels indo-européens à Rome*, p. 8 and other works of the same author.

7. In the translation of the Ṛgveda hymn X.83 analysed by G. Dumézil *Jupiter Mars Quirinus IV* ("Un hymne à Manyu"). L. Renou, *Études védiques et pāṇinéennes*, XV, Paris, p. 172 ff., renders *ójas-* and *sáhas-* differentially as "enormous-power" and "dominating-power" respectively.
8. According to the observations of E. Brunius-Nilsson, *Daimonie. An Inquiry into a Mode of Apostrophe in Old Greek Literature*, Uppsala, 1955.
9. E. Benveniste, *Noms d'agent et noms d'action en indo-européen*, Paris, 1948, p. 62 and more recently J.P. Vernant, *Catégories de l'agent et de l'action en Grèce ancienne*, in *Langue, discours, société. Pour Émile Benveniste*, Paris, 1975, pp. 365-366, cf. 368. It would appear that the presence of such a noun is the condition for the analysis undertaken by Horowitz to be perfectly satisfactory; but Skt. *kṣatríya* is obviously not an agent noun.
10. At least, this is Geoffrey S. Kirk's opinion, *War and the Warrior in the Homeric Poems*, in *Problèmes de la guerre en Grèce ancienne* (edited by J.P. Vernant), Paris—The Hague, 1968, pp. 115-116.
11. G.S. Kirk, *War and the Warrior in the Homeric Poems*, p. 113.
12. For a quick but instructive summary, see also G. Dumézil, *Les rois romains de Cicéron* in G. Dumézil, *Idées romaines*, Paris, 1969.
13. One does not readily admit an Indo-European origin to the Vedic *reṇú* (IE. **e/or-* enlarged by *nu-*) "dust", see Mayrhofer, *Kurzgefasstes etym. Wb. d. Ai.*, III, p. 73.
14. In other Indo-European languages, direct and indirect evidence shows that phrases were easily adopted to express the idea "to think of combat, to cause the combat" or "desire the combat" and "create the combat". Some examples: according to I. Gershevitch, *Amber at Persepolis* in *Studia Classica et Orientalia Antonino Pagliaro Oblata*, II, 1969, p. 228, the Elamite probably has conserved an ancient Iranian proper noun **razma- čana* "desiring the combat", cf. p. 246 for another hypothetical proper noun **yauda-manah*, "who thinks of the combat", in which are found the Iranian reflexes of two epithets of Indra *yudhmá-* "combatant" and *manyumáttama* "possessor of the greatest warlike fury", and in which can be recognised the same term *manyú* discussed above. If Il.3. 7 says *kakén érida prophérontoi* "they (the Trojan army) propose a combat with no quarter", the Phrygian inscriptions of conjuration often have the corresponding phrase *kakoun addaket* or *kakoun abberet* "(who) will use violence" or "(who) will bear violence" respectively, their equivalents in Greek inscriptions being close to the Homeric expression *kakà phérein tiní* (Il.2. 304), cf.

kakón ti prospoieîn (O. Haas *Die phrygischen Sprachdenkmäler*, Sofia, 1966, pp. 80-81); note the identity of Phrygian phrases and the expressions in the Iliad supported by etymology: *abbaret = ad+beret* cf. Skt. *bhar-* "carry", Gr. *phérō*. See also Indra *khajakṛ́t* and *ājikṛ́t* "creator of combat" as well as the derivatives in **er-* in Sanskrit which have acquired the meaning "hostile agression": *ṛtī-ṣáh-* "triumphing over the aggression", *irasy-* "to be wickedly jealous" ("neidisch sein", Grassmann), *íṛṣya-* same meaning, cf. Av. *arəšyant*. In Old Slavic, the proper names such as **Ratibor*, with its Old Slavic elements *rat'* "combat", related to Skt. *ṛti* "attack", Av. *ərəti* "energy" and **bor*, action noun of the Old Slavic verb *brati* "to combat, to wage war", or such as **Ratimil* "to whom the combat is dear", perhaps attest the same effort to create phrases having similar meanings to the one being studied.

The same line of thought can be applied to information available in Ossete folklore. In the Iron dialect, there is a hero named Tyxost or Tuxwast as he is known in Digor. Tyxost/Tuxwast has as first member the word *tyx* (or *tux, tuxä*; this is how the word is transcribed by V. Miller *Jazyk osetin*, Moscow-Leningrad, 1962, p. 34 who stresses the absolute ending in *a (oe)* thus differentiating between the two Ossete dialects, for only the Digor dialect uses it]; this is the Av. root *tav-*, Ved. *távasvant* "strong", related to the IE.* *tū* "to swell" (Pokorny, *Idg. et. Wb.*, p. 1080); the second element is *wac-/ w̄az-* "speech" in which can be found the Iranian **vāc* (Ved. *vā́c-*). The hero resembles Vedic Indra, not only because he is a fighting god but also because his speciality is to rush to the aid of those whom he protects when they are attacked by their enemies and call out to him for help, cf. ṚV 4.42.5 quoted earlier. In his *Romans de Scythie et d'alentour*, Paris 1978, p. 72, G. Dumézil says, "it is this attribute that made him worthy of . . . . . . the genius of . . . *foedīs (foedes)*"; according to V. Abaev, *Istoriko-etimilogičeskij slovar' osetinskogo jazyka*, I, 1958, p. 429, this word means "alarm, pursuit", "all the people who go to the place of alarm"; the primary meaning of this word would be (according to Abaev, *ibid.*) "pursuit by the traces", and refers to alarm raised during war attacks. Once it has been established that this word belongs to the vocabulary of war and war-hunts, it is very suggestive that in Ossete folklore are found the expressions *foedīsy coewyn, foedīsy acydysty* translated by Abaev as "to go to the alarm", "they went to the alarm" (I have quoted from the same page of Abaev's dictionary). These translations are justified considering the modern language, but the very construction allows for the following reflections. In his *Études sur la langue ossète*, 1959, pp. 22-25, and *Titres et noms propres en iranien ancien*, 1961, p. 123, É. Benveniste has established that the meaning of the Ossete verb *caewyn (caeun)*"to go"—and probably other meanings too as attested by Abaev, p. 307—came only much later in the evolution of Iranian to Ossete which took place in such a way that from the Iranian **čyav-* to the Avestan *šyav-*, the semantics changed from "set in motion, shake up" to "to go"; there were intermediate stages in this evolution, for in Gathic Avestan, the meaning of *šyav-* was first "to undertake, to accomplish", and in so-called recent Avestan, *šav-* means "to start off" which finally becomes "to go". Thus it is in Iranian dialect, continued by Ossete, that *čyav-* maintained its etymological meaning the longest before limiting itself to the notion of "going" (É. Benveniste, *Etudes sur la langue ossète,* p. 25). Further, it was only after this semantic and formal evolution that the ancient Iranian verb could no longer be used in transitive constructions (*Titres et noms propres en iranien ancien,* p. 123). By reconstituting the primitive meaning of the Ossete construction *foedīsy coewyn* which contains the verb and the noun in the inessive case, a very clear parallel can be seen in these Vedic constructions in which Indra shakes up men so that they fight (see ṚV 2.21.3 which says of Indra *janabhakṣó janaṃsáhā́ś cyávano yudhmó... vṛtámcayáḥ* " (he) who devours men, who triumphs over men, who shakes up, who fights, who gathers the armies" (Renou, *EVP,* Vol. XVII, p. 67); add the translation of *sáhurir* "who dominates", revealing the social value of the warrior-god), cf. also *aj- vṛt-* "urge the army to fight" in ṚV 1.174.3 (hymn to Indra). The Vedic has the compound *pṛtanā́j* whose meaning becomes clear as it contains the vestiges of the ancient phrase corresponding to "create the combat". Like its derivative *pṛtanā́jya* "war race" this compound is based on **āj-pṛtanām* (non-attested) cf. however *sam-āj- spṛ́dhaḥ* "urge to face-to-face combat" (ṚV 6.25.9). Indeed Benveniste has pointed out that, contrary to the Avestan in which is found the construction *pəšana az-* "wage battle" (Yt. 9.30 and Yt. 13.37), the Vedic retains only a vestige in the shape of the compound (É. Benveniste, *Phraséologie poétique de l'indo-iranien* in *Mélanges à la mémoire de L. Renou,* pp. 74-75). It can thus be considered that the compounding process translates the formular meaning of the phrase attested in Avestan.

15. F. Vian, *La fonction guerrière dans la mythologie grecque* in *Problèmes de la guerre en Grèce ancienne,* pp. 57-58, cf. Jupiter Feretrius of the Romans who gives victory not by direct intervention (he never fights) but by throwing the enemy forces into disarray (G. Dumézil, *Les dieux des Indo-Européens,* Paris, 1952, p. 28).
16. In fact, *mēdomai érgon* means "to be preoccupied with feats", "to premeditate on feats", with the idea of the ancient verb **med-* whose primary meaning "take. . . the measures necessary for a

present difficulty, bring back to normal. . . a definite trouble" was noted by É. Benveniste (*Vocabulaire des institutions,* II, p. 129). In the Iliad, *médomai,* doublet of *mēdomai* is also used to mean "to be preoccupied with the fight", "to think of resisting valiantly" (É. Benveniste, pp. 128-129). It can be considered that Achilles disapproves of the fact that Ulysses, by going down into Hades, has gone beyond the measure of antagonism between the world of the living and that of the dead.

17. Cf. J. Irmscher, *Götterzorn bei Homer,* Leipzig, 1930, p. 13.
18. *skhétli' epeì xeínous oukh'ázeo...esthémenai* (Od. 9. 478-479) and other examples have been interpreted by A. Cheyns, *La signification religieuse du verbe* ázomai *dans les poèmes homériques* in *Travaux de la faculté de philologie et lettres de l'Université catholique de Louvain III. Recherche de philologie et de linguistique,* 2nd series, Louvain, 1968, pp. 129-134. In the song 5 of the Iliad, the idea of not respecting somebody, expressed by negative constructions using the verb *ázomai* is related to the idea of excessiveness and insolence that can take a human hero, for example, beyond human limits (pp. 114-115); on the other hand, no respect is given to Ares, the god of War, since his exactions are hostile to men. This hostility, whatever form it may take, leads to the necessary over-stepping of usual norms.

    Further, it has been noted that the action of Polyphemus who devours Ulysses' companions, is parallel to the threatening acts of revenge by enemies of the heroes and gods of the Iliad, among whom can be recognised the war heroes (Hera, Hector, Achilles); threatening to devour someone (or devour his liver, see Il.24.212-213, as Hecuba says of Achilles) is considered in the works of Homer as the promise of an extreme act, bordering on barbarism (see S.L. Schein, *Odysseus and Polyphemous in the Odyssey* in *Greek, Roman and Byzantine studies,* Vol. ii, 1970, n. 2). Another passage of the Odyssey (an interpolated one, according to V. Bérard), 21.26-30, makes Herakles into a *skhétlios* because he kills his host Iphitus without respecting divine providence or his guest's table. According to G. Dumézil, *Heur et malheur du guerrier,* Paris, 1969, pp. 91-92), this crime of Herakles would be the one which characterises the hero as a person having a warrior role, and compares him to Vedic Indra.
19. T.K. Dasgupta, *Der Vajra. Eine vedische Waffe,* Wiesbaden, 1975, p. 16, for a discussion about Indra's weapon.
20. I refer to the third chapter of G. Dumézil's *Heur et malheur,* pp. 103-104 in particular. The importance of initiation into a larger social sphere is also highlighted by J.P. Vernant in his Introduction to *Problèmes de la guerre en Grèce ancienne,* pp. 14-16.
21. This is perhaps a reply of an archaic procedure of Indo-European

poetry technique by which a couple of elements were linked by the particle *$k^w e$ but in other conditions. Regarding the inherited nature of constructions using this particle, see R. Schmitt, *Dichtung und Dichtersprache in indogermanischer Zeit*, Wiesbaden, 1967, pp. 269-272.

22. É. Benveniste, *Vocabulaire des institutions indo-européennes*, II, pp. 19-22. For the notation of Old Persian, see M. Mayrhofer-W. Brandenstein, *Handbuch des Altpersischen*, Wiesbaden, 1964, p. 126.
23. M. Mayrhofer, *Kurgefasstes etym. Wörterbuch d. Altindischen*, I, p. 284 and M. Mayrhofer-W. Brandenstein, *Handbuch des Altpersischen*, p. 126.
24. But in ṚV 1.136.3 is found *jyótiṣmat kṣatrám āśāte adityā́ dā́nunas pátī* "they have attained the luminous k., the two Āditvas, protectors (possessors) of the (celestial) gift". The proposed translation is closer to Geldner's in *Der Rig-Veda*, I, Teil, Cambridge, Mass, 1951 than to Renou's in *Ét. véd. et pāṇ.*, Vol. V, p. 75. The former's translation is "sie haben die lichtreiche Herrschaft erreicht, die beiden Ā., die Herren des (Himmels)-gabe" with the "celestial gift" explained as "rain", and seems to give a better understanding of the contents of the verse: those who have made themselves the protectors of the gift have done so thanks to their mastery of the field which dispenses this gift. This favours the hypothesis that this line represents an echo of **kṣatrám pā* (note that in the series of Indo-Iranian clichés given according to Schlerath, the verbs have a reconstructed form known as "arisch").
25. The translations vary: "verleihen, gewähren" (Geldner), "to exercise" (Renou). Schlerath, *Königtum...*, p. 130 feels that in Avestan *xšathram dā-* corresponds to "arisch" *kṣatrám dhā-*.
26. According to C. Kiehnle, *Vedisch* ukṣ *und* ukṣ/vakṣ, Wiesbaden, 1979, p. 144 the Avestan parallel Y. 31.6 *xšathrəm vaxšat* imposes the choice of the translation "make the k. grow".
27. See B. Oguibénine, *Structure d'un mythe védique*, Paris—The Hague, 1973, pp. 89-101.
28. I have explained this: *Structure d'un mythe védique*, pp. 123-130.
29. As is also the case with another socio-religious Vedic term *vṛjána* which originally indicated a territory which contains a social group, and could therefore indicate a social group or a religious sect (see Renou, *Ét. véd. et pāṇ.*, III, pp. 19-20 and IV, p. 69). As an analogy, I refer to my study *Un modèle conceptuel pour l'étymologie du slave commun* vorgŭ *'ennemi'* in *IJSLP*, 23, 1981, pp. 13-23, in which is recalled the related and close term *vrajá* which has a collective value and stands for the enclosure as well as the herd of cows. It is also possible to show that the *rāṣṭra* of a *kṣatríya* ("the realm of a warrior-king") also extends to the meaning of the mass, the totality of the royal subjects, ṚV 4.42.1: *máma* . . .

rāṣṭrám kṣatríyasya "it is to me that... the temporal-realm (belongs), to me, the temporal chief", followed by an explanation: *rā́jāmi kṛṣṭér upamásya vavréḥ*" I reign over the people of the highest stratum" (Renou, *Ét véd. et pāṇ.* V, p. 97, cf. *Ét. véd et pāṇ.* VII, p. 78 on the relationship between *kṣatríya* and sovereignty). Despite the translation proposed by Schlerath, p. 42 ("Ich herrsche über das Volk der obersten Hülle=der Erdoberfläche"), it would be tempting to relate this highest stratum to what the Ṛgveda itself refers to as *(kṣayád) vīra-* "(Herr uber seine) Mannen" (Schlerath, pp. 13 ff. and p. 124), and the Greek as *etaîroi*, the acolytes closest to a warrior chief, his companions at arms (and at the table in Homer).

30. G. Dumézil, *Les dieux souverains des Indo-Européens*, Paris, 1977, pp. 74 and 76.
31. G. Dumézil, *Fêtes romaines d'été et d'automne*, Paris, 1975, pp. 115-138, cf. some remarks made after this study of royal rituals by which god Indra's hostile acts are related to a primitive form of rituals that are subsequently more elaborate, in my summary of the conference of 1975-76 (*Annuaire de l'École Pratique des Hautes Études, Sciences Religieuses*, Vol. LXXXIV, pp. 205-209).
32. J.C. Heesterman, *The Ancient Indian Royal Consecration*, 's-Gravenhage, 1957, pp. 133-135.
33. I refer to a very enlightening study on the preponderance of spatial oppositions in universal models created from systems of human signs: T.V. Tsivjan, *O nekotoryx sposobax otraženija oppozicii vnutrennij/vnešnij* in *Strukturno-tipologičeskije issledovanija v oblasti grammatiki slavjanskix jazykov*, Moscow, 1973, pp. 242-261.
34. G. Dumézil, *Tarpeia. Essai de philologie comparative indo-européenne*, Paris, 1947, p. 12.
35. Reaffirmed with supporting examples by E. Campanile, *Studi di cultura celtica e indoeuropea*, Pisa, 1981, pp. 19-20.
36. I am particularly reminded of V.N. Toporov's review of *Indo-European and Indo-Europeans: Papers presented at the Third Indo-European Conference at the University of Pennsylvania*, published by G. Cardona et al, Philadelphia, University of Pennsylvania Press, 1970 (*International Journal of Slavic Linguistics and Poetics*, 1975, pp. 71-89).

CHAPTER 2

Aspects of Sacrifice in the Ṛgveda

2.1. Structure and Expression of Conflict Between the Sacrificer and the non-Sacrificer

2.1.1. The Role of Indra, the Warrior God

When dealing with gods the Vedic man believed that he belonged to a privileged species which was defined by its opposition to another species namely, the non-sacrificers. This is because, in his eyes, sacrifice was the focal point of the life of a pious man who had to multiply signs of his devotion to gods, but a pious man who could outdo his peers, rivals and especially his enemies. Numerous instances have been found to which very little attention has been paid in the explanations of Vedic religious values: the Vedic sacrificer's adversary, his competitor and his rival whom he has to combat in order to satisfy (*juṣ-*) or invigorate (*vṛdh-*) his deities are often confounded with his enemy. One thing should however be made clear: this deliberate confusion is the product of his desire to distinguish his species from an openly hostile one; what is more, it is proof of his concern for imparting greater purpose to the sacrificial act conducted in a manner that will please the gods.

Two facts are of constant importance to the religious life of a group of Vedic sacrificers: the act of sacrifice by which they seek to distinguish themselves in the eyes of the gods, and the sacrifice itself which by its merits and effectiveness surpasses the sacrifice of a rival. By the former, the sacrificer distinguishes himself from a non-sacrificer and by the latter, from a less worthy sacrificer. Thus, it is all a question of degree and also something more because it allows for the unravelling of tangled values as well as metaphors which are more than the expression of these values, endowed as they are with significant religious connotations.

Let us take the case of Indra. A warrior god par excellence, he is nonetheless involved in areas which define the religious interaction between humans and gods in the Ṛgveda. This is what makes him such a fascinating study.

What follows does not aim to explain the entire nature of Indra; I will however furnish some facts that help in evaluating the religious aspect that obviously goes beyond the equally religious significance of the warrior aspect.

Indra is primarily called upon to distinguish the sacrificers from the non-sacrificers; here his role is to maintain order in an area which is not exactly identical to a war situation: "Distinguish the Aryans from the Dasyu. By thy orders let those who do not obey the laws be delivered to the one who performs the sacrifice; be strong, encourage the one who conducts the sacrifice (*bhava...yájamānasya coditā́*)! During public banquets I rejoiced in all that came from thee " (1.51.8). But this kind of involvement on the part of Indra is not without its consequences; characteristic of Vedic hymns, it merges with its other form, that of the warrior. 1.33 gives some important details which enable us to establish that the basic distinction between the sacrificers and the non-sacrificers has important consequences.

1.33.4 (As in other instances, the non-sacrificer's name is *dásyu*; this however is not his only name) "Yes, thou hast felled the rich *dásyu* with thy weapon; ... From this place, from above and below, they have dispersed in all directions; the Sanakas who do not sacrifice have gone to the beyond!"

1.33.5 "... (the Sanakas) who do not sacrifice are competing with those who do...Thou hast with thy breath blown away these lawless people from both the worlds."

1.33.7 "Thou hast fought with these hostile beings who were crying and laughing...thou hast burnt this *dásyu*... thou hast lent assistance to the song of one who presses soma, the one who praises the gods."

1.33.9 "...Thou hast won against those who do not join in the prayers of those who pray, O Indra! thou hast, with thy breath, crushed the *dásyu* by joining the brahmins."

From this brief description the following should be retained: (a) all violent acts of god are directed against the non-sacrificers who are also called the lawless people; (b) the opposition between the sacrificers and non-sacrificers is such that the mere comparison of the two is rendered by a reference to a war-like confrontation (here the verb root is *spṛdh-, spūrdh-*, which denotes the act of fighting as well as the act of competing with a rival); and (c) that god is on the side of those who practise different forms of sacrifice—they extract soma for the gods, they praise the gods with their songs or address their prayers to them.

It would be worthwhile to first examine (a) and (c) before trying to clarify the meaning of (b) which is more profound and unexpected than its usual explanation in essays dealing with the interpretation of this aspect of Vedic religion.

Moroever (a) and (c) are closely connected. In fact by citing a few examples, this kind of behaviour of a god frequently portrayed as a person solely committed to war, is as follows.

When faced with his devotee, he is reminded of his desire to destroy foes who in the conceptual system of the Ṛgveda are opposed to the sacrificers: 10.49.1 "I have given the poet the best wealth, I have created the edifying word, my strength, I have become the inciter of the sacrificer, I triumphed over the non-sacrificers in every confrontation." The characteristic feature is the grouping of Indra's actions which bring about the division of his oneness: he is at once the provider of wealth (*vásu*) desired by the poet-priest, the creator of brahman or the poetic language, the one who intervenes on behalf of the person conducting the sacrifice and lastly the powerful protector of the sacrificer (*áyajvanaḥ sākṣi* "I triumph over the non-sacrificers" says Indra; the verb is *sah-* "to defeat, to triumph over", which is very typical of this god). But this division in his oneness is only apparent. When seen from the point of view of the god himself, the creation of a discourse strengthening the gods (*várdhanam*) ensures that the officiant fulfills his duty by providing him with the means to do the same; he is also obliged to reward the poet-priest by acting through the patron of the sacrifice. The latter is encouraged by the god to be generous with the officiating poet-priest for it is by his generosity that the patron of the sacrifice is integrated into the sacrificial act. One thus sees that the act in its totality is reconstituted by its terms and basic relations—the officiating poet-priests pray, the gods prove to be liberal, the patrons of sacrifice give the dakṣiṇā to the officiants. The cohesion of the elements and the constitutive acts of the sacrifice is better defined by opposing the act to that which is both external to the sacrifice and is finally introduced in it: the fruits of the existence of the non-sacrificer, his riches that are taken away from him after a confrontation with the sacrificer.

This distinction is often highlighted and made use of, particularly when it concerns Indra's pacts which help him in warding off the non-sacrificer (5.34.5: "he does not wish to form a group of five or ten, he does not join forces with the one who does not extract soma, however wealthy he may be"). Having vanquished the non-sacrificer, Indra is generous with favours toward his devotee [further on in the same stanza: "he defeats him in his manner or kills him with his rustling breath and gives the devotee (his due) in the cow's stable"; refer to the stanza 6 of the same hymn: "He is powerful, he blocks wheels during a combat; he is hostile to the one who does not extract soma, he invigorates the one who extracts soma; Indra the master of all, the Terrifying One, the Ārya, he manipulates the dắsa to his will"]. This dắsa or the non-Ārya who does not extract soma or perform any sacrifice, who is a foreigner to the religion because of his inactivity, finds himself integrated into it inspite himself; for, in his concern to protect the sacrificer, Indra dispossesses the non-sacrificer or the miser, refer 5.34.7 "he drives the wealth (the cattle) of the miser (to herd together) to take them away from him and he gives the precious wealth to his devotee" and this, as we see in numerous examples, is naturally for the benefit of the sacrificer. What is most characteristic of Indra is that it is rare for the dispossession of the non-sacrificer to take place without reference to a conflict; we have two more examples to add to 5.34.7 in which the robbery is only a mitigated version of a conflict.

1.81.9 "O Indra, here are the people who make swell the best possessions for thee. But thou canst perceive the wealth of the people and of the chief; bring us the wealth of the people who do not honour thee.!"

7.19.1 "Indra is he who offers the wealth of each one who does not honour (the gods); thou givest this wealth to one who extracts soma best." Refer also 8.45.14d and 15.

(b) Often however the integration of the non-sacrificer into the sacrificial process is necessary because, as much as the other elements, it is intended to ensure the smooth conduct of the sacrifice; and this is accomplished through violence: Indra is then exhorted to kill "those who do not extract soma and uproot the misers who are not willing to give" (6.44.11) to kill the non-sacrificer who is accessible only when dispossessed and finally to behave towards him like a highway robber who robs the rich.

However as Indra's violence makes, in its own way, a distinction between the sacrificer and the non-sacrificer, it finds its echo and in fact its use during conflicts revolving around the essential object of contention in confrontations described in the Ṛgveda i.e. cattle. An apparently war-like conflict in which Indra the god of war intervenes, but since of the two parties only one gains the benefit of Indra's alliance and since its thematic framework suggests that the poet-priest is deeply involved, there seems to be very little doubt over the specific religious aspect of the conflict. This is the case where the generous Indra has to favour two prosperous but warring groups, "the two groups being fully provided with troops..., he makes one of them his ally, he the Terrible, aided by his warriors and with a thundering sound, makes the (other's) herd come out [of the stable]" (5.34.8) and where according to stanza 9, the poet-priest proclaims himself to be the defender of his patron Śatri Āgniveśi. Geldner (*Der Ṛgveda*, II, p. 34) rightly points out that the people (or the group) chosen by Indra as his allies have the advantage of the intervention of the god on behalf of his group and that the scene is like a battle between two tribes. But given the necessity of sharing the disputed wealth and particularly, given Indra's obligation to join one of the two groups and given the fact that the poet-priest anticipates his share by virtue of his recourse to a dānastuti (a reminder of the credit that goes to him in any sacrificial act) the benefit of this distinction and this alliance going to the sacrificer and not the non-sacrificer should not pose any problem.

In other words, if in a conflict between two parties, Indra enriches one through the riches of the other, the beneficiary of these riches (i.e. the sacrificer) is undoubtedly the one who takes for his own the possessions of the impious.

Since we are talking about the type of conflicts that take place to ensure the successful completion of the sacrificial act (for that is their fundamental aim) it would be useful to compare the presentation of the conflicts in the hymns 1.131 and 2.23.

We will be able to clearly see the structure of the conflict, a structure that moreover we will have no difficulty in recognising as a constant that is reproduced at times when it is necessary to evaluate the obviously forced participation of a non-sacrificer in the sacrifice as compared to a sacrificer protected by a god. I will first give the entire contents of the first hymn 1.131 in an analytical form:

1. The Sky and the Great Earth have paid homage to Indra; all gods make Indra their chief. He shall receive all the soma-juice as well as the offerings, both being the fruit of human effort.

2. When extracting the soma, men wishing to attain their share of the supreme wealth[1] attack Indra; these men are *vṛ́ṣamaṇyavaḥ* "who are inflamed with the fury of a bull" (they thus seek to imitate the ancient exploit of Indra himself. See Renou, *Sur quelques mots du Ṛgveda*, p. 84). Sacrificers who compare themselves to Āyu (another reference to the ancient times) wish to make the god the theme of their song of praise, a way of saying that it is to him that the hymns are addressed.

3. Warring pairs of combatants fight over Indra: they seek his favours and would like to reach the enclosure where the cows are kept. At that moment Indra takes a hand—he joins the two groups of humans who are on the quest of the supreme wealth i.e. the herd of cows (*yád gavyántā dvā́ jánā svàr yántā samū́hasi*).

Though it may pose a few problems and despite Geldner's reservations, the verb *sam-ūhati* belongs to the war vocabulary. Let us consider the stanza following the one that dwells on the war-like nature of the conflict between the opposing parties thrown against one another by Indra, the mediator (Geldner admits this). It says: *āvíṣ kárikrad vṛ́ṣaṇaṃ sacābhúvaṃ vájram indra sacābhúvam* "(you bring them together for the confrontation) by openly and powerfully brandishing thy taurean vajra that is thy companion, O Indra, thy companion". The war context is undisputable particularly because of the mention of Indra's weapon.[2] It appears that the translations of Renou and Geldner are not accurate enough because these authors have apparently thought of gatherings where no conflict is involved (Renou: "Thou gatherest the two clans, the seekers of the cows who are leaving (to conquer) the sun"; Geldner: "da du die zwei auf Rinder ausziehenden Völker, die in (denKampfum) die Sonne ziehen, zusammenbringst").

The context clearly confirms that it does indeed have to do with the confrontation of adversaries with conflicting interests: Indra helps one of them in a war that has at least two principal features: it is fought against an adversary (which is obviously a common point) and what is more specific to the *samohá* warriors, it is fought with the intention of enriching Indra's favourites. It is remarkable that among Indra's favourites is the sacrificer or his double, the poet-priest. It is enough to see the *samohá* mise-en-scènes: we will see that it concerns a group of facts governed by a rigorous logic where details do not appear at random.

Using figurative language 1.8.6 says that the men (the warriors, the *nṛ́*[3]) have triumphed in a combat (*samohé*; Geldner's "im Schlachtgewühl" is definitely preferable to Renou's "gathering of the warriors"). Firstly, this combat is over the issue of descendants (male and potential warriors: *samohé...tokásya sánitau*). This combat is then explicitly compared to competition where inspired orators *(víprāso vā dhiyāyávaḥ)* have a hostile confrontation. It is these people who are called *dāśvāṃs* (the root *dāś-* means "to worship, to honour") who can later enjoy the benefits of Indra's protection (1.8.8 and 9)

8. *evā́ hy àsya sūnṛ́tā*
virapśī gómatī mahī
pakvā́ śā́khā ná dāśúṣe.

"In fact his generosity is bounteous, rich in cows, it is immense; it is like a ripe branch (offered) to one who worships (honours) (this god)."

9. *evā́ hi te víbhūtaya*
ūtáya indra mā́vate
sadyáś cit sánti dāśúṣe.

"O Indra, thy help is so powerful (for someone) like me; it is instantaneous for he who worships (thee) (or: honours thee)."

Let us examine the content of these passages: in a confrontation which is a trial of strength between two hostile parties, the combatants who are comparable to the poet-priest, constitute the party that is favoured by Indra. [The beneficiaries of his help can however only be poet-priests who honour this god or who openly offer sacrifices: It is true that only poet-priests (who are spokespersons of humans in general) are presented in these two stanzas by means of an elliptical process, like an elliptical dual which involves two members of a dvandva: *pitárā* "father and mother".]

Thus, it is not surprising that 4.17.13, an extract from a hymn dedicated to Indra should mention division of wealth between two parties in a war situation where one is dispossessed for the benefit of the other: *kṣiyántaṃ tvaṃ ákṣiyantaṃ kṛnotī́yarti reṇúm maghávā samóham/ vibhañjanúr aśánimāñ iva dyaúr utá stotā́ram maghávā vásau dhāt*: "He acts so that the other (the adversary) who had a home is without a home, he raises dust, the Generous One, he provokes a combat, he who breaks (the enemy's resistance), wielder of the mace, like the sky; the Generous One places the worshiper in the midst of wealth." Indications of a war-like situation are numerous: the previous stanza uses a war vocabulary (4.17.12 *yó yasya śúṣmam muhukaír íyarti* "(Indra) who sets off his (combative) fury with war cries"); this vocabulary becomes more subtle in 4.17.13 where *íyarti réṇum (ar- reṇúm)* is probably a reproduction of an Indo-European expression **He/or-er-nu* that is rendered by Greek *órnumi érin*" to provoke, to incite a combat" (Od. 3.161) and is used in another expression which is less ambiguous, *kr̥-ājím* "to create a dispute" (4.42.5 *kr̥nómy ājím maghávāham índra íyarmi reṇúm abhíbhūtyojāḥ* "I create the combat, I, Indra the Generous One, I raise dust, I who possess a superior strength", cf. 1.56.4 *yó dhr̥ṣṇúnā śávasā bā́dhate táma íyarti reṇúm br̥hád arhariṣváṇiḥ* "he who drives back the gloom of his daring forces, he raises dust with a loud cry "hurrah", refer EVP p. 22.[4] This then is the *samohá*, a combat[5] held under the auspices of Indra who is not to be dissociated from the rewards of poetic labour, from the share of wealth given as reward for the poet's effort.

4. It concerns a real combat, an act of war; it is difficult not to see the violent nature of Indra; he has destroyed the rival forts (*púro avā́tiraḥ*) and this indeed is the accomplishment of a strong man (*asyá vīryà*). But this exploit has already been presented as a meeting of adversaries and has similar consequences—beneficial to one and devastating for the other. The distinction between the sacrificer and the non-sacrificer is maintained: *śā́sas tám indra mártyam áyajum śavasas pate* "O Indra, thou hast punished the mortal who does not sacrifice, o most Powerful One;" above all, it is still the party hostile to the sacrifice who is dispossessed (*mahī́m amuṣṇāḥ pr̥thivī́m imā́ apó mandasānā́ imā́ apā́ḥ* "Thou hast deprived him of the great land and these waters, having become intoxicated with (the soma), these waters."

But this robbery committed by Indra naturally benefits the sacrificer as seen in 5.34.7 (*sám īm paṇér ajati bhójanam muṣé ví dāśúṣe bhajati sūnáraṃ vásu* "he drives the wealth (the cattle) of the miser (to herd together) in order to take them away from him and he gives this precious wealth to his devotee", see above); other texts on this subject have been quoted by Schmidt, *Br̥haspati und Indra*, pp. 188, 221, and 226 and in particular, 10.67.6 and 10.68.10. Refer especially 2.20.5 *só áṅgirasām ucáthā jujuṣvā́n bráhmā tūtod índro gātúm iṣṇán/muṣnánn uṣásaḥ sū́ryeṇa stavā́n áśṇaṣya cic chiṣnathat pūrvyā́ni* "Pleased with the songs of praise of the Aṅgiras, Indra gave strength to the chant when he sought a path for it; stealing the dawn and the sun, after being worshiped, he reduced to rubble the old fortress of Aśna."

It is of interest to note that among the objects stolen by Indra, one finds cosmic elements, especially the Great Earth which pays homage to him and thus plays the role of the sacrificer (see 1), the dawn as well as the sun. This is the wealth taken from the non-sacrificers, wealth that the Vedic authors intentionally confuse with the sacrificers to whom it will be distributed in the form of war-booty and dakṣiṇā.

5. The rest of the hymn shows a rare but appreciable continuity because, contrary to other examples in the Ṛgveda, not only is there no break with the preceding element but the accents are also distributed in the same manner. Those who have glorified the exploits of Indra, the Uśij, friends of Indra *(sakhīyántas,* those who constitute a circle of friends devoted to one god) have a right to his help and it is for them that he arranges the outcome of battles and assures them of victory (*cakártha kārám ebhyaḥ pṛ́tanāsu právantave*). More generally, it involves favours dispensed by Indra among his devotees "who seek renown" *(śravasyántaḥ*: this is the renown of the persons conducting the sacrifice, obtained for them by the poet-priests); favours that ensure victory to one and defeat to the other. Both victory and defeat revolve around the cows given by Indra to the Uśij. This is explained in 2.21.5: by means of their sacrifice the inspired poets Uśij stimulate their own thoughts (*dhíyo hinvānā́ uśíjo manīṣíṇaḥ*) and obtain cows and other riches with the help of Indra. Here one cannot maintain that it is a strictly a war victory won by Indra and his followers.

6 and 7. The last two stanzas suggest that at the most, the language of war is used possibly because the situation involves a sacrifice held under the auspices of a warrior god. In reality, the hymn should be read by seeing the similarity between a war-like confrontation and the rivalry that is triggered off by any sacrifice, be it verbal or mate-

rial. For, in the form of a routine exhortation at the end of his praise, the poet-priest multiplies his appeals to that aptitude of Indra which is a kind of intuition by which the god listens to the poetic discourse and simultaneously takes pleasure in receiving an offering (*arkásya bodhi havíṣo hávīmabhiḥ* "be ready to receive our song and our offerings which are accompanied by our appeals"). The fact is that these appeals, these entreaties are addressed to Indra with a view to make him listen to the poet-priest; the latter (he calls himself the new organiser of the rite, *návīyo vedhás*) offers them to Indra by exalting the worth of his discourse ("O Indra, if it is thy wish to destroy thine enemies, ... listen to this poetic offering!"). He later touches upon the warrior qualities of the god who, once invigorated (*vāvṛdhānó*), will have the duty of eliminating any mortal who does not behave like a friend (in other words the evildoers) and of keeping all evil intentions at bay.

Thus, the discourse of the poet, if it reaches its target is the means which, accompanied by offerings, strengthens Indra for the purposes of the poet-priest who desires above all the success of his prayers and the defeat of his adversary. The poet who sings is of course the officiant of the sacrifice and his adversary here is the non-sacrificer. Their opposition is very clearly defined and is beyond any doubt. But the Ṛgveda also contains degrees of this opposition that gives us more information about the similarities between war and poetic activities.

2.1.2. Bṛhaspati, the Poet of Poets

This is the lesson to be learnt from 2.23, one of the hymns which presents the god Bṛhaspati, "the poet of poets" (*kaví kavīnā́m*, 2.23.1) and the "supreme king of the Bráhmans" (*jyeṣṭharā́jā bráhmaṇām*), in such a way as to give a clear picture of his actions as protector of officiating poets.

The fact that the controversial and competitive aspects of these actions are described is not only striking, but also typical of the concept of the officiating poet as given in the hymn.[6]

1-2. These lines virtually define the god Bṛhaspati; for example, the sentence which calls him the poet of poets or the creator of the individual *bráhman* of the poets (2 *víśveṣām íj janitā́ bráhmaṇām asi*). The composition of the poet, the Brahman, is certainly the back-bone of the sacrifice, as Schmidt points out (p. 110). But can we agree with him that the hymn deals with the problem of the relationship between the king and the officiant, the former being represented by Indra who according to verse 18 is his ally, whereas the latter is also his ally (10 *tváyā ....bṛ́haspate...yujā́* "thanks to thee, O Bṛhaspati, the ally")?

From verse 3 onwards, the adversary of Bṛhaspati's protégé is attributed various names, all of which are mentioned by Schmidt, but it is equally important to review them as it is to consider the fate that the author of the hymn wishes upon the adversary of the poet.

Given below are the individual verses with (1) the references to the adversaries or the hostilities and punishments that await them or the defence against them; and (2) some traits of Bṛhaspati which correspond to remedies against the enemies and their hostile actions.

3. *ā́ vibādh- parirā́pas* "drive back and dis(perse) the calumnies" (and after that Bṛhaspati must ascend the chariot of the *ṛtá* which will destroy all kinds of adversaries, kill the demons, scatter the cattle and procure the sun; one is reminded of Lüders who rightly saw a song of praise in the formula *rátham ṛtásya*).

4. *brahmadvíṣas tápano manyumī́r asi"* thou art (Bṛhaspati) the one who burns the enemy of the bráhman, and diminishes his warrior (fury)".[7]

5. *(ná) tám áṃho...titirur ná dvayāvínaḥ...víśvā íd asmād dhvaráso víbādhase* "neither distress...nor treacherous beings have defeated him...thou dost push away (far) from him all harmful forces".

6. *yó no abhí hváro dadhé/svā́ tám marmartu duchúnā*

hárasvatī "and the one who has assailed us with his harmful deed, may his own powerful evil reduce him to nothingness"!

7. *utá vā yó no marcáyād....arātīvā́ mártaḥ...vṛ́kaḥ/bṛ́haspate ápa tám vartayā patháḥ* "and the one who would deal us a lethal blow...the mortal (who is) hostile (to us), the wolf, O Bṛhaspati, remove him from our path!"

8. *bṛ́haspate devanído ní barhaya* "O Bṛhaspati, bring down those who scorn the gods (this is Renou's translation EPV XV, p. 53).

9cd. *yā́ árātayo 'bhí sánti jambháyā tā́ anapnásaḥ* "the hostilities which are greater (than us), seize them (violently) they that (do not offer) any benefit"!

10. *mā́ no duhśáṃso abhidipsúr īśata* "let not (the man) of evil words, who seeks to destroy (us) overpower us"!

11. *níṣṭaptā śátrum pṛ́tanāsu sāsahíḥ/ási satyá ṛṇayā́ bráhmaṇas pata ugrásya cid damitā́ vīḷuharṣíṇaḥ* "(thou) who dost consume the enemy, who art powerful in battle, thou art the true avenger of wrong doings, O Bṛhaspati, vanquisher of the terrifying (adversary) who bristles with his massive resistance". (I have but slightly modified Renou's translation: EVP XV, p. 54; the translation of *ṛṇayā́* as "avenger of wrong doings" and of *vīḷuharṣín* as "who bristles with his massive resistance" is taken from Renou).

12. *ádevena mánasā yó riṣaṇyáti śāsám ugró mányamāno jíghāṃsati/bṛ́haspate mā́ práṇak tásya no vadhó ní karma manyúṃ durévasya śárdhataḥ* "The one who brings (us) grief, (armed) with a mind (which ignores) the gods, who would like to destroy (us), and believing himself to be strong, (obeys) (false) commandments, O Bṛhaspati, let his weapon not attain us! May we destroy the (warrior) fury of the evil-doer who seeks to be victorious through force!"

13. *bháreṣu hávyo námasopasádyo gántā vā́jeṣu sánitā dhánaṃ-dhanam / víśvā íd aryó abhidipsvò mṛ́dho bṛ́haspátir ví vavarhā ráthāñ iva* "He whom we must invoke during battles, whom we must revere with homage, who moves there where (we obtain) the prize-of-victory, who wins riches after riches,

(that) Bṛhaspati has snatched away all the harmful deeds of the *arí*, such as the wheels (of an enemy chariot)."

14. *téjiṣṭhayā tapanī́ raksásas tapa yé tvā nidé dadhiré. . . / . . bŕ̥haspate ví parirā́po ardaya* "with the most searing fire, sear the demoniacal (enemies) who have exposed thee to calumny!...O Bṛhaspati, liquidate the utterers of evil"!

Particularly in (17) the emphasis is on the ability of Bṛhaspati to destroy falsehood. (17d *druhó hantā́*); (16) contains a request to Bṛhaspati not to deliver his disciples to thieves and treacherous rogues who dwell in iniquity (16a *mā́ na stenébhyo yé abhí druhás padé nirāmíṇo ripávaḥ*). This verse also specifies the nature of the adversaries *ná paráh sā́mno viduḥ* "who know (nothing) beyond the sacred melody" (Renou, EVP XV, p. 55). Renou asks a question about them which is in fact the best solution to the problem that he presents: "Did the poet mean," they know of no effective means against the *sā́man*=against Bṛhaspati, as he is the bearer of *s°*"?

What is also significant is that the hymn evokes the desire of its author to be given human riches thanks to Bṛhaspati's help. (9ab *tváyā vayáṃ suvŕ̥dhā bráhmaṇas pate spārhā́ vásu manuṣyā́ dadīmahi* "Through thee, O Bṛhaspati who hast grown in stature, may we obtain the desirable human riches!" cf. 13 above; 15 *tád asmā́su dráviṇaṃ dhehi citrám* "such splendid wealth, give it to us!"). Reference is obviously made to Vala's narration in which Bṛhaspati frees the herd of cows and, helped by his ally Indra, liberates the waters that had been imprisoned by the darkness (18).

If an objective comparison is made of the concept of war activities and sacerdotal (poetic) activities as given in 1.131 and 2.23, a certain unity is seen in their composition which is quite repetitive. Moreover, it is this redundancy that clearly brings out their meaning.

At first, the two hymns seem to be the opposite of each other. 1.131 seeks to explain the nature of the warrior-god (Indra) who helps his disciples, the latter being the sacrificers who have to be distinguished from the non-sacrificers.

That is to say that the religious aspect, or rather, the nature of the god who is the patron of the sacrifice is a counterpoint to his warrior aspect. This other nature reveals his role thanks to the motives that evoke the sacrifice, just as the mention of the sacrifice make it possible to understand Indra's deeds of war.

2.23 describes the main aspect of Bṛhaspati's actions. It would be going too far to agree with Geldner that here Bṛhaspati is the protector of the poets against the intrigues of their rivals and the dishonesty of the patrons of the sacrifice, and that the author of the hymn refers to his personal disappointment. Schmidt has rightly pointed out that (p. 109) this would be an incomplete interpretation of the hymn.

The composition of this verse is both richer and more ambitious and this is precisely due to the almost systematic contrast between the description of Bṛhaspati's and Indra's respective actions. There certainly is no question of trying to find an imaginary text which would be the source of the two hymns. I do think, however, that they have common contents when describing the war between sacrificers and non-sacrificers as well as the rivalry between the worthy and not-so-worthy sacrificers, and how a sacrifice must be conducted in accordance with the objectives of Vedic man and to satisfy the gods.

The contrast between Bṛhaspati's and Indra's actions serves to create an opposition between the two gods *as they are presented here*. For, when all is considered, it is clear that the god Indra remains a divine warrior, whereas his deeds help the sacrificers, and that the god Bṛhaspati is the god of prayer whereas the entire hymn 2.23 is composed in such a way as to give a completely warrior-like aspect to the specialist of the prayer invoking Bṛhaspati. I do not think that there can be another explanation for the profusion of verbs that denote the fierce hostility against the enemy of the officiating poet who seeks the protection of Bṛhaspati; the semantics of the verbs leave no room for doubt: most of them refer to the pure and simple physical destruction of the poet's adversary, while the rest suggest the idea of destruction, but their meaning clearly indicates that elements which are extraneous and harmful to the sacrifice are limited to the exterior (these elements are eliminated or repulsed when they are not annihilated; see further on the difference between the interior and exterior in the behaviour of the patron of the sacrifice).

Thus, the first set which contains the larger number of verbs includes *tap-* (4 and 14) or *niṣ tap-* (11) "to burn, to sear completely", "to consume" (when dealing with the destruction of the enemy or of demons: *brahmadvíṣ, śátru* or *rakṣás*); *mar-* (6) "crush; (int.) powerfully crush"; *ní barh-* (8) "bring down"; *ja(m)bh-*(9) "snatch, grasp"; *dabh-* (in *abhidipsú* "which seeks to harm"); (10), *sah-* (as in *sāsahí* "very powerful", having in its meaning "to be powerful, to dominate, to overpower" a definitely warrior-like connotation[8] (11), as also *dam-*(11), "to subdue, master (the enemy); *ní kṛ-* 'to fell'; *ví vṛ-* (13) "to tear away"; *ard-*(14) which can be translated as "to liquidate"; and finally *han-* (17) "to destroy" which is found in the agent noun *hantṛ́*.

The second set consists of three verbs: *ví badh-* (3 and 5) "push back (to the exterior)"; *mī-*(4) "diminish (the enemy warrior's fury)", which is found in the adjective *manyumī́r*; *ápa vṛ-*(7) "to turn away"; *mā īś-*(10) "not to dominate", could be a negative expression of the desire to see the enemy yield.

How can one evaluate the relationships between sacrificial deeds that are given a war-like slant and the systematic use of the vocabulary of war when speaking of sacrifice? I feel that, in conclusion, the generalisation of a type of conflict can be done only by resorting to symbolic Vedic thought; this generalisation is effected by comparing the confrontation on religious ground to the confrontation in war. The resulting metaphor must have been stable and used several times over.

Hymn 2.23 probably deals with the confrontation between sacrificers and non-sacrificers, as does 1.131, but since our interest is to generalise and find a *type* of conflict, it is also plausible that there is a confrontation between two rival sacrificers.

That one of the sacrificers should be the officiating poet and the other the patron of the sacrifice is not very important.[9] The two protagonists clash (either with a rival, in which case the conflict is within the act of sacrifice, or with a non-sacrificer, in which case the conflict is defined according to the contrast between the interior and the exterior); the element that is permanently repeated is the very principle of the conflict which reflects the violence of the opponents. Thus, the degree of differentiation of these latter is scarcely perceptible, yet their conceptual value is not lost—the sacrificer is opposed to the non-sacrificer, and therefore, the external enemy, in the same way as the worthy sacrificer protected by a god or seeking protection of a god is opposed to the rival sacrificer, his enemy within who threatens him by his possible success in the art of sacrifice.[10]

An author has fortunately stated the following, although he has studied a subject quite different from mine: "Mythological battles, human wars, racing contests and professional rivalries are, in the ṚV, dealt with by means of a terminological 'pool' to which all these themes contribute and on which they all draw promiscuously[...].[11]

The difference between a sacrificer and a non-sacrificer subsumes the difference between a fortunate and an unlucky sacrificer; let us retain what is essential: the conflict, the rivalry, the contestation of the power of the rival sacrifice which is considered as a destroyer and which one tries hard to destroy; hence the similarities between ways of presenting the sacrifice as such and the war which will benefit the sacrifice.

We shall immediately see how the concept of war undergoes transformations brought about by the need to give more importance to sacrificial activity.

2.2. The Warrior and his Integration in the Sacrifice

In Vedic sacrifice the practice of dakṣiṇā is the result of symbolic obligations which ensure that the sacrificial act is cohesive (see *Indo-Iranian Journal*, vol. 27, 2, p. 90 and p. 207 of this book). The wealth given as dakṣiṇā represents wealth which can be dissociated from the mass of wealth obtained by men and distributed so as to give a fraction to the officiants as a reward for their efforts in the sacrifice.[12]

The warrior's violent deeds are oriented towards the conquest of wealth which is different from that obtained by men from the gods as a compensation for what they sacrifice to them (but it is noteworthy that the divine gifts largely surpass man's initial investment in the sacrifice), namely, speech and food, one meant to express truth at cosmic level, the other to satisfy the gods at the sacrificial repasts. The wealth conquered and stolen from the non-sacrificers has the purpose of benefiting the sacrifice, for the officiant can offer sacrifice once the patron warriors have conferred this wealth on him. The *yájamāna*, the warrior who is the beneficiary of the sacrifice, the patron who orders the sacrifce, thus disposes of a part of his wealth. It is imperative to avoid any misunderstandings which could eclipse what is essential—if the patron of the sacrifice transfers a part of his wealth to the officiant, this is done at the beginning of the sacrifice and serves to give an initial incitation to the proceedings. The wealth thus conferred is quite apart from the dakṣiṇā which is given to the officiant at the closing stages of the sacrifice.

These two stages mark the patron's effort to integrate himself in the sacrifice. The first one, which starts off the sacrificial proceedings precedes the initial gesture of the officiant who will make his offering in any one form, notably the verbal form, and thereby take on his role of intermediary. The second one affirms the participation of the patron in the sacrifice, in particular, his role of instigator of the sacrifice.

The various aspects of the integration of patrons in the sacrifice have to be studied to elicit a reply to the question: do the patrons of the sacrifice offer sacrifice?

The ways of finding an answer to this question were by no means easy because of the considerable lacunae in all that is by nature foreign to the sacrifice. Hence, looking for information about the patrons of the sacrifice who were but incompletely integrated in the sacrifical procedings involved hypotheses rather than well-documented conclusions. It was, however, possible to distinguish several cases, each of which seems to be eloquent enough, but which are better studied together for they present configurations which complement each other and have amongst them various relationships of contrast, inversion or transformation.

The ideas of the Ṛgveda present in a contradictory manner (but this is not the only contradiction and, like many others, it must have meaning): (1) the apparent indistinction between the officiants and the patrons of the sacrifice; and (2) and the distribution of the benefits of the act of sacrifice amongst the officiating poets, supposedly isolated. It must be explained that the first point gives the impression of an incertitude to which either the Vedic authors or the religious institutions which these authors described must have been prey. But in order to understand the institutions themselves as well as the mentality of Vedic authors, it would apparently be more interesting not to limit oneself to merely taking note of the contradictions, but to make best use of them.

It has been seen that the sacrificer (where "sacrificer" means a person who serves the gods, although his precise human function, officiant or patron of the sacrifice, has not been made explicit) is in contrast to non-sacrificer. This opposition which takes on the form of a conflict, as generally mentioned in the Vedic religion, works in such a way that the sacrificer is assured of the benefit of maintaining the *ṛtá*, whereas the non-sacrificer on the contrary, is doomed to dispossession and destruction. At this point it is necessary to examine the fact that these tendencies do not cover the entire range of modalities which contribute to re-establishing the image and the role of the two persons involved, viz. the sacrificer and the non-sacrificer.

Let us remember an essential principle. If the personality of the non-sacrificer takes on importance, if it always seems useful to stress on the meanings of metaphors or figures of meaning which present in their own way the Vedic religious reality, it is because there is always a series of metaphors more complex and more important than other metaphors. The wide difference between the various kinds of metaphors as also the divergence of the metaphors from the reality of the Vedic cult is in relation to a certain background, ever present, but it would be wrong to think that this background is that of reality presented as it was. For we are dealing not with documents which could provide evidence free of all inflections dictated by the need for a clear and concise presentation of facts, but with a discourse in which there is liberal use of metaphors, and in which the desired clarity is replaced by mythological concepts which contain richer information than any attempted non-metaphorical discourse.

Having taken these precautions we can define the role of the patron of the sacrifice in the sacrificial proceedings. This role can be reasonably described only in relation to that of the officiant. The roles of the officiant poet and the patron of the sacrifice are fairly clearly related but they are often combined and therefore merge. This merging is justified, but only in relation to the proceedings of the sacrifice. They show the momentary affinities envisaged by the Vedic poets; they also show how these authors respected the integral structure of the sacrificial act.

By studying the theme of relationships between the patrons of the sacrifice and the officiant poets from the point of view of the patrons, it can be shown that the latter integrate themselves in the sacrifice in order to become what they were not at first, that is, sacrificers of a quite different nature from the officiants.

This difference in the nature of the sacrificer is expressed very clearly in the Vedic poets' affirmations on the fundamental division of human beings into two groups which are functional and closely interdependent.

Let us first consider the division. It is evoked many times, as much for its own sake as for revealing the fact that wealth won by each group is differential.[13] The verses which speak of the division are often at the end of the hymn and thus have a functional role: the end of the hymn is frequently reserved for the *dānastuti* which notify the donor; they not only indicate his act of rewarding but also his identity. It can be considered that the verses which terminate the hymns and which make a distinction between the functions of the two human groups are connected to the *dānastuti*, or at least reproduce their most pertinent elements, viz., the opposition or juxtaposition of two bodies each one of which has a part to play in the sacrifice. Composed by poets who are themselves conscious of the need for differentiation, these verses often tend to emphasise "we ourselves" with which are associated the patrons of the sacrifice included as a sort of sub-group of this "we ourselves". It is difficult to believe that the choice of vocabulary in these sentences is purely accidental (or arise from a technical rule which justifies the use of a collective pronoun rather than a noun with a concrete reference; to assume the contrary would imply underestimation of the importance of the lexical choice).

Take the example of 7.20.9 and 10 (the second verse is the final one). "The desire to grow rich has come upon thy bard; thou, O powerful (Indra), thou canst offer us riches" (*rāyás kā́mo jaritā́ram ta ā́gan tvám aṅgá śakra vásva ā́ śako naḥ*). The "us" is all the more differentiated as it follows the term by which the poet names himself (*jaritā́ram* vs *naḥ*)—here there is a deliberate anacoluthon which expresses the train of thought—whereas verse 10 makes everything clear, the separation of the two groups being explicit: "This being so, O Indra, mayest thou prepare us to enjoy what thou offerest; the generous patrons (as for them) become animated themselves."

7.26.4d-5ab (again the final verse): "May the pleasant favours (of Indra) be imparted to us. This is how Vasiṣṭha sings of Indra at the pressing, the bull of the people, so that he may lend his assistance to (our) men (i.e., the patrons of the sacrifice)."

This division is no doubt most often proclaimed in order to emphasise only one fact: the officiant poets pray on behalf of the patrons of the sacrifice, all the time giving the impression that they obtain wealth without the help of the latter. But it seems evident that often when the two groups are deliberately named, the Vedic authors wish to maintain the very idea of the division to the extent of rejecting the notion of services rendered by the poets. What transpires is that the Vedic authors were preoccupied with a question in addition to many others, and which had its own conceptual value—is it the activity of the officiant poets or that of the patrons of the sacrifice which ensures the sacrificial proceedings? Or, as proved by numerous examples, is it not true that the action of the officiant poets, however essential it may be, is not sufficient to ensure these proceedings, and that the activity of the patrons of the sacrifice is equally indispensable?

The authors have taken care to define the two groups in relation to one another.

Along with the distinction made in the word "us" (humans opposed to or in confrontation with the gods), they present the group of officiant poets in confrontation with the gods separately from the patrons of the sacrifice. Thus as in 2.2.12 (second last verse), "we, the ones and the others, O Jātavedas, (poets) celebrators and patrons of the sacrifice, O Agni, may we be under thy protection"! (*ubháyāso jātavedaḥ syāma té stotā́ro agne sūráyaś ca śármaṇi*), in the same way 5.65.6 (final verse), "You two, O Mitra (Varuṇa), you put together this group of men, you guide it. Leave not outside your attention either the generous patron or ourselves, the poet-seers!" (*yuvám mitremám jánam yátathaḥ sáṃ ca nayathaḥ mā́ maghónaḥ pári khyatam mó asmā́kam ṛ́ṣīṇām*).

The second case is different from the first in that it stresses on the two human subgroups of a large group (*jána*) subject to the power of the two gods (cf. 5.65.2: the two divine kings are shown facing the *jána,* see Renou's commentary on the collective meaning of *jána*), while each of the subgroups is susceptible to obtaining its share of divine consideration.

Then in order to show that the distinction between the two human groups appears to be the initiative of the officiant poets, let us consider 5.64.4 and 5. The group of officiant poets intends to present a spokesman from their midst by using the voice of one of them who will state the same distinction between the human groups. ["To you two. O Mitra—Varuṇa, I.would like to give through my hymn the best of all that is meant for the contest in the dwelling of the generous patrons and the officiant celebrators. (Come) towards us, O Mitra—Varuṇa, with your luminous inspirations, so (that we may) assemble together, so that we may gain strength in our own dwelling of the generous patrons and of our allies!"]

As for the poets invoking the god Agni[14], one finds here also some hints about one individual member of the whole poets' group who speaks on his behalf but clearly taking into account the group's attitude and desires.

This individuation which goes to the extent of exalting a single officiant (cf. 5.65.1 *yáś cikéta sá sukrátur devatrā́ sá bravītu naḥ* "the one who is learned, who has a powerful spiritual strength, may he speak for us among the gods!") seems to be part of a plan. This plan is realised when the apportioning of human roles is taken further and when each of the groups is given its share of riches and success.

There is a basic element which is essential in Vedic religion—the words of the officiant guarantee that the humans will get the common riches which have to be distributed so that they are transformed from virtual into real and thus gain religious values. The distinction between the benefits of the officiant poets and the patrons is interesting in that, by repeating the separation of the two groups, it defines the forms of the riches obtained by characterising their *differences*.

When the gods are invoked, when favours are being asked of them, these are subdivided according to whether they are meant for the officiant poets or for the patrons of the sacrifice. Even if requests are formulated as a whole and contained in one or two verses, the authors are remarkably unanimous—they never request the same thing for themselves and their patrons.

In a general manner, the poet says (6.44.18), addressing Lord Indra: "In these confrontations (with the enemy), procure for us, O generous (god), large space and easy passage. In the obtaining of waters, descendants and progeny, O Indra, see to it that our patrons are gifted only half (of the benefits)," followed by 6.17.15 which is a sort of summing up: "may we conquer, by means of this song, the prize-of-victory bestowed by the gods, may we rejoice for hundred winters!" (*ayā̂ vā̂jaṃ deváhitaṃ sanema mádema śatáhimāḥ;* this final request is applicable to the poets as well as the patrons).

Whatever be the modalities dictated by various circumstances, the poets' requests stress on the distinction of the wealth accruing to the two groups: to the patrons, a great renown; to the poets, riches and the ritual delectation (5.86.6 *tá sūríṣu śrávo bṛhád rayíṃ gṛṇátsu didhṛtam íṣaṃ gṛṇátsu didhṛtam*); to the patrons, domination and ability in conquest; to the officiant poets, the favours of Indra and a greater strength equal to that of the god himself (6.26.7 *ahám caná tat sūríbhir ānaśyāṃ táva jyā̂ya indra sumnám ójaḥ* "I would like, O Indra, to obtain, (I) and the patrons, thy favour and thy strength superior (to that of others)" and 8. *prā́tardaniḥ kṣatraśrī́r astu śréṣṭho ghané vṛtrā́ṇām sanáye dhánānām* "the son of Pratardana (the patron of the sacrifice) who makes his domination brilliant, may he be the best in the killing of the enemies, in the gaining of riches!"). While it is true that in 6.26.7, the poet associates himself with the patron of the sacrifice (*ahám caná ... sūríbhiḥ*), it is not rare to see, as in the example quoted above, 6.17.15, that the benefit is requested for the entire humankind: the criteria for the distribution are either implied or stated in what precedes or what follows.

Another series of verses included in a hymn to the god Agni alternates the requests of the poet for himself and for the patrons of the sacrifice (7.16.6-12): he prays Agni to bless the patron with a fortune (*kṛdhí rátham yájamānaya*), but does not deprive himself of a more personal favour (*ā́ na ṛté śiśīhi víśvam ṛtvíjam suśámso yáś ca dakṣate* "make us more capable (of the relevant sacrificial act) of the *ṛtá*, (make also) each officiant capable of brilliant speech and clever!"); then an intervention on behalf of the patrons of the sacrifice: may they be loved in the god Agni, they who command other human beings and who distribute the pasturage of the cows (7. *tvé agne . . . priyā́saḥ santu sūráyaḥ / yantā́ro yé maghávāno jánānām ūrvā́n dáyanta gónām*); there follows another exhortation as much for the benefit of those who protect the oblators (descriptive way of naming the patrons of the sacrifice) as for "ourselves" (8. "those in whose dwelling the offering is made, protect them...from all calamities, from all blame, assure us the protection of wide-spread renown!"); and finally, after two verses invoking Agni for the benefit of the patrons of the sacrifice, (9. "Agni, come with wealth to our generous patrons" and 10. "those who give gifts consisting of horses, presents, they who are motivated by the desire for great renown, make them pass beyond the narrow passage"), the conclusion is a brief statement in which the distinction, even though it has been mentioned many times, disappears, for the statement refers to the benefits of those who serve and worship the god Agni (*dádhāti rátnaṃ vidhaté suvī́ryam agnír jánāya dāśúṣe* "Agni gives the fortune consisting of elite men to these humans who serve him and who show their devotion").

From these somewhat repetitive texts similar to many others in the Ṛgveda, certain general principles can be formulated. They can take the form of permanent presuppositions which seem to follow each other and are organised into a system. As we have seen, the requests of the poets are made in a distributive manner, for even if they amalgamate here and there, it is because of the nature and the substance of the solicited benefits and favours (for example, when the delights obtainable by the rituals, the *íṣ-*, are desired sometimes by one group, sometimes by the other, cf. above); otherwise the separation is resumed, and different things are solicited for different groups.

But it would be difficult to distinguish the groups according to the nature of wealth that they wish to receive, except for the rather isolated case of *śrávas* "repute, renown, glory", for which the patrons have a predilection. Of course, domination over the enemy and the so-called elite men (no doubt in the warrior sense) are intended for the patrons of the sacrifice, just as the reactivation of the aptitude for eulogy or clarification of spiritual powers are requested by the poets. But at the same time, protection, a long lease of life, riches in the general sense and naturally the background of the universe ordered according to the *ṛtá*, represent the benefits meant for all collectively. Since it obeys the inherent logic of the Vedic cult, the imperative need for the distribution of wealth and favours is expressed not so much in terms of their qualitative differences, which are expressed by the differences in the articulation of the requests, but by the very fact of the differential dissimilarity in the wealth to be distributed, and which is an important detail, *within the limits of the same concrete solicitation,* at a given time.

In other words, even if generalisations can be observed that are additive in nature, that represent a sum total of respective wealth of human groups as opposed to the gods rather than spontaneous amalgams, the tendency to individualise as has been mentioned earlier is also expressed otherwise: individual requests never club together wealth or favours of the same kind. To distinguish these at a given moment is to understand the *functional contrast* which their differentiation bears, veiled as it may seem at other times. It is also to accentuate the contrast between the respective human groups. But the second contrast is not subsumed by the first, for even though they are determined by similar methods of reflection, these contrasts are not of the same nature. The contrast between wealth and favours is established, as already seen, in space and at a definite moment during the Vedic prayer; on a common symbolic base, divisions are made that are punctual and no doubt temporary, for what is given to the poets at one point of time will be given to the patrons of the sacrifice at another. Moving as they do from one moment to another, the Vedic authors seem to pay little heed to the contrast. This leads one to suspect that the second contrast, that is, the one between two human groups, is of a more permanent nature and is independent of the vicissitudes of the invocations that are subjected to the effect of the time taken for the sacrificial proceedings.

It is however a fact that the second contrast could not be conceived otherwise than by retaining the references to the wealth and favours solicited differentially. For its stable and clear-cut nature is far from excluding the interdependence of the two human groups. Moreover, nothing more than the way the two varieties of divine wealth pass from one to the other clearly and regularly proves that the elements of the contrast between the two groups must undergo fluctuation. This can be understood even better if the hypothesis of interdependence of the two groups is accepted, as also if it is agreed that the contrasting of the respective wealth obtained is done considering their common source. There would thus be an indirect confirmation of the fact that the momentary and punctual contrast in wealth is manifested only under the conditions of an isolated invocation. It was necessary to distribute the mass of wealth acquired by men. But the functional interdependence of their two groups made the distribution fluctuate in respect of the nature of the attributed wealth, so much so that this wealth, contrary to appearances, became *interchangeable* (it has also been said that it would be difficult to define the nature of each group based on the allotted wealth).

8.59.7 very probably gives an example of this interchangeability, seeing that the riches usually given to the ones are asked for the benefit of the others. "O Indra—Varuṇa, confer on the patrons of the sacrifice a favourable and lucid mind, as also abundant wealth. As for us, confer on us progeny, prosperity and well-being, prolong our life span so that we may attain a long life span!"

Hence it appears that the interchangeability of these riches given to each group translates a state of affairs contrary to the distinction of these same riches; it must be once again emphasised that this distinction is operated in the space of the moment of the invocation. In this I see no contradiction or inconsistency of thought; it is more correct to see a method of style, and then, since it seems that the style of the Ṛgveda rarely has no conceptual end, to evaluate the bearing of this method which has the value of a symbolic operation having a deep meaning; by this conception of this apparent contradiction, one will see the inversion of previously established relationships. These relationships in which the differentiation was primary, find themselves as if effaced, but their suppression must not signify their gratuitous abolition, for it seems that Vedic thought meant to provide a reply to the questions formulated above and which concern the role of the patron in the sacrificial proceedings.

In the place of a distinction which seems unconditional, being made in order to confirm a principle of considerable importance, comes the attestation of the interdependence of the two human groups. This is expressed by using a unique term for the sacrificer *(yájamāna)*; by this, it is as if the distinction ceased to exist.

The term *yájamāna* thus denotes the one who sacrifices in an impressive number of cases. It loses its initial meaning owing to its formation in *-māna* on the root *yaj-* and refers to man in general, to man as a sacrificer, man confronting the gods, as if with the support of the interchangeability of the obtained wealth, no distinction were made between the officiants and the patrons.

Despite a commonly accepted translation of the term *yájamāna* as "lay-sacrificer" (Renou in his *Études védiques et pāṇinéennes*) it would appear that this term means the sacrificer in general and not the patron of the sacrifice, the sacrificer who has the characteristics of both the officiant and the patron.

In several parts of the Ṛgveda, this term can be understood with its new meaning (assuming that the primary meaning is "the one who offers a sacrifice for his own benefit"), which is often distinct from that of the proximate terms: 8.31.16 *ná yájamāna riṣyasi ná sunvāna ná devayo* "thou dost not suffer any grief, O sacrificer, O presser of soma, O thou who art devoted to the gods"! (it is however quite plausible that it is the same person presented first by a general term, then by a qualificative having a general value); 5.77.2 also stresses on the importance of the sacrificer, or rather the one who first offers sacrifice (*pū́rvaḥ-pūrvo yájamāno vánīyān* "the earlier one offers sacrifice, the more one gains"), while the last verse of the same hymn repeats the theme of sacrifice in general without detailing its function or use (5.77.5 *yó bhū́yiṣṭhaṃ nā́satyābhyāṃ vivéṣa cániṣṭham pitvó rárate vibhāgé* "the one who has offered the most to the Nāsatya, who has given them the best share of the food when the distribution was made....."); when a god is invoked to ensure the success of the sacrifice, the sacrificer is referred to in a general way (for example, 6.15.16 *savitré yajnáṃ naya yájamānāya sādhú* "lead (O Agni) the sacrifice towards Savitar, as is usual, for the benefit of the sacrificer"); also, when a wish is made for the prosperity of the sacrificer by using the common formula *dhā- śáṃ yóḥ* "to confer health and happiness",[15] it does not seem to be directed to a particular group of those who conduct the sacrifice, but to all the sacrificers without differentiation, and therefore to all humans (1.93.7, 3.17.3, 10.182.1 etc.).

There are, however, certain cases in which it would be difficult to make a clear-cut distinction (is it the patron of the sacrifice or the sacrificer in general?). This is especially true of cases in which Lord Indra is the one who incites the *yájamāna*. 1.51.8 *ví jānīhy ā́ryān yé ca dásyavo barhíṣmate randhayā śā́sad avratā́n / śā́kī bhava yájamānasya coditā́* "Discriminate the Aryans and the Dasyus, deliver by punishing them the lawless people to the one who possesses the sacrificial litter; be powerful, be the inciter of the sacrifice" (see a somewhat different translation in Renou *EVP*, XVII, p. 15, in particular the term *yájamāna* rendered by "the lay-sacrificer"); 10.49.1 *ahám bhuvaṃ yájamānasya coditā́yajvanaḥ sākṣi víśvasmin bhāre* "I have become the inciter of the sacrificer, I triumphed over the non-sacrificers in every confrontation" which obviously cannot be separated from the beginning of the same verse in which Indra proclaims: *aháṃ dām gṛṇaté pū́rvyam vásv ahám bráhma kṛṇavam máhyam várdhanam* "I have given the poet best wealth, I have created the edifying word, my strength."

It can be accepted as very probable that there is, besides the contrast of the patron and the officiating poet, the contradistinction which modifies and complements the first, i.e. between the sacrificer in general and the ungodly who do not offer sacrifice. It is enough to compare the texts quoted above to evaluate both the imprecision (in fact, misleading) of the term *yájamāna* and its revelatory amplitude. It denotes, on the one hand the sacrificer who is carefully segregated from the non-sacrificer, and on the other hand, it is opposed, here at any rate, to the term which refers to the effective performer of the sacrificial ritual.

What is the significance of this merging, and can it be imputed to the awkward turn of the expression? Indeed, the term *yájamāna* shows itself to be a veritable synthetic *signifiant* arising from the intersection of the two human groups together opposed to the non-sacrificer. It can therefore be considered that it is this latter opposition that gives a fluctuating meaning to the term *yájamāna*. Denoting the patron of the sacrifice, it retains its primary meaning, then this meaning is broadened and it denotes the sacrificer in general, thus including the officiant as well as the organiser of the sacrifice. Thus it would seem that nothing could better express the idea of the synthesis of the functions associated with the one and the other. This synthesis above all serves to establish the interdependence of the two, which when expressed, modifies the essential content of the term *yájamāna*.[16]

But in Vedic hymns, denominations have only a limited value. Not that it is reasonable to deny them the role usually given to key words in religious practice, but in the case of the term that has been studied, a certain number of expressions in the hymns show that the authors thought of giving it consistence and vigour by a simple method. This method is nonetheless effective for it consists of a confrontation between the two concerned protagonists in a sort of narration which, like most of the narrations in the Ṛgveda, is brief and does not go beyond an allusion, an outline or a simple sketch of a narration.[17] It sometimes provides veritable explanations regarding the causes of the interdependence of the officiants and the patrons which is so necessary for the efficiency of the sacrifice.

Lord Indra whose deeds ensure that the combative aspect of the sacrificers is manifested, sees to it that those who are invested with the two human functions of the sacrificial act reveal themselves. 6.23.10 (final verse) *evéd índraḥ suté astāvi sóme bharádvājeṣu kṣáyad ín maghónaḥ / ásad yathā jaritrá utá sūrír índro viśvávarasya dātā́* "Here Indra has just been honoured during the pressing of the soma by the Bhāradvāja. He has power over the generous (patrons); (this power ensures) that there is a patron of the sacrifice for the singer. Indra is the donor of wealth desired by all."

In hymn 6.24, Indra is said to be worthy of praise by songs addressed however to valorous men (1. *arcatryò maghávā nṛ́bhya ukthaír*); then it is explained that he listens to the invocation of the poet and gives him assistance (2. *śrótā hávaṃ gṛṇatá urvyū́tiḥ*), feeds him and after being honoured, distributes the prizes-of-victory (*kārúdhāyā. . . stutó vidáthe dāti vā́jam*); if he is further honoured he gives in neither to the persistent nor to the strong, even though they may be a powerful enemy impelled by the Dasyu (8. *ná vīḷáve námate ná sthirāya ná śárdhate dásyūjūtāya stavā́n*).

In short, when Indra is depicted as "the starting point of poetic art and of the cult", according to the apt description of Geldner (see his note on 6.24.6), in other words, when this god is represented as the protector of the officiant poets who prepare for their functions at dawn [9cd *sthā́ ū ṣú ūrdhvá ūtí áriṣanyann aktór vyùṣṭau páritakmyāyām* "hold thyself erect with thine assistance protecting (us) from (the traps) at the hour when the darkness clears, at the decisive hour (before the confrontation of the officiant poets)!"], the final verse of the hymn acquiring the value that is often allotted to it, especially *after* the explanations about the role of the poet and of the god. It recalls the importance of the assistance of Indra which is desired for the sacrifice (10. *sacasva nāyám ávase abhī́ke* "follow closely the one who conducts and lend him thy assistance at the time of a face-to-face confrontation!").

In this regard, an analysis like the one given here cannot do without the invaluable reference of 6.25. What interests us directly is given at the end of verse 7 but it would be useful to see how its contents, coming after a series of rigorously articulated arguments throughout the preceding verses, are related to the series and give it a sort of conclusion.

The following is a summary of the various aspects of Lord Indra protecting the sacrifice of his devotees against their adversaries. The rivalry of the sacrificer and the non-sacrificer is very clearly shown by explaining the meaning of the participation of the patrons in the sacrificial act:

(1) The officiant poet speaks on behalf of the group. Indra must assist them in their efforts to break the enemy opposition by awarding them the prizes-of-victory.

(2) His group, favoured by Indra, opposes another which must suffer defeat, since the former is helped by the god; the rival group thus represents a particular case of the opposition. "With thy helpers, shatter the adversaries who contest us, by protecting (us) from grief, (shatter) the hostile fury of the enemy, O Indra! with these helpers, fell all the adversaries by scattering them in all directions and cause the *dāsá* tribes to be at the mercy of the Aryan group!"

Let us accept that (according to a discussion on the terms *ā́rya* and *dāsá* by Dumézil, *Les dieux souverains des Indo-Européens,* pp. 231-251), on the one hand, an *ā́rya* group is defined by its internal solidarity even though it opposes other identical but rival groups, also called *ā́rya,* and that this dual definition of the solidarity corresponds exactly to the degree of opposition of the sacrificer and the non-sacrificer, for the latter can be a member of the poet's group (he is the rival and ineffective sacrificer) or outside his group (in this case, he is a more formidable adversary, the *dāsá*).[18]

(3) The same exhortation to Indra to help the poet's group, but with this detail that the hostility they face is on two levels simultaneously. On the one hand, the adversaries are the relatives, the kin, or should we say, the poets' ilk who have an affinity for them, their doubles (*jāmáya* plural of *jāmi,* "the co-sanguinous", with this important comment by Renou, *Études sur le vocabulaire du Ṛgveda,* p. 49, that the co-sanguinity expressed by *jāmí* when not considered in its

absolute state is to be taken in the plural as referring to the interior of a group, cf. p. 50: "in a broader way, *j.* is the "relative" as opposed to the outsider...*ájāmi* to which can be compared *víjāmi* "false or bad relative"). On the other hand, the adversaries are the *ájāmayo* or "false relatives", or, which is more apt given the context of this hymn, adversaries not related to the poet and his group. This once again shows in a different way the antagonism between the *ā́rya* and *dāsá* groups (between the non-related) and the rivalry within the *ā́rya* group (between the related).

Considered in the light of these fresh details which in no way clash with the contents of the preceding verses, the poet's request for Indra's protection can easily be seen to belong to the sphere of rivalry having sacrificial value, and of war activities, one being within a group of connected people, the other falling outside the group.

(4) This being acquired, this verse corroborates the certitude that the two levels are superimposed. It deals, in a recapitulative way, with the confrontation between two strong men (*śū́ro vā śūraṃ vanate. . .táruṣi yát kṛṇvaíte*), probably two warrior heroes. The violent encounter in which each wishes to prevail over the other (this is the meaning of *táruṣi yát kṛṇvaíte*, freely translated as "when both act in such a way as to demonstrate their superiority"), is not unrelated to the traditional stakes of the sacrificial act. This is made clear in the second part of the verse which enlarges on the importance of the combat and makes the two heroes the representatives of the rival groups who quarrel loudly (*ví krándasī brávaite*; the value of *krándas* explained in Grassman's note in *Wörterbuch*, p. 356-357, is a tributary of the verb *krand-* "shout loudly": "die gegenüberstehenden Schlachtreihen als die laut rufenden"); there is a sudden but explicable change when the two clashing groups seek to acquire what is currently obtained from a successful sacrifice: descendants and progeny, cows, water and fields (*toké vā góṣu tánaye yád apsú ví krándasī urvárāsu bravaíte*).

It is worthwhile to refer to 6.19.12-13 and 6.31.1.6.19.12 is in fact an appeal from an individual poet but he expreses his being part of the group of which he is the spokesman: *jánaṃ vajrin máhi cin mányamānam ebhyó nŕ̥bhyo randhayā yéṣv ásmi / ádhā hí tvā pr̥thiviyāṃ śū́rasatau hávāmahe tánaye góṣv apsú* "That man (or those men, if the term *jána* is taken to be a collective noun, as said earlier), may he think he is great, deliver him to the mercy of these valorous men of whom I am one, O thou bearer of thunderbolt! For we invoke thee in (our) combat to (obtain) the (entire?) earth, progeny, cows and water."

The implicit idea immediately perceptible is certainly the war confrontation in which the stakes are the benefits and wealth demanded by the poet who addresses Indra, but the usual complexity of the discourses of the R̥gveda is such that a second reference cannot be ignored. The adversary of the poet is not found only on the warrior level cf. 6.19.13: *vayáṃ ta ebhíḥ puruhūta sakhyaíḥ śatroḥ-śatror úttara ít syāma,* "May we be above every enemy whoever he may be, thanks to thy friendship, O thou whom we often invoke!" The following part indicates the presence of two types of adversaries: *ghnánto vr̥trā́ṇy ubháyāni śūra rāyá madema br̥hatā tvótāḥ* "quelling the resistance of both, may we, O hero, rejoice in the great wealth, being under thy protection!" [cf. verse 8 of the same hymn which adds more details to the vocabulary of 6.25.3 which has just been explained: *yéna váṃsama pŕ̥tanāsu śátrūn távotíbhir utá jāmī́ṅr ájāmīn,* "(armed) with this courage, we wish to triumph over the adversary in combat, thanks to thy help, over related and non-related (adversaries)!"].

In 6.31.1 *ábhūr éko rayipate rayīṇā́m ā́ hástayor adhithā indra kr̥ṣṭī́ḥ / ví toké ápsu tánaye ca sūré'vocanta carṣaṇáyo vívācaḥ* "thou, O master of riches, thou hast become it alone, thou hast taken the population in thy hands, the opponent human groups have quarrelled over descendants, water, progeny and the sun"; the stakes are the very ones looked for in the sacrifice and it would appear that the quarrel is the verbal one suggested by the sequence *vi...ávocanta vívācaḥ* made from an etymological figure *ví-vāc vi-vac* "the contender contests (with his adversary)".[19]

It is very obvious, as Kuiper suggests, that the verbal contest even though it began with the confrontation between two pieces of poetry, goes far beyond mere oratorical contests (whereas Renou stressed on their intrinsic value considered independently of the sacrifice, and this was refuted by P. Thieme). It is also obvious that the verbal contests (*vívāc*) were intended to bring order to the universe, and its corollaries such as the riches offered to two kinds of sacrificers (the officiant and his patron).

But by considering the hymns in the perspective of rivalry constantly mentioned by the officiant poet, it can be believed (which complements Kuiper's theory) that this rivalry brings face to face the Vedic sacrificer (in the general sense, that is, the officiant and his patron) and *two kinds of adversaries.*

These adversaries can be distinguished according to whether they belong to the group of poets or whether they are outsiders and external to the group. At the moment when it is known who is the adversary who is confronting him, the sacrificer is given a definite form (*yájamāna* in the general sense). This is how the adversaries are subdivided into internal and external adversaries.

A lot can be said about the vocabulary of the Ṛgveda which often describes in non-univocal terms the internal and external rivalry (even the word *sūrí*, patron of the sacrifice, thus acquires the meaning "patron-of-the-contestants, the *sūrí* opponent" according to Renou, *EVP* II, p. 109-111), but for the moment let us restrict ourselves to referring to what Renou has established in these pages regarding the self-description of Vedic social groups; *arí* (cf. *ārya*), *arí* qualified as unfavourable would denote, he says appropriately, the *arí* whose hostility is "internal", coming from the same clan as his rival, as well as an *arí* whose hostility is "external" since it comes from afar and from an outsider; further, and I continue to quote Renou, "the notion of "speech" (*víp*), of "oratorical contest" (*ājí*), of the "prize of the winner" (*vā́ja*) dominates in the passages referring to unfavourable *arí*, and "whenever a feat of strength or armed combat is involved, everything points out to one meaning: "literary contest" (p. 109).

Leaving aside for the moment the "literary contest" as stressed upon by Renou, (for I think that the import of Vedic contests goes beyond this end in itself which is determined by using speech outside the sacrifice), what can be considered is the bifurcation of the principle stated by him (to continue what has been put forward by him). Hostility is conceived as a practice involving both the officiant poets and professional warriors, and the combat thus takes on a metaphorical meaning (which is expressed by superimposing the rivalry of the poets and the war hostilities). The bifurcation and the metaphor are possible only if it is understood that the officiant poet is up against his ilk within the Vedic social groups and that the warrior fights in his own way against his counterpart from outside.

These two levels of hostility have been created as analogies. They call for two types of adversaries corresponding to two types of sacrificers (cf. earlier, the general value of *yájamāna*).

The articulation of the two aspects of the sacrificer can be seen thus: as combatant and antagonist, he has recourse to words of praise when he is dealing with his internal counterpart (which is probably denoted by the word *vívāc* when it refers not to the act of contesting, but to the agent of the contest or the verbal controversy, by a transfer usually found in the Ṛgveda in a certain number of cases). He is a *warrior* when his actions are combative and seek to eliminate his external counterpart. Since poetic speech is nothing but sacrificial speech, and is both an offering and a sacrifice, and as Kuiper has often indicated, since the practice of verbal contest cannot be isolated from other war practices, Kuiper's submission regarding the close link between the Vedic verbal contest and the seasonal sacrifice (just when the New Year begins) can be complemented in this way precisely—the two activities are conceived at a level which unites them and mingles them, but whereas the verbal duel (as also the chariot races which are generally associated with it) is an event which affects the Vedic human group from within, the war combat (perhaps an imitation of the cosmic combat) concerns it from without.[20]

Let us continue our analysis of 6.25.

(5) This verse declares the unsurpassable superiority of Indra invoked by the poet on behalf of the sacrificer, but whether this is the officiant or the patron is not made clear. It also echoes the first verse which praises the bountiful help given by Indra to humans. It is said again that no hero (*śū́ra*) or combatant, however powerful he may be, is capable of defeating him (*nahí tvā śū́ro ná túro ná dhṛṣṇúr ná tvā yudhó mányamāno yuyódha*), yet it cannot be claimed that judging by the vocabulary which has a war consonance, it deals only with Indra, god of war, to the exclusion of all other faces of the same god who also manifests himself by his assistance to the officiant poets (cf. earlier 6.24.2 *śrótā hávaṃ gṛṇatá urvyū́tiḥ* "he heeds the invocation of the singer, gives him his powerful assistance", cf. also 1.78.3).

The very imprecision of this exaltation of Indra gives more credibility to the hypothesis that Indra is considered a hero both in a war situation and in a situation of ritual dispute between poets. Being endowed with this quality Indra is capable of intervening in either situation. Hence such a generalisation about the roles of Indra who patronises the sacrificer in the most general sense of the term, can be related to the synthetic value of the designations of the sacrificer, as they have been shown earlier. Thus both represent the interdependence of the officiant poets and their patrons.

(6) This seems to be a redundant summary of Indra's

presiding over the two kinds of combat, the sacrificial confrontation and the external combat (8. *sá patayata ubháyor nṛmṇám ayór,* "he possesses the strength of the violence of these two", probably refers to the strength of the two groups of men). Both these groups pursue their respective objectives (line c shows only the objective of the human group attacking enemy territory, whereas the confrontation within the group of officiants is referred to by the same word *vṛtrá-* "resistance (in the general sense)" which has already been seen in the compound *vṛtrahátya,* noun of action, which must be understood not as "murder of Vṛtra",[21] but rather as "destruction of resistances" without clarifying the nature of the latter).

In 6cd it is said: *vṛtré vā mahó nṛváti kṣayé vā vyàcasvantā yádi vitantasaíte,* "when on growing the two (adverse groups) confront (intensely) each other either during the combat or in order to obtain a great dwelling-place for (their) valorous men". The god is called upon to help during the confrontations by the *vedhás,* the orderers of the sacrificial rites who are probably with the officiant poets, or simply a subgroup of poets (b: *yádī vedhásaḥ samithé hávante* "when the orderers of the rites call out during the combat" which can be related to 4.42.5: *mā́ṃ vṛtā́ḥ samárane havante / kṛṇómy ājím maghávāhám índraḥ,* "it is to me, when they are encircled in the combat, that they call out; I create the combat, I, Indra, the generous one").[22] There is very little doubt that the group of men seeking to conquer this territory which will become their dwelling place can be directly compared to the group of patrons of the sacrifice.

(7) This invocation seems to be the most relevant to the problem being examined. Here we see once more the constant that we had discerned in the previous verses, i.e., the parallel, and here, simultaneous evocation of the two human groups for whom the poet solicits the protection of the same god Indra. It must be acknowledged that the interpretation and even the translation of this verse is some-

what difficult. This is how I see it: when the human groups which are first designated by a general term (*carṣaṇáyo* pl.) begin to move, let Indra be their guardian and protector; it is more probable that the human groups not yet differentiated in their functions represent precisely these two functional social groups formed by officiant poets and the patrons of the sacrifice, and this is confirmed by what follows: our patrons, the valorous men, have put us in front, we the *arí* (*asmā́kāso yé nṛ́tamāso aryá índra sūráyo dadhiré puró naḥ*).[23] Despite some doubts regarding the grammar of the line quoted above, I see in it what the entire hymn from beginning to end seems to teach: the close interdependence of the officiants and the patrons of the sacrifice expressed by their co-operation which is revealed in the motive for inciting the officiants to take on their role of mediators by the action of the patrons expressed by the verb *purás dha* "to put in front".

(8) This is a final injunction and has the value of a summary encompassing the whole hymn. Its meaning becomes clear very easily if one considers the two kinds of adversaries whom the two human groups are supposed to confront: "During the combats, O Indra, gather together our adversaries, deliver (to us) the opponents who have no gods!" Indra is asked to act in such a way as to fell the two kinds of adversaries, but only after making the distinction between the two groups on behalf of whom the poet sings the praises of Indra. The corresponding distinction between the adversaries should arise from this, but there is insistence on the details of the fate that one wishes to inflict on particularly fearsome adversaries, those who oppose the two human groups in the same way as do sacrificers and non-sacrificers (*evā́ na spṛ́dhaḥ sám ajā samátsv índra rārandhí mithatī́r ádevīḥ*).

The hymn that has just been analysed is a somewhat exceptional case. Elsewhere are found short phrases or sentences which reveal the common task to be fulfilled by the officiant poets and the patrons of the sacrifice.

Whatever be the interpretation of verse 7.92.4 which poses similar difficulties as in verse 6.25.7 (because of the ambiguity of the use of the word *arí*), there is no doubt that it also deals with the co-operation between the poets and the patrons of the sacrifice, their association in a war which can never take place on an entirely external plane: "(the patrons), devotees of vā́yu, who intoxicate Indra, devoted to the gods and the generous, the Aryan (patrons), with these other patrons, these warriors, may we destroy the opposition by overcoming our enemies in combat"! (*yé vāyáva indramā́danāsa ā́devāso nitóśanāso aryáḥ / ghnánto vṛtrā́ṇi sūribhíḥ syāma sāsahvā́ṃso yudhā́ nṛ́bhir amítrān*). It would be limiting to agree with P. Thieme (*Der Fremdling im Ṛgveda*, pp. 20-21) that in *aryáḥ* is found an example of the genitive singular,[24] that its general meaning is reduced to an expression of desire by the followers of the cult of the god vā́yu to overcome their enemies, a meaning that could be summarised as "may we triumph, as we are pious". The aspect of solidarity that is seen in this verse seems to be explained not only by its content but also, and perhaps even better by what is said in hymn 7.92 before and after.

There is indeed a connection between those loyal to vā́yu and this god, which is undoubtedly traditional and characteristic of the Vedic sacrifice which is materialised by the offerings made to the god, and inversely, by the wealth obtained from it by humans. A thousand gifts are "harnessed" for him, he is also offered the intoxicating soma-juice (1. *sahásraṃ te niyúto. . ./ úpo te ándho mádyam ayāmi*, cf. 2). vā́yu himself comes to the dwelling-place of his worshipper bearing "harnessed-gifts", and he is requested to "harness" bountiful riches and generous gifts consisting of elite men, cows and horses; after the verse in question [4], in the final verse, there is a reiteration of the contents of the previous verse by inviting the guest to become intoxicated during the pressing of the soma, which has already been invoked.

Thus, it is the sacrifice and its desired effects that are at the core of the relationship established in this way, and it is good that the poet, with this tendency so frequently shown, comes back to the integral, even integrative nature of the sacrificial process which cannot do without the active role of the patrons of the sacrifice. Referring once more to Thieme, it could be said that, when considered in the perspective of the whole hymn, 7.92.4 further supports the idea that is badly forgotten if one has to evaluate the sacrificial act by the personalised efforts of humans clearly divided into two interdependent categories: "may we triumph, for we act along with the patrons of the sacrifice who are devotees of vā́yu".

Sometimes the integration of the patrons in the work of the poet is presented as a sort of lesson at the end of a hymn, and this didactism has an explanation, for the verses that follow were very obviously meant for the end of the sacrifice.

In 5.44.11, the sacrifice is over, the officiants prepare to go to each one of the patrons of the sacrifice (Viśvāra, Yajata, Māyin) for they know that their reward awaits them (*sám anyám-anyam arthayanty étave vidúr viṣā́ṇaṃ paripā́nam ánti té*; this indeed refers to the end of the sacrifice: *viṣā́ṇa* is exactly the "release"—remember *vimócana* "the release" or "the liberation" of the dakṣiṇā conferred by the steed (3.53.6); *paripā́na* reminds you of the distribution or the circulation of drinks, see Renou, *EVP* V, p. 27). 5.44.12 is immediately linked, and underlines the participation of the patrons of the sacrifice. Other names are invoked (according to Geldner, the patrons are assembled in a sort of sacrificial union and I give the names as he does)—Bāhuvṛkta, Śrutavid, Tarya as well as Yajata, already named and referred to as the ever generous donor whose responsibility it is to destroy the enemies (*sadāpṛṇó yajató ví dvíṣo vadhīd*). Though what follows is vague, one can think that the person referred to is Yajata: "he goes forth to meet the two objects of the wishes (no doubt the dakṣiṇā and the drink), he shines when he comes, he joins the group (of officiant poets armed) with good guides" (*ubhā́ sá várā práty eti bhā́ti ca yád īm gaṇám bhájate suprayā́vabhiḥ*).

What better proof can be found to show that when the sacrifice ended and another was to follow, it is through the dakṣiṇā that the patron of the sacrifice hoped to join the group of officiants? Moved by the same desire, he must receive the officiants on his sacrificial litter (this is evident from the call of the hotṛ, the invocator of the gods to the adhvaryu, the one who manually performs the sacrifice: 3.53.3 *édám barhír yájamānasya sīdā́thā ca bhūd ukthám índrāya śastám* "take thy place on this ritual-litter of the patron of the sacrifice, may the hymn of praise to Indra be chanted!"). Further, it is the officiants who seek the welcome of the patron in order to avoid ills: [5.45.5 *éto nv ádyà sudhyò bhávāma prá duchunām inavāmā*[25] *várīyaḥ/āré dvéṣāṃsi sanutár dadhāmā́yāma prā́ñco yájamānam ácha* "Come ye there! May we have today good intentions-for-the-sacrifice, may we chase away misfortune to the distance; may we push hostilities as far away as possible; (thus) have we come towards (our) patron of the sacrifice!"]. Similarly the patron of the sacrifice will accept in the sacrificial fire the favours arising from the works of the officiant poets [3.3.3 "The inspired-orators celebrate with their thoughts the luminous-signal of the sacrifice, the one which causes the ritual distribution to come to an end, (lord) Agni; they have composed in him their works, their songs, it is in him that the patron of the sacrifice accepts the favours"].[26]

There is perhaps nothing else that better illustrates the necessity of associating the words addressed to the gods with the words of the patrons of the sacrifice than the verse 1.24.11: "It is for this that I go toward thee, paying (thee) homage with my formulated words, it is this that wishes for himself the patron of the sacrifice with the oblations (that he orders); be without wrath (towards us) O Varuṇa, (thou) for whom the song (resounds) in the distance!" (*tát tvā yāmi bráhmaṇā vándamānas tád ā́ śāste yájamāno havírbhiḥ / áheḷamāno varuṇehá bodhy úruśaṃsa*). The dilemma is clearly posed: the officiant poet uses the sacrificial words (*bráhman*), the patron makes use of the words for his personal ends. The words of the patron are uttered for himself (*ā́ śāste*), and not for the gods to whom the words of the officiant are generally addressed, and the oblations necessarily complement them. In this verse can be seen the prefiguration of what the Ṛgveda expresses in a more complex and convoluted way; but here it is simpler, since the prayer to the three gods (Agni, Savitṛ and Varuṇa) in hymn 1.24 is reduced to a request to Varuṇa which is repeated in the rest of the hymn (12-15).

This request is diversified in the continuation, and expresses the desire to escape from the punitive wrath of the god who has the power to undo human sins. This diversification reveals the means that men have at their disposal.

Men are presented through two essential and functional categories with respect to their gods: there are the men who officiate by their words and those who *make others* officiate by their sacrificial offerings. It is because men are primarily represented as an undifferentiated human entity (*jána, mánus*) with no functional charges, that when it comes to allotting the functions according to the objectives of the sacrifice, these functions are named in conjunction as in 1.24.11.

But the interest lies not only in seeing the two human functions recalled one after the other by bringing out their contiguity and their solidarity, it also lies in the manner in which the sacrificial words of the poet are compared to the words of the patron. Each is defined in relation to the other and shows different directions which only serve to underline their respective objectives. The poet's words are directed towards god [*yā-*, both "to go (towards) and "to implore", "to pray" cf. L. Renou, "Sur quelques mots du Ṛgveda", p. 79 ff.: *yā- bráhmaṇā vándamāna*, "to go (or "to pray"), paying homage with (or by) words" is thus the expression of two aspects of the Vedic cult, i.e. the verbal and the gestual]; whereas the words of the patron are directed towards himself (*ā́ śās*, in the middle voice, translated by L. Renou in *EVP* V, p. 94 as "the lay-sacrificer wishes himself", rightly expresses this movement of the words); as they lack the scope of the officiant's words, they are complemented by oblations (*havís*). It is rather natural that in 1.24.14 are briefly mentioned the two human activities that the poet attributes to "us", once again and momentarily synthetic, but which these two sacrificial activities alone are capable of articulating. More exactly, this penultimate verse elegantly puts together the elements of the sacrifice by giving terminology which is simultaneously concrete, specific and general: "we approach (thee) O Varuṇa with our homage, our sacrifices and our oblations so that thy wrath (may be) spared to us" (*áva te hélo varuṇa námobhir áva yajnébhir īmahe havírbhiḥ): námas* must be considered as a gesture accompanying the verbal homage, *havís* as denoting the material oblation and *yajñá* as a comprehensive name for both kinds of sacrifice. Thus, it is seen to what extent the two sacrificial roles are really interdependent.

But the instances quoted above also bring out a less evident aspect of the speech proffered during the sacrifice. Far from being undifferentiated as to its functions and uses, it is bipartite and thus corresponds to the functions of officiant and patron.

This is how the *degree* of integration of the patron in the sacrifice is manifested.

While the words of the poet contribute to the starting of the sacrificial act and serve to announce it to the gods, the patron of the sacrifice does not use words with the same objective. What includes him in the sacrifice is the material gifts and oblations. His words, centred on himself, brought towards himself, only help indirectly in the sacrifice. The words of the poet are true to his sacrificial vocation, whereas the words of the patron are insufficient in themselves; the dakṣiṇā and the oblations that he orders are two auxiliary and necessary elements of the sacrifice on the whole, and thus serve to define the nature of the participation of the patron.

Thus what we have established regarding the respective positions of the officiant poet and his patron is confirmed. The former who confronts his rival within the sacrifcial community is as if destined to use the means that he himself has, i.e., words; the latter who has to combat the external enemy is, on the contrary, forced to maintain his place in the sacrificial proceedings because his nature condemns him to direct himself outside the sacrifice (cf. earlier, the opposite directions of the essential activities of the two human persons in Vedic sacrifice). Right now, it would appear that the use of words by the one and the other is revelatory since they are differentiated in direction and hence correspond to the dichotomy of verbal activities and war activities, assimilated and related in the thought of Vedic authors, but also different precisely because of the role of words in each of them.

2.3. *vā́ja* and dakṣiṇā: A Contrastive Analysis

The word *vā́ja* denotes an important concept in Vedic sacrifice. Its role brings out more subtly the articulation of the concept of war. In the analysis which follows, the relationship between *vā́ja* and *dakṣiṇā* assumes importance because of the parallelism and identical articulation of the essential values of poetry contests and war. When considering the meanings of the term *vā́ja*, it will be noted that it stands for "victory",[27] "prize of victory" (Renou, *L'Inde fondamentale*, p. 53),[28] "prize of poetic victory" (L. Renou, *EVP*, I, p. 17, cf. *EVP*, IV, p. 29). The apparent difference in the three meanings notwithstanding, the basic meaning can be reduced to "prize of victory" as Renou had already discerned, for when *vā́ja* is evoked, it invariably refers to gain or benefit obtained through violence irrespective of the methods and aims of the latter.

Thus, it is not surprising that *vā́ja* is on the same plane as reward, riches and the fruits of sacrifice sought by all the sacrificers. A hymn such as 7.93 however shows some interesting nuances in the concept of riches designated by the word *vā́ja*. The poets ask for it as they ask for any other riches, without making any distinction regarding its orgin or, at first sight, its functional value, for both have their importance in the organisation of Vedic sacrifices. 7.93.1cd "I address my vigorous request to you, the two of you (Indra and Agni), (gods) whom we call easily, who are generous donors (conferring) immediately the *vā́ja* to the one who desires (it)" (*ubhā́ hí vāṃ suhávā jóhavīmi tā́ vā́jaṃ sadyá uśaté dhéṣṭhā*). At the ceremony for the distribution of the riches, those who seek to obtain their *vā́ja* (7.93.3a *úpo ha yád vidáthaṃ vājíno gúr*) come forward as poets interested in the riches which, in this hymn, are given the names of *rayí* and *deṣṇá* (thus underlining the ordinary nature of the riches acquired as *vā́ja*, cf. 7.93.4).

It seems however incontestable that these riches simultaneously called *vā́ja, rayí and deṣṇá*, especially when the poets'requests are formulated in the hymn in which the term *vā́ja* is the key-word, are not entirely equivalent to either the riches gained by the sacrificial act, or the fraction of wealth represented by the dakṣiṇā. 7.93 gives some details which are clear if attention is given both to the place occupied by these evocations of *vā́ja*, and also to the contents of these evocations.

From the very beginning of the hymn, it is seen that the ambience in which Indra and Agni are invoked is one of a war confrontation. The two gods are *vṛtrahánā* (this term has two accepted translations, either "(gods) who assassinate Vṛtra", or more generally, "(gods) who fell opposition", but in either case it is probable that the allusion is to a war ambience). From the work of Benveniste and Renou on Vṛtra and Vrθragna, we know that the word *vṛtrá* can also take on the meaning of "fight, combat", which is only one aspect of the meaning of "defence". It is particularly interesting to see the two terms *vā́ja* and *vṛtrá* in an invocation to the warrior god Indra, from which can be clearly inferred the nature of the association between war and *vājakṛ́tya* "war with a view to taking booty": 10.50.2 *víśvāsu dhūrṣú vājakṛ́tyeṣu satpate vṛtré vāpsv àbhí śūra mandase*, rendered by Renou in *Vṛtra et Vrθragna,* p. 99 as "in all the harnesses (=combat on chariots?), in the taking of booty, O true master, or else in the battle, in the waters, O hero, thou rejoicest" (on the word *vṛtrá* and its given meaning, see p. 98 of the same book).

Despite Renou's doubt, since the war of destruction of enemy opposition and the war for profits (the taking of the booty) are similar, it does not seem accidental that this equivalence is strengthened by the reference to combat on chariots. Nothing is more usual for Vedic authors than to refer simultaneously to chariot races and war battles, when this is not just implied.

This is a permanent source of metaphors. Thus we have here the evocation of war for profits, war alone, and the chariot contest which is frequently compared to poetry contests. This is not forgotten in the hymn 7.93.

It recalls the nature of the two gods invoked by accentuating their power to allow man to win what is beyond present human possessions, i.e., abundant riches, pasturage and also *vā́ja*. 7.93.2d *pṛṅktáṃ vā́jasya sthávirasya* "Satisfy (us) with a powerful *vā́ja*." "To allow to win, to cause to win" is expressed here by a word derived from the root *san,* "to win, acquire at the end of a war confrontation" (*sānasī́* "you two who-can-cause to win", according to Renou, *EVP,* XIV, p. 55). The expression *san vā́jam* "win the booty (of war)" is also known, and attested in a significant context: there is a very precise reference to what happens to the worshipper of Indra-Agni—once his worship is over, he is capable of crushing his enemy (bearing a generic noun, depersonalised *vṛtrá*, see Renou, *Vṛtra et Vrθragna*, p. 96) and, as a natural consequence, of winning his booty (6.60.1 *śnáthad vṛtrám̐ utá sanoti vā́jam indrā yó agnī sáhurī saparyā́t* "He is capable of crushing a *vṛtrá* and winning his *vā́ja*, he who will honour Indra and Agni (these two gods) who dominate." With the help of examples such as 8.38.1 *sásnī vā́jeṣu kármāsu* "(You are, O Indra and Agni) the winners of the prize of victory, in (war) deeds," it can be accepted that war and the acquisition of *vā́ja* are closely linked when they are seen in relation to each other.

Indeed 7.93.3 *úpo ha yád vidátham̐ vājíno gúr dhībhír víprāḥ prámatim ichámānāḥ / árvanto ná kā́ṣṭhām̐ nákṣamānā indrāgnī́ jóhuvato náras té* "the *vā́jin* (those who seek to obtain their *vā́ja*) have come to the ceremony for the distribution (of riches), (these) inspired-orators (armed) with poetic thoughts, seeking (your) protection, just as steeds arrive at the bar, these men who invoke with passion Indra and Agni", while maintaining the ambiguity, specifies that the officiant poets desirous of obtaining the *vā́ja* are easily likened to the steeds of the ritual races.

That the chariot races are rich in war connotations is well-known. This verse therefore accentuates a familiar idea which originates from a metaphor that links representations of war confrontations to all kinds of contests. Only here, and this is again confirmed in 7.93.4, the two series of representations are treated from the point of view of the result desired by the participants of poetry contests. This result is, so to speak, the terminal point and the end of a confrontation, i.e., the *vā́ja*.

It is perhaps not by chance that the entire hymn is articulated in two parts, 7.93.1-4 and 5-8. Verse 5 thus appears by its position to be central to the hymn which is remarkable by its particularly general contents, for the theme of confrontation is treated in a way that is almost speculative. It is a kind of summing-up, with references to the great Vedic theme of violent encounters between two adverse parties (5ab *sáṃ yán mahī́ mithatī́ spárdhāmane tanūrúcā śū́rasātā yátaite,* "when in positions of rivalry two great enemy factions fight against each other, with shining bodies, in order to win the battle of the heroes"). While it is no doubt true that the verb *saṃ-yat* denotes the gathering organised to be the theatre for war and oratorical contests (for the root *yat-* see Renou, *Études sur le vocabulaire du Ṛgveda,* pp. 44-46 in which 7.93.5 is not taken into account, but in which Renou stresses on the fact that the contests among the poets does not exclude the meaning "military"), it is also true that it is not at all possible to state with certainty that the quoted sentences refer to a single type of conflict. This is precisely because of the skill of the Vedic authors who manipulate two series of concepts, the concept of war and the concept of poetry contests, both of which have sacrificial overtones. It is however probable that a certain degree of inaccuracy (which is due to the fact that the verb *mith-* could denote all kinds of quarrels, see again Renou, *Études sur le vocabulaire du Ṛgveda,* p. 47) is vaguely seen in the second half of the verse. There is a more direct reference to the war conflict, in which can be recognised the theme of the defeat of the non-sacrificers, and capture of booty which will be distributed by the gods Indra and Agni helped by their devotees (5cd *ádevayuṃ vidáthe devayúbhiḥ satrā́ hataṃ somasútā jánena,* "Fell, with a single blow, the impious ones during the distribution (of riches) helped by pious men and men who press the soma!"). But the meaning contained in the two sentences remains quite general, as we can see; it refers to the conditions of acquisition of the *vā́ja* obtained thanks to the assistance of Indra and Agni (7 and 8).

In other words, the *vā́ja,* tinged with symbolism of war, and tending to mean "war booty", does not lose its connection to the sacrifice itself. So it is necessary to correct one of the accepted translations of the term *vā́ja.* It does not designate only the booty; like many other Vedic terms, it has a much richer meaning by virtue of its belonging simultaneously to two semantic fields—that of poetry contests with their sacrificial connotations and that of war. The former belongs to the within of the sacrificial proceedings and the latter is outside them. These two fields correspond respectively to the activity of the officiant poet and the patron/warrior.

One of the difficulties that Vedic thought had to contend with is the nature of the *vā́ja* and its connection to the sacrifice of the officiant poets and to the essential moment of the sacrifice when the dakṣiṇā is to be received.

It can be presented in this way: amongst all the practices included in the sacrificial proceedings the officiant poets receive two kinds of rewards, the dakṣiṇā and the *vā́ja*, both given to them by the patrons of the sacrifice. Take 1.122.12: *etám śárdhaṃ dhāma yásya surér íty avocan dáśatayasya náṃśe/ dyumnā́ni yéṣu vasútātī rārán víśve sanvantu prabhṛthéṣu vā́jam*, "After having obtained the *daśataya*, they said: we would like to form the cohort of this patron! May all those in whom the splendour of prestige and wealth are pleased win for themselves the *vā́ja* during the (sacrificial) ceremonies!" It must undoubtedly be understood that the officiants who obtain their reward in the form of a repast "characterised by the number ten" (the somic drink produced by the ten fingers of the one who prepares the soma, see Renou, *EVP*, IV, p. 290) wish that the patrons of the sacrifice are always victorious in the combats and that they carry off the booty, a share of which will be given to the officiants. Here, this share is called *vā́ja* but the usual procedure is to make things shorter by an ellipsis, for on another occasion there is this explanation 1.180.6 *préṣad véṣad vā́to ná sūrír ā́ mahé dade suvrató ná vā́jam* "May he be pleasant, may he go in front like the wind, (he who) like a patron of the sacrifice, keeping his vow, has taken possession of the *vā́ja* in order to give it generously!"

Hence one of the first questions is to find out exactly what is the relationship between these two kinds of rewards.

The hymns contain an ambiguity comparable to the subject of the dakṣiṇā and its sources—it comes from both the wealth obtained by the sacrifice as well as the war booty. While the hymns suggest that the *vā́ja* which crowns the success of the officiant poets during the sacrifice is the prize of victory won by the patrons of the sacrifice for their own benefit, as well as for the officiants, it can be considered that this is one of the forms of co-operation between the patrons and the officiants. 4.41.8 shows that the *vā́ja* is the prize awaited by the poets in such a way that, according to the characteristic metaphoric usages for images of war, the war combat and the poetry contest are in association with each other: *tā́ vā́ṃ dhíyó 'vase vājayántīr ājíṃ ná jagmur yuvayū́ḥ sudānū / śriyé ná gā́va úpa sómam asthur índraṃ gíro váruṇam me manīṣā́ḥ* "these poetic thoughts that seek to obtain the *vā́ja* (as well as) yourselves went towards you, O (gods) of fine gifts, as (one goes) to combat, in quest of your assistance. The songs and my inspired thoughts approached Indra and Varuṇa for their glory as cows approach the soma".

The nature of the *vā́ja* can indeed be explained taking into account its dual purpose as well as its relationship with the dakṣiṇā. Since the *vā́ja* is conferred on the poets by the patrons of the sacrifice, it is clear that, as in the case of the dakṣiṇā, the officiants can obtain this kind of reward only through the patrons; thus there is one more analogy with the dakṣiṇā.

Another question can be asked: while accepting that there can be two kinds of rewards reaped by the officiants, hence two kinds of interaction between the two groups participating in the ritual (and two kinds of integration of the patrons in the sacrifice), can one infer their identity and even their redundancy in the context of the symbolic system of the Ṛgveda? It can indeed be seen that the points of resemblance are easy to observe and can be recapitulated in this way: *won by the officiant poets and coming from and through the patrons of the sacrifice, the dakṣiṇā and the vā́ja are given to the officiants as a reward which crowns their para-warrior efforts and ensures the solidarity of the two groups involved in the sacrificial ritual.* But not only is it improbable that a religious system would have recourse to two almost identical symbols which fulfil the same function, the hymns also provide sufficient information for the differences in the treatment of the two symbols not to be neglected. These differences appear when it is noticed that their opposition is the subject of speculation by the Vedic authors who present this naturally in the form of allusions.

First, 6.33.2: *tvā́m hìndrā́vase vívāco hávante carṣaṇáyaḥ śū́rasātau / tvám víprebhir ví paṇī̃r aśāyas tvóta ít sánitā vā́jam árvā* "it is thee, O Indra, that the people who confront each other call to help when the heroes fight. Thou, (acting in concert) with the inspired-poets hast destroyed the Paṇi. The steed wins the *vā́ja* thanks to thy assistance".

Two kinds of sacrifice are related to each other. The war sacrifice during which the Paṇi demons are defeated, thereby making the Aṅgiras (evoked here as *víprāḥ* "inspired-poets") deserve their dakṣiṇā, and the poetic sacrifice which is referred to by the image of the steed obtaining its *vā́ja*. These two kinds of sacrifice are related and compared but they remain disparate because of their different natures.

On another occasion Lord Indra is presented as an instigator of the dakṣiṇā: as a god, he is compared to a generous patron of the sacrifice; then the perspective is modified and the patrons come in as mediators [6.37.4: *váriṣṭho asya dákṣiṇām iyartī̃ndro maghónāṃ tuvikūrmítamaḥ/ yáyā vajrivaḥ pariyā́sy áṃho maghā́ ca dhṛṣṇo dáyase ví sūrī̃n* "Indra the most active amongst the generous (patrons), powerfully sets his dakṣiṇā in motion; it is with this that thou dost inflict a defeat on misery, O bearer of thunder, when thou dost distribute among the patrons of the sacrifice (thy) generous gifts, O strong (god)!"]. In the next verse Indra is made a donor of abundant *vā́ja* by having his true warrior nature restored to him (6.37.5).

But who is the beneficiary of a *vā́ja*? 6.7.3 provides an answer which without being a definition of the origins of the beneficiary, enables one to decipher the statements on the acquisition or distribution of the *vā́ja*: *tvád vípro jāyate vājy àgne tvád vīrā́so abhimātiṣā́haḥ*, "It is from thee that the inspired orator is born, the steed, O Agni, from thee (are born) the valorous men, capable of defeating hostile intentions." Thus a *vípra* "inspired-poet" is destined to win the *vā́ja*, thus he gets the name *vājín*, just as *vīrā́ḥ*, "the valorous men", "the warriors " have the task of defeating the enemies. In this can be seen the opposition of the two functions, as well as their relationship which arises from the fact that each is confronted with his own adversary (cf. Renou, *EVP*, XIII, p. 127: "the *vípra* linked to the *vā́ja*, prize of the sacred contest, the *vīrá* linked to the *abhímāti*"). The poetry contest and the war confrontation are related just as in 6.33.2 quoted above. Here, the warrior impact of the *vípra* is enhanced because his success as a competitor for a prize is very close to victory which bears the stamp of war more clearly presented by the *vīrā́ḥ*, the professional warriors. It will be noticed that the series of metaphors is created from the linking of typical images of Vedic religion—the officiant poet, the steed, the warrior. Their relationship is explained by the intention to highlight this warrior aspect taken on by the officiants of the sacrifice on whom the *vā́ja* will be conferred. The allusion to the difference which separated the dakṣiṇā of the poet and his *vā́ja* can be discerned. The first is his reward within an internal confrontation, the second is his reward presented from the point of view of the war conducted outside.

Geldner is proved to be right, but with a modification of his stand on the opposition between the reward of the poets and the prize that is awarded at the end of a chariot race. In order to bring out this opposition, he refers to 1.27.9, 2.2.10, 6.45.12 and 8.2.36 (see his note on 6.33.2 in *Der Ṛgveda*, II, p.

131). On re-examining these examples individually, it can be seen that it is impossible to separate them from their contexts (bearing in mind that it is now currently accepted that the hymns are of a fragmentary nature and it would be useless to look for links between the mantras).

First 1.27.9 [*sá vā́jaṃ viśvácarṣaṇir árvadbhir astu tárutā / víprebhir astu sánitā* "May (he who is) known to all peoples (to all rivals?) conquer for himself the *vā́ja* (helped) by the steeds! May he conquer (it) helped by the inspired-orators!"]. There is little doubt that this is the continuation of wishes formulated earlier for the benefit of a mortal, (probably the poet) with the help of Lord Agni: 7. "the mortal that thou shall help, O Agni, during his combats, he whom thou shall incite for the prize of victory, he is the one who will obtain endless pleasures", and 8. "None shall surpass him, whomsoever he may be, O powerful (god); may the *vā́ja* which confers renown (be his!)." The person referred to is the person singing of Agni and likely to win the *vā́ja* at the end of the poetry contests [cf. 8.19.9: *só addhā́ dāśvàdhvaró 'gne mártaḥ subhaga sá praśáṃsyaḥ / sá dhībhír astu sánitā* "the mortal who honours (the gods) by rites, O Agni, O benevolent (god), he is worthy of praise: may he win by his poetic thoughts!"].

So if it is the officiant poet referred to in 1.27.9, it can be seen how the victory of the inspired orator and his acquisition of the *vā́ja* (which is possible if he is seconded by steeds), complement and oppose each other; if an officiant poet is to be successful with the sacrifice, that is, with an effort to pronounce the sacrificial words, he can be imagined either as a warrior or as a steed. This is what the poet of 8.2.36 seems to express when he presents Indra successively as an orator helped by steeds (in Vedic thought, belonging to a group implies possessing qualities enabling one to be part of this group), then as a warrior.

The opposition and the resemblance between the poetic victory and the victory crowned by the *vā́ja* often takes on the appearance of an alternative: 2.2.10 *vayám agne árvatā vā suvī́ryam bráhmaṇā vā citayemā jánāñ áti* "May we (win) O Agni, with (or thanks to) the steed, abundance in men, or may we surpass with our speech the brilliance of people(= our rivals)!" (cf. Renou, *EVP*, p. 96 on "the two basic and often undistinguishable competitions, the horse race and the oratorical contest"). This alternative happens to result in a complex representation, with a continuation of the linking of metaphors indicated above 6.45.12 *dhībhír árvadbhir árvato vā́jāñ indra śravā́yyān / tváyā jeṣma hitáṃ dhánam* "(may we vanquish) the steeds with (our) poetic thoughts, with the steeds (may we win) the prize of victory which confers renown, O Indra, may we conquer the riches named by thee (as the object of the competition)"! In order to build up the metaphor, the figures used are the officiant poet and the steed between whom one can make a choice because both of them are necessarily associated with war. The opposition between the reward of the officiant poet and the prize won at a chariot race is then clearly diminished for what is involved is, finally, two kinds of contests having a war character. It is now necessary to focus on the conditions of the conquest of the *vā́ja* as compared to the conquest of the dakṣiṇā.

The latter is desired by the officiant poet as such, and he wins it by remaining within the sacrificial proceedings; the *vā́ja* is won by the same officiant, but in order to receive it, the poet must take on the appearance of a steed. It is also by this rhetorical procedure that the likening of the poet to a warrior becomes possible (this procedure is more significant than is generally believed, like most procedures which arise from pure style).

Coming back to the question posed earlier (why are there two kinds of rewards for the officiant poet?), we have seen that these two forms are in opposition, but in a singular way, since this opposition is in fact an alternative. The solution to this apparent redundancy reaffirms the hypothesis stated earlier: the two alternative forms of reward for the sacrificial activity of the poet, the dakṣiṇā and the *vā́ja*, are differentiated according to their point of attachment, the first being inside and the second outside the sacrificial proceedings.

A certain explanation is however called for. Whereas the dakṣiṇā places itself only within the limits of the internal fight between the officiant poets, the *vā́ja* translates a *tendency* to create a link between the sacrificial act and the war conducted outside. Both the forms of reward originate in the war of the patrons of the sacrifice who capture booty, but the dakṣiṇā is the objective of the competition between the officiant poets and this competition can be likened to war only by a metaphor, because of the confrontational aspect of the competition. But the *vā́ja* is more clearly involved in the facts of war as perceived in a non-metaphorical manner. There is thus an essential difference between the two rewards, which lies in the quality of their opposition which takes the appearance of an alternative or a progressive opposition: the dakṣiṇā incarnates an effective relationship between the patrons of the sacrifice and the officiant poets, it is a relationship which is imperative to the very institution of the sacrificial act. The *vā́ja* is not exactly a relationship, for the interaction between the patrons of the sacrifice and the officiant poets is made possible precisely by the giving of the dakṣiṇā. In the system of Vedic symbolism, the *vā́ja* seems to be introduced as a kind of reply to the dakṣiṇā, thus enabling the nuances of the war connotations of the latter to be discerned. It is in this sense, and in this sense alone, that the *vā́ja* can be accepted as the double of the dakṣiṇā, while possessing a distinct value. This was possible only because the symbol used for this purpose was loaded with war significance in as particular a way as is the *vā́ja*, the warrior's reward in the precise sense of the word.

Once this information regarding the problem of the relationship between the dakṣiṇā and the *vā́ja* is provided, it is easy to understand why 8.40.2 exalts Indra, protector of the poet in his dual aspect, first appearing as the winner of a prize of victory, then only as an officiant poet, having no connection with the *vā́ja*, but as a participant in a contest which will get him a dakṣiṇā [8.40.2cd *sá naḥ kadā́ cid árvatā gámad ā́ vā́jasātaye gámad ā́ medhásātaye* "May he come to us someday with a horse (as a gift), may he come so that (we may) win (this horse) as a prize, so that (we may) win when our poetic faculties (are manifested)!"]. To these two aspects correspond on the one hand, the involvement of the officiant poet in the interior of the sacrificial act, and on the other hand, his deeds which make him a warrior-like figure. It is also possible to understand, but only to a certain extent—for, what this episode narrates is drawn from an obscure legend—the meaning of the co-operation between Indra and Kutsa.

Indra and Kutsa are two *kaví* participating in a chariot race, but the *vā́ja* figures in the episode only because their co-operation is also for the purpose of their victory over the demon Śuṣṇa. For this reason the alliance of the *kaví* takes on the aspect of a war waged against an external adversary who is defeated at a decisive moment on the day of the race [4.16.11: *ṛjrā́ vā́jaṃ ná gádhyaṃ yúyūṣan kavír yád áhan pā́ryāya bhū́ṣāt* "seeking to keep the two horses, like the prize of victory that one wishes to possess, so that the seer (*kaví*) may be ready (with the needful) at (the decisive hour) of the day"; further, it is Indra the warrior god assisting Kutsa, who is praised as the donor and provider of the *vā́ja* 4.16.16 *tám íd va índraṃ suhávaṃ huvema yás tā́ cakā́ra náryā purū́ṇi / yó mā́vate jaritré gádhyaṃ cin makṣū́ vā́jam bhárati spārhárādhāḥ* "This Indra (who is) easily invoked, we would like to invoke for you, he who hath accomplished numerous feats worthy of a man, who rapidly carries to a poet like me a *vā́ja* that one seeks to possess, he who possesses enviable wealth"].

Thus my conclusion is that the dakṣiṇā and the *vā́ja* are distinguished in the same way as the inside of the sacrifice is distinguished from the outside of the sacrifice. Just as the sacrificial act cannot be realised unless there is concurrence between these two zones, the giving of the dakṣiṇā can take place only if the officiant poet is metaphorically imagined as a warrior rewarded with a *vā́ja*. This comparison must follow the path already traced by the symbolic comparison of the poet to a warrior.

This comparison is dual because of the nature of Vedic sacrifice which has two clearly defined aspects. The sacrifice consists of a competition between poets, and conceals the war that is waged against the adversaries of the sacrifice who are excluded from the world of the sacrifice. Further, it must not be forgotten that the competition is akin to war all the more because, from the Vedic point of view, it involves a principle common to all competitions, i.e., the elimination of the competitor. By considering the dakṣiṇā and the *vā́ja* as two complementary and opposite versions of reward for the officiant poet, the progressive nature of the opposition can be understood. It is progressive since the terms in opposition imply, as he already been seen, that one or the other has to be chosen. With the *vā́ja* and its greater association with war than the dakṣiṇā, there is further strengthening of the tendency to make use of the *vā́ja* to confirm the connection between the sacrificial act and war in the literal sense.

In other words, the *vā́ja* as well as the dakṣiṇā are expressions of the inside of the sacrificial act, but to unequal extents. The former tends to be associated with the outside rich in war references, whereas the latter does not step out of its zone of origin and is associated with war only in a relative way by virtue of the competition between the officiant poets.

It is also because of this tendency noted in the concept of *vā́ja* that cases are produced in which a symbol like that of a cow, generally used to denote the dakṣiṇā, can appear, although in a modified sense, to denote the *vā́ja*. Their closeness construes their relationship, while at the same time showing their opposition based on the war connotation of the *vā́ja*, which the dakṣiṇā also has, but to a lesser extent. 3.36 presents Indra first as the god of war using his talents as a poet which serve to conquer the cows [5ab *vāvṛdhe vīryā̀ya samā́cakre. . .kā́vyena* "he has grown for himself with the aim of accomplishing his virile deed", i.e., his warrior deed which is alluded to by the Indraic term par excellence *vīryā̀*—"he has assembled for himself (the cows) thanks to his power of poet"]. He is then presented as Bhaga distributing the cows as *vā́ja*, which is possible because of his qualities of warrior, and as dakṣiṇā, which is possible by virtue of these same qualities and which is the normal obligation of a warrior. [5cd *índro bhágo vā́jadā asya gā́vaḥ prá jāyante dákṣiṇā asya pūrvī́ḥ* "Indra is Bhaga, his cows are those that are given as *vā́ja*, his generous (or plentiful) dakṣiṇā are born of him"]. The task of the warrior is divided into two: he must overcome the enemies who possess wealth that will serve as *vā́ja* [compare 3.37.6 *vā́jeṣu sāsahír bhava. . .índra vṛtrā́ya hántave* "be the dominant one at the moment of conquering (the booty) of the *vā́ja* (*san- vā́jam*, "win the booty of war" must have been the base for the expression *vā́jeṣu sāsahír*) O Indra, to fell thine enemy]; that is his proper war duty, but the warrior makes war only to satisfy his second vocation by associating himself with the sacrifice by giving dakṣiṇā to the officiants. It is however necessary to clarify that the one was not possible without the other and it is perhaps because they wanted to make clear the warrior origins of the wealth given as dakṣiṇā that these were deliberately mixed with the origins of the *vā́ja* (5.1.3 *ā́d dákṣiṇā yujyate vājayántī* "the dakṣiṇā is harnessed, which has for its source the *vā́ja*"). The progressive or gradual character of the symbolic structure of the two closely related terms is thus brought out all the more clearly.

2.4. The Quest for Booty and Meaning in Vedic Sacrifice

I now intend to present the results of my research pertaining to war expeditions as they are portrayed in Vedic hymns. Three inevitable questions arise that have to be answered: (1) What is the religious and social significance of the movements of Vedic warriors? (2) Since the ideology of the hymns seems to be centred around sacrificial activity, what is the connection between the war expeditions and the sacrifice itself? (3) It is obvious that, as far as comparatism is concerned, one is once again confronted with the problems of links between a religious function and at first sight, but only at first sight, an eminently warrior-like behaviour; thus the question that arises is whether the sacrificial and war aspirations of Vedic Indians correspond to similar ideas of other Indo-Europeans.

I shall begin by a Vedic lexical evidence. Firstly, there is the expression *apáso náviṣṭi* "seeking the new in (literary or poetical) work" attested in ṚV 8.2.17. Secondly, there is a compound with the same element *-iṣṭi* derived from the verb *iṣ-* "to desire", *gáviṣṭi* "seeking cattle", or more exactly "seeking cows". L. Renou had suggested the reconstitution of a compound **bhariṣṭi* "seeking the material booty, the cows":[29] in fact, in ṚV 4.40.2 is found *sátvā bhariṣó gaviṣó* "he (Dadhikrāvaṇ) is (like) a warrior who seeks to win booty, who seeks to win the cows" (the noun *bhariṣá* is visibly based on *gaviṣá*).[30] These two kinds of quests are easily related by virtue of their rhyming endings *-iṣṭi*[31] and are not together merely by chance. For, other than what can be considered the unique connection between them because of their context, these expressions simultaneously translate the concepts of the Vedic warrior and the Vedic officiant poet. The warrior (*sátvā*) who seeks booty and cows, and the poet who seeks the new in his creation, reveal their permanent intentions. The poet who seeks the new follows a direction whereby his new compositions are different from old and existing works, and in addition, from those of his rivals. So by creating a *gír* (an extemporaneous song) as opposed to *pitṝṇā́m...mánman* (inherited and memorised poetry dating back to ancestors), the *náva (návya)* in contrast to the *sána* (the new to the ancient),[32] the Vedic poet has even further objectives, not very evident at first, but which have to be taken into consideration. By his improvisation the poet no doubt moves away from tradition but he does not entirely break away from it, for his action is in keeping with the rules of the cult of traditional sacrifice. This cult commands him to compose poetical works which are in fact sacrificial works that the poet offers to the gods to obtain their favours and blessings for the patrons of the sacrifice and for himself. This is one definition that can be given to Vedic sacrifice as seen by one of the humans participating in the sacrifice. But this definition is incomplete as we shall see shortly.

The sacrificial work of the poet addressed to the gods attains yet another objective which consists of surpassing the poet's rival in the sacrifice and rendering this rival's work ineffective. A large number of phraseologisms in the hymns show to what extent the notions of rivalry and victory desired over the rival permeate the basic ideas of poetic and sacrificial creations found in the hymns. It must be noted that the poet's success earns him a sponsor, the patron of the sacrifice; this remuneration is technically known as dakṣiṇā and mostly consists of a cow or a herd of cattle. It can easily be understood that the quantity of dakṣiṇā varies according to the extent to which he has pleased the gods whom he has praised and to whom he has offered his poetical work. The Vedic warrior for his part is also exposed to rivalry, only it is found elsewhere. In the Vedic religious ideology in which sacrifice has a dominant role, the warrior uses and draws inspiration from the notions of sacrifice, and duly discharges his duties so that he may make his contribution to the sacrifice. Since he lacks the means that the officiant poet has for offering sacrifice, he has a symbolic way of doing so which is adapted to his nature, and which can be found in the hymns. The warrior's nature is remarkable in that it is not a fixed one, but changes according to the needs of the sacrificial work in the Vedic community. His foremost task is to attack those who do not offer sacrifice, to dispossess them of their wealth, usually herds of cows. After that, he has to be integrated in the cult, for which he has to change his nature and become a patron (*yájamāna*). To do so he has to order the officiant poet to perform the sacrifice. Although the hymns do not provide many details on this subject, it is possible to imagine two ways in which the sacrifice is promoted—either the instigation comes from the patron who has attacked the non-sacrificers and thus helps to enrich the community of sacrificers, or the poet who is to officiate at the sacrifice takes the initiative himself. These two options are probably provided for in the Vedic religion, but it must be noted that the person central to the sacrifice is the officiant poet. He has priority over the warrior-turned-patron, for his movements subsume during the sacrifice those of the warrior who has helped the sacrifice by his razzia and by his giving the booty to the sacrificers.

The end of the sacrifice is the time of *viṣā́ṇa* "releasing" (ṚV 5.44.11)[33] or *vimócana* "unharnessing" (ṚV 3.53.6.).[34] This is a significant moment because it shows how the patron of the sacrifice, the former warrior, is finally integrated in the sacrifice. This is the moment when the dakṣiṇā is given; thanks to the dakṣiṇā, the patron joins the group of officiant poets, as is very clearly stated in ṚV 5.44.12 *ubhā́ sá vārā práty eti bhā́ti ca yád īm gaṇám bhájate* "He goes before the one and the other object-of-desire (that is, the dakṣiṇā and the drink that he distributes), he shines when he joins the group (of poets....)." We thus see a clear-cut series of contrasts between the patron of the sacrifice and the officiant poet, but these contrasts are evidently complementary. Firstly, it is seen that the patron of the sacrifice is a figure unclearly defined in relation to the sacrifice itself. This lack of precision, probably deliberate, arises from his being given a fundamentally ambiguous and varying status. He is not exactly a warrior nor a patron of the sacrifice but takes on one or the other of these two roles. At first he is projected outside the conceptual sphere of the sacrifice performed by the officiant poets; at that time he takes an essential step for himself and for the sacrifice by taking away from the external enemy (*dāsá, dásyu*) wealth which is needed for the sacrifice. Secondly he effects the conversion of this wealth into riches which he places at the disposal of the community of sacrificers. He thus enters from the outside to the interior of the field where the sacrifice takes place, and which is defined as the conceptual sphere of the sacrifice. By these movements he shows his bivalent nature as opposed to the univocal and constant nature of the officiant poet who is not required to go out of the conceptual sphere of the sacrifice, either in the literal sense or in the figurative sense.

The second difference between the patron of the sacrifice and the officiant poet lies in the kind of enemy they confront. The poet's enemy is his rival when he formulates his prayer or his personal *bráhman* which must overcome the *bráhman* of the rival poet (see ṚV 1.152.7 *asmā́kam bráhma pṛ́tanāsu sahyāḥ* "may our *bráhman* triumph in the combats", cf. another translation "may our mystery triumph in the combats" proposed by L. Renou, *L'Inde fondamentale*, p. 64); since the warrior becomes the patron of the sacrifice, his enemy is an external one who threatens the institution of sacrifice. The two conflicts are related many times by their symbolism so much so that an entirely certain value is given to the lines of the war conflict, which thus is not really a war in the strict sense; it is a conflict which takes on a greater war significance when the hymns highlight the patron of the sacrifice, and a greater religious and sacrificial significance when the officiant poet is given importance.

The last difference between the two persons lies in their manner of offering sacrifice. The poet uses his inspired mind and words of praise. The warrior/patron is forced to perform two kinds of sacrifice by the very fact that he tries to integrate himself in the sacrifice. He must attack the external enemies and reward the officiant poet for his oratorical services by giving him in exchange for his verbal offering the cattle-dakṣiṇā seized during his razzia victories.[35]

Thus the Vedic sacrificer cannot be called unitary and simple. From the point of view of concepts realised by the totality of notions of Vedic sacrifice, it can even be said that this person is virtual insofar as he is not actually in the form of the complementary persons, the officiant poet and the patron of the sacrifice. Sacrifice is therefore a comprehensive activity, it is practically the only activity to which the hymns give a religious meaning. In order that the functions of the officiant poet and the patron of the sacrifice be accorded their proper place, this activity is required to be split into two by breaking up its illusory nature of oneness. Consequently, the two ways of offering sacrifice complement each other and include each other only in the complementary perspective of the components of the sacrificial act.

This complementary aspect can be further seen in the hymns which make use of a kind of symbolism whereby the officiant poet behaves like a warrior when he competes with his peers, and the warrior is represented in such a way as to liken him to an officiant poet.[36] Thus in ṚV 1.163.7, the poetic mind is shown as the path to the razzia. The sacrificial horse is addressed but reference is made to the war feats of the Aśvamedha steed: *átrā te rūpám uttamám apaśyaṃ jígīṣamānam iṣá ā́ padé góḥ* "I have seen thy highest form, the one which seeks to conquer wealth in the steps of the cow." Interpreted in a double way, *padé góḥ* is seen to be the poetic speech that poets usually associate with the conquest of the cow.[37] It will also be said that Lord Indra has discovered the enclosure of cattle for the benefit of the Aṅgiras, the officiant poets. This is an eminently warrior movement together with another that can be anticipated, i.e., delivering to the sacrificers an angry law-breaker, that is, a non-sacrificer. (ṚV

1.132.4 *yád áṅgirobhyó 'vṛṇor ápa vrajám índra śíkṣann ápa vrajám / aíbhyaḥ samānyā́ diśā́smábhyaṃ jeṣi yótsi ca / sunvádbhyo randhayā káṃ cid avratáṃ hṛṇāyántaṃ cid avratáṃ)*. Now these movements, those of a warrior for several reasons, are made by Indra who is described in the same hymn in the same manner as the steed Dadhikrāvaṇ (ṚV 1.132.3 *sá ghā vide ánv índro gavéṣaṇo bandhukṣídbhyo gavéṣaṇaḥ* "Indra is in fact known as the one who seeks to fight (in order to take possession) of the cows for the benefit of the *bandhukṣít*." The *bandhukṣít* are the Aṅgiras so-called because they reside or live in *bándhu* "relationship, spiritual relationship, correlative link"; they are thus linked to Indra by a spiritual relationship and they know the correlative links.[38] Indeed, the aim of the poets is precisely to show an aptitude better than their rivals' (note that, according to Renou, *L'Inde fondamentale*, p. 149 ff., the links to be indicated pertain to various kinds of phenomena—microcosm and macrocosm, rites and myths, human and divine, the fields to which the Vedic poet gives greatest importance in his analysis).

The quest for booty and the quest for cows are fundamentally identical when they are made by the warrior. Now that we have seen that the officiant poet's behaviour is linked to that of a warrior, it can easily be accepted that the poet's quest for the dakṣiṇā, in particular the cow-dakṣiṇā, could not be imagined differently in relation to the razzia for cows. Just as the person of the Vedic sacrificer can take the dual form of the officiant poet and the warrior, Vala's narration brings together Indra, the warrior god, and the officiant poets, the Aṅgiras. Helped by these poets, Indra with a violent warrior movement opens the enclosure holding the cows. The poet is also considered as having the power to open by destroying the cows' hiding-place, by virtue of his words as well as of his *bandhútā* (ṚV 4.4.11 *rujāmi bandhútā vácobhis*; Geldner refers to ṚV 4.1.15, 4.2.15 and 6.39.2 by which the connection of these words to the verses relating Vala's story can be seen). Here, the *bandhútā* "relationship, close connection, correlation" is not merely "family connection and affinity"[39] of the poet to his father Gotama (4.4.11 goes on to say: *tán mā pitúr gótamād ánv iyāya* "this came to me from my father Gotama"), it is both the means and the result of the effort of the poet who must discover and also invent and *understand* the essential links, the correlations, the equivalences and even the causal and genetic relationships between the phenomena.[40] As Renou has remarked, it is thus that the Uśij, the singers or model officiant poets, claim *bandhútā* "(spiritual) relationship" with the Ṛbhu, but it is not only because of this relationship which ensures their connection or symbolic equivalence to the Ṛbhu that the Uśij came to imagine how these first craftsmen succeeded in obtaining their share of the sacrifice. It is also their *mánas* (effort) of the (poetic) mind and their *védas* "science or wisdom" that they have contributed (ṚV 3.60.1 *mánasā bandhútā nara uśíjo jagmur abhí tā́ni védasā...yajñíyam bhāgám ānaśá*, cf. 3.60.2 *yáyā dhiyā́ gā́m áriṇīta cármaṇaḥ yéna hárī mánasā niratakṣata téna devatvám ṛbhavaḥ sám ānaśa*). Besides the correspondence of the *mánas* of the Ṛbhu and the Uśij, note that the *dhī́* "inspired (poetic) mind" of the Ṛbhu corresponds to both the *bandhútā* and the *védas* of the Uśij.[41]

The knowledge of the system of correlations "will enable the poet to shine in sacrificial competitions" (Renou, *JAs*, 1953, p. 173); it is also during the sacrifice by his speech which becomes like a competition with his rival that the poet creates his work crowned by the reward of the dakṣiṇā; his sacrificial work is however primarily an effort to understand mysteries and symbolic connections. These are the fundamental elements which though contradictory are nonetheless enlightening, for the hymns while seeming to ignore the apparent incompatibilty between two objectives of poetic sacrifice, establish a symbolic equivalence between the poet's words at the sacrifice and the cow. The formula ṚV 4.5.3 *padáṃ (na) góḥ*, "word (or name, trace, abode) of the (Cosmic) Cow"[42] only presents in a summary way, in a conceptual metaphor, the effect of these words which are likened to a cow that the officiant poet will win by snatching it from his rival thanks to his brilliant expression, his *bráhman.*[43] Thus it is by means of rationalisation, by placing on the same plane the means (the words) and the prize which these means can obtain (the cow) that the hymns create this metaphor which has often puzzled readers of the Ṛgveda.

We see now that its roots can be found if the stages of Vedic speculation on the value of the words are re-established. It is from the point of view of this speculation that one should consider the correspondences between the poet's words expressed by *padā́. . .gúhyāni* (ṚV 10.53.10, cf. 1.72.6) and *padā́ni. . .gúhā* "the secret traces (or the secret abodes) of the word" which ṚV 1.164.45 describes as Cosmic Cow. This Cow-word states things that cannot be expressed (ṚV 8.100.10 *vā́g vádanty avicetanā́ni*); the young poets of ṚV 1.152.5 on their part enjoy the inconceivable mystery (*acíttam bráhma*)[44] when they celebrate the *dhā́man* (the "plane" or "situation", according to Renou, *JAs*, 1953, p. 174) of Varuṇa and Mitra; in this can be seen the revelation of the *bráhman* (enigma consisting of posing a correlation, a correlative identification, according to Renou), in this specific case, the correlation between the solar horse without feet (RV 1.152.3 *apā́d...gárbha,* "the embryo...without feet") and the steed that this horse becomes after the defeat of the *ánṛta* ("the Disorder, the non-Truth") thanks to the *ṛtá* (the "Order, Truth").[45]

The story of Vala and the Aṅgiras who destroy his hiding-place and free the penned-in cattle is read, according to Lüders (*Varuṇa*, pp. 521-528) like a *Namenzauber*, the evocative magic of the secret names of the freed cows. In the perspective presented here, it seems evident that the revelation of the secret names corresponds to the technique of Vedic poets who are equipped with their knowledge of connections which they establish between their words and the concealed names of the cows (*gúhya, apīcyà*),[46] just as they correlate their *padā́...gúhyāni* to *padā́ni ...gúhā.*

But with regard to my aim, I must point out that the Aṅgiras are the poets at Indra's service, and although in Vala's story Indra is given the power of speech, it is the Aṅgiras whose songs are effective whereas Indra is a warrior who gives them the dakṣiṇā, the cows that he takes from Vala's cave. Indra the warrior is the *yájamāna,* the patron of the sacrifice which he entrusts to the Aṅgiras. From the various versions of the story contained in the hymns, one can sometimes deduce that the institution of the officiant king was known in the most ancient Vedic religion[47]. I think however that, given the fundamental difference between the warrior patrons and the officiant poets, there is a superimposition of the officiant function and the warrior function which is due to the complementary ways of offering sacrifice, one typical of the warrior and the other of the officiant poet. This superimposition or secondary interpretation was no doubt facilitated by the symbolic exchange of the functions caused by the recourse to the notions of war and rivalry which take on specific nuances according to whether dealing with poetic sacrifice or war waged outside the sacrifice. It can even be considered that the appropriation of cattle, one of the principal subjects of the hymns, is submitted to two different and complementary interpretations, one pertaining to war proper, and the other to sacred rites, but both undergo a conceptual re-interpretation. This reinterpretation is significant in Vala's story, in which the sources of the cows given as dakṣiṇā are identified since the warrior action of Indra, which alone would suffice to destroy Vala, is combined with the sacrificial chant of the Aṅgiras who obtain the cows as dakṣiṇā from Indra. The importance of this reinterpretation lies in the fact that it is based on the exploitation of one of the two major themes of Vedic poetry, whereby the power of recognising and formulating symbolic connections is attributed to the words, the *bráhman* of the officiant poets. The conquest of the cattle is achieved by a twofold war—the stylised war of the rivals in sacrifice and the actual war waged outside the sacrifice. The war razzia is thus echoed in the main supports of the theory of the hymns about the dakṣiṇā. In the concept of sacrifice taken as a whole, the dakṣiṇā is the symbolic value of the sacrificial words; as Renou has said, it is connected to the words just like the other known symbolic connections in the hymns. Thus, the patrons of the sacrifice are the *vā́jabandhu* associated with the *vā́ja*, the booty (ṚV 8.68.19): the generous patrons must be protected from calumny (*ná yuṣmé vājabandhavo ninitsúś caná mártyaḥ avadyám ádhi dīdharat* "may no envious mortal, O ye who are associated with the *vā́ja* attain you with his reproaches!"). It is clear that the poet identifies those who have gratified him with the *vā́ja*, this form of booty and riches which is won in competitions of war or poetry. Similarly, Lord Agni is *yajñábandhu*, characterised by his connection with the sacrifice of Manuṣ, of the first man who is distinguished by his aptitude to offer sacrifice (ṚV 4.1.9): *sá cetayan mánuṣo yajñábandhuḥ. . .sá kṣety asya dúryāsu sā́dhan devó mártasya sadhanitvám āpa,* "it is (Agni who) causes to be distinguished (the men, being) connected to the sacrifice of Mánas.... He dwells-in-peace in the dwelling of this (mortal), when he brings to its finish (the sacrifice); being a god, he has obtained for the mortal the right to be taken with (him to heaven)"—translation according to Renou, *EVP*, XIII, p.2.

The sacrificial horse is *devábandhu* (ṚV 1.162.18 *vājín devábandhuḥ*) "associated with the gods"; according to the commentary of Uv. of VS 25.41, this is because once immolated, "the horse will become the friend of the gods". This is a typical interpretation of commentaries, frequently resulting in reflections coming from an intellectual milieu quite different from the original milieu which suggests a more coherent vision with all the nuances of the meaning of the word *bándhu*. The horse achieves its relationship to the gods and this is because of its *mánas* turned towards the gods at the moment when it arrives at the place of immolation (ṚV

1.163.12 *úpa prā́gāc śásanaṃ vājy árvā devadrī́cā mánasā dī́dhyānaḥ*); it is thus likened to the poet endowed with *mánas* and related to the gods (see Renou, *Hymnes spéculatifs du Veda,* p. 19; *EVP,* XVI, p. 88 and J. Gonda, *The Vision of the Vedic Poets,* p. 207).[48]

Lastly, the Marut are *góbandhu* (ṚV 8.20.8): *góbhir vānó ajyate sóbharīṇāṃ ráthe kóśe hiraṇyáye / góbandhavaḥ sujātā́sa iṣé bhujé mahā́nto na spárase nú* "The song of the Sobhari is anointed (with the milk) of the cows, on the chariot, on the golden casket. These (Marut) who have the cow as a relation, the high-born, the great, (may they help us) to benefit from the delight, by winning (it)!" (according to Renou, *EVP,* X, p. 49). The quoted verse has at least two meanings. One is derived from the naturalist interpretation. The Marut bring the celestial waters to reward the song of the Sobhari, hence they are able to procure blessings for men who praise them with their songs (Lüders, *Varuṇa,* p. 377, n. 2); the other meaning is based on war connotations. The Marut help the singers to enjoy the delight (*iṣé bhujé*) and to earn it (*spṛ-*). Now, *spṛ-* is a verb with a war connotation (ṚV 5.44.10 *spṛ-vā́jam,* see Renou, *EVP,* X, p. 107, and a good number of other uses of the verb). The verse also appears to contain a double meaning concerning the source of *gó-* meaning both "milk of cows" and "cow". The double meaning once again conveys the incertitude, common in Vedic hymns, regarding the origin of the dakṣiṇā, for on the one hand, it is said that the cows of the dakṣiṇā are a part of divine favours, and on the other hand, that they are part of war booty. Here it is the first idea that is touched upon, by accepting that the cows are given as remuneration for the song, but the second is also suggested, since the singers hope to gain from the military or para-military conquest by addressing the Marut who are connected to the cow. Importance is thus given to the correspondence between a dakṣiṇā won in the form of a cow by means of rival songs of praise, and the cattle won thanks to the help of the Marut, the warrior gods. It must be remembered that the internal fight between the officiant poets and the war waged outside by the patrons of the sacrifice have analogous structures.

The razzia of the cattle is thus a Vedic theme in the hymns which make use of the idea of symbolic connections in a manner that can be understood only if one takes into account the relationship of correspondence between the power of the poet to establish and formulate the connection between words and the cow, and the power of the warrior to loot cattle. The two kinds of power are most often oriented towards cattle, especially the cow, and the hymns lay greater emphasis not on their possession but on their movement from outside the sacrifice to within it.

The Vedic authors present the officiant poet as one who takes care to establish connections by correlation (and Renou has often emphasised this; see *JAs*, 1953, p. 174). With regard to this human protagonist central to the sacrifice, the ideology of sacrifice gives more importance to the sacrifice of the poet by his words rather than by oblations. It can therefore easily be deduced that by virtue of the specific relationship between the sacrificial words and the cattle, as well as the position of the symbol "cow" in the Vedic world, or more exactly, in the warrior version of this world, what is involved is as much the cow, stripped as it were of its symbolism, therefore the animal obtained or conquered, as the movement of the symbols. The Vedic poet "wages war" against his competitor in order to succeed in establishing the connection (his *bráhman*) between his words and the cow, while the warrior, on his part, attacks the non-sacrificers to establish the same connection since he will have to give the officiant poet his cow-dakṣiṇā in order to be able to enter the sacrifice. By doing so he fulfils a need imposed by socio-religious considerations. He succeeds in joining the sacrifice, establishes his own symbolic connection which valorises the poetic speech. In Vedic sacrifice, words and objects revolve around the poetic speech and the metaphor linking speech to cow (*dhenú*

ṚV 4 1.16, *gó* ṚV 9.87.3, *usrā́* ṚV 8.41.5) concealed like its *nā́man* "name", subject of Vedic formulations,[49] acquires such an importance that it alone provides the warrior the justification to loot the cattle, rather than the reasons for rewarding the poet, and the need for offering milk products. And, much more than a justification, this metaphor bestows a meaning on the interaction of the warrior and the officiant poet each of whom offers sacrifice in his own way using the means available to him.[50]

Can we then pose this oft repeated query: Is the Vedic cow clothed with an exclusive metaphorical meaning, is it a symbol or, on the contrary, is it an animal exalted as such in the hymns? In other words, are the looted cows uniquely these animals considered necessary for a sacrifice using milk products, and which the warrior must give the officiants? Or are they the material which served to conceptualise the sacrificial world? The Vedic hymns do not seem to have concerned themselves with making this distinction[51] which is absolutely needed for an analytical categorisation, but which was alien to their authors. If this is understood, one cannot restrict oneself to saying that "a human undertaking as natural as the looting of cows" was considered in a metaphorical perspective thanks to "the symbolic character of the Indian *ṛṣi*", to "a leap in their speculative thought".[52] To maintain such a viewpoint is to abandon forever the serious study of the contents of the hymns, religious works in which the purpose of symbolism most certainly is not only to lend charm to poetry which must be removed from the hymns in order to attain the social reality, that is, in the case studied here, the use of cows in sacrifice. I think I have shown that the religion of the hymns has made a decisive choice by opting for the cow as a substitute for the offering (for poetic thoughts and words are identified with the cow in the phraseology of the hymns), and by associating it with words by means of a symbolic correlative link.[53] This fact is often neglected, as well as another, which is that the offerings to Vedic gods are varied and follow a hierarchy. They are varied because they are separated into food offerings (of which not all are taken from milk products or the cow itself; it must not be forgotten that it is not at all certain that the cow was immolated in this religion) and non-food offerings, such as hymns of praise, poetic speech and inspired thoughts. The hierarchy is established because on the one hand the hymns show a tendency to diminish the importance of food offerings and on the other hand all the Vedic gods do not consume food offerings. For example, the goddess Uṣas is one of those who accept only poetic speech as an offering.

Under these circumstances, a model of Vedic razzia which is inspired by a more general model, supposedly Indo-Iranian and Indo-European, according to which cattle are looted by warriors perhaps to be given to the officiants if the warriors have not used them for their own benefit,[54] does not correspond to the reality of the religious aspirations of the hymns. The cattle (particularly cows) are no doubt given to the officiant poets, as is attested by the institution of dakṣiṇā, but for what purpose? In ancient Vedic sacrifice, this purpose seems to have been determined by the symbolic value first attached to the cow, then by the link that had to be established between the cow and words in order to give a meaning to their being pronounced.

Of course there remains the question of compatibility between the symbolic value of the cow and the cattle acquired (or found) by the poet and won, looted by the warrior. I have emphasised the fact that the warrior's undertaking to appropriate the cattle outside the sacrifice was given a meaning which was conceptualised by the officiant poet within the sacrifice. This meaning when seen from the point of view of the hymns and Vedic sacrifice, is imposed on the warrior by the poet who takes over the cattle according to his skill in pronouncing the sacrificial words. The sacrificial words are equal to the cows as has already been seen; the warrior amasses the cattle, the poet amasses the words.

In the study of the history of thought which aims at examining the socio-religious reality of societies, it is extremely important to separate the study of objects which are taken into account by this thought, and their conceptualisation. Nevertheless we have seen from the examples provided by Vedic facts that the expelling of information pertaining to symbolism could cause errors in the evaluation of a socio-religious reality. It seems worthwhile to remember that if Vedic thought reserves a special place for the officiant and his sacrifice, it is because the ideology of sacrifice was oriented in such a way as to include the warrior's sacrifice in that of the poet. On the other hand, it is wrong to explain that the Vedic razzia was an activity which had to promote the sacrifice by bringing cattle to be sacrificed. This conclusion not only contradicts the evidence provided by the hymns but also belies the relationship between the ideology of sacrifice and the ideology of war which, in this case, is incorporated by the former.[55] Is this not an outcome of the effort to use social and religious symbolism as an instrument of analysis, which is much more effective than any other socio-religious presentation of Vedic sacrifice in which a careful distinction is made between cows in the sacrifice and the symbolic value?[56]

REFERENCES

1. *svàḥ sanisyávaḥ*: here, *svàr* is translated according to a suggestion of Renou, *Sur quelques mots du Ṛgveda* in *Journal of the American Oriental Society*, 85, 1965, pp. 83-85. This word expresses a more abstract idea (not merely the sun), that of an ill-defined happiness which has a greater value in the aspirations of the Vedic poet-priests.
2. For the nature of the *vajra* see B.Schleraṭh, *Vedisch* vajra "die Keule des Indra" in *Orbis*, XXIV, 2, 1975, pp. 493-518 and *Orbis*, XXVI, 1, 1977, pp. 133-134 and W. Rau, *Erwiderung auf B. Schlerath: Vedisch* vajra "die Keule des Indra" in *Orbis*, XXV, 2, pp. 356-358.
3. Retaining G. Dumézil's emphasis on the distinction between the *nṛ́* and the *vīrá*. L'homme: *ner-* and *uiro-*, in *Idées romaines*, pp. 226-241.

4. For the war vocabulary and symbolism associating combat and the throwing up of dust see pp. 34-36 of this book. To the interpretation of the war vocabulary and symbolism I would like to add two points: one concerns ṚV 8.1.7 *álarṣi yudhma khajakṛt puraṃdara* "Art thou excited, O Warrior who creates the combat, O Destroyer of citadels?" P. Thieme proposes another translation: "Du wirst stark (= immer starker), du Kämpfer, du Khajakṛt, du Wallzerbrecher" (*Kleine Schriften*, II, Wiesbaden, 1971, p. 789); it is true that the word *khajakṛt* is "leider dunkel" as remarks Thieme, but I have assumed that the parallelism *yudhma khajakṛt*, two nouns in the vocative case being the agent nouns, would suffice to establish that the second word also signifies "doer of combats". I however admit that the solution is arbitrary enough.

 The other point concerns a remark in C. Haebler's article, Pa. *iñjati*, buddh. h. *iñjate*: ved. *ṛñjate*—eine mittelindische—vedische Isolexe in *Pratidānam. Indian, Iranian and Indo-European Studies Presented to F.B.J. Kuiper on his Sixtieth Birthday*, The Hague—Paris, 1968, pp. 283-296. Dadhikrā, the steed in ṚV 4.38.7 is truly a replica of a combatant, reproducing the behaviour of a warrior or a poet undergoing the test of a competition, a role no different from the former: both confront their rivals but the type of rivalry is the same: *vājī́ sáhurir... samaryé / tū́raṃ yatī́ṣu turáyann ṛjipyó 'dhi bhruvóḥ kirate reṇúm ṛñján* "winner of prizes, the master ... in a combat, quickly darting between the drivers (of chariots) advancing in a straight line, he kicks up dust violently (which rises) up to the eyebrows, (he who) rushes (straight) (touching) the dust". In *túraṃ... turáyan* "running swiftly" and *ṛjipyó...ṛñján* "launching himself in a straight line" Haebler sees two symmetrical stylistic figures which have identical syntactic and semantic internal structure. These two stylistic figures are joined by a third one (* *He / or-* * *er-nu-*) associating two reconstructed elements based on the account of *(kirate) reṇúm ṛñján (reṇúm)*; the second accusative *reṇúm* is added by virtue of the syntactic valence of the verb *ṛj-* on which may depend a direct object. See Haebler, p. 296. "To rush (straight) (touching) dust" is a metaphorical expression used to describe the warrior-like behaviour of the steed: it corresponds to two other expressions of stanza 6 that are otherwise obscure, in which the steed *reṇúṃ rérihat kiráṇaṃ dadaśvān* "(he rushes) forcefully licking the dust, biting the dust"(?). Cf. Renou, *EVP*, XV, p. 163 for discussions and the problems of translations.
5. Not "a lot of dust" (See Geldner's translation of 4.17.13: "er treibt den Staub in dichten Haufen auf") for one should differentiate between *samohá* and *samūhá-*; the former means "feindliches Anrücken, Zusammentreffen" and the latter "Anhäufung, Schaar,

Menge" (O. Böhtlingk, *Sanskrit-Wörterbuch in kürzerer Fassung*, Vol. VII, St.Petersburg, 1889, pp. 67-68).

6. This hymn has been presented and analysed by H.P. Schmidt in his *Bṛhaspati und Indra* (pp. 104-113). I would add very little to his observations if our conclusions were not so divergent, which is explained by the difference in the way we deal with the problem of the king and the officiant in the Ṛgveda.
7. But Renou (EVP XV, p. 52) translates *manyú* as "the bad-thought". It is a fact that the translations of this term vary extremely from one author to another and in one context and another. (In this regard see Ch. Malamoud, *Manyúḥ Svayambhūḥ*, in *Mélanges d'indianisme à la memoire de Louis Renou*, Paris, 1968, p. 495.) The god Manyu is certainly the divine form of (warrior) Fury, and if I feel that it is possible to stress on the war aspect of the hostility that Bṛhaspati combats, it is because on the whole the vocabulary of these confrontations accentuates this tendency.
8. On *sáhas* derived from *sah-* and its war values, see pp. 30-31.
9. Cf. H.P. Schmidt, *Bṛhaspati und Indra*, pp. 111-112.
10. I cannot take a positive stand regarding the existence, during the time of the hymns, of the forms of adjacent sacrifices, incompatible with the widespread forms. Nevertheless read H.P. Schmidt, *ibid.*, pp. 111-112. I think that there was rivalry between those who practised the *same* form of sacrifice, who followed the *same* sacrificial doctrine.
11. S. Migron, *Ṛgvedic* van: *An old hunting term?* in *Indo-Iranian Journal*, vol. 22, no. 4, 1980, p. 274, cf. p. 280, n. 68.
12. For more details see my essay *La dakṣiṇā dans le Ṛgveda et le transfert de mérite dans le bouddhisme* (The dakṣiṇa in the Ṛgveda and the transfer of merit in Buddhism) in *Indological and Buddhist Studies.Volume in honour of Professor J.W. de Jong on his sixtieth Birthday*, Canberra, 1982, pp. 393-414.
13. A. Bergaigne in *Religion védique* I, p. 126, points out in particularly explicit terms that the distinction between officiants and patrons of the sacrifice was already known in the Ṛgveda, but this is not universally accepted as information of prime importance. He has, however, explained it in his own way, and with perspicacity:

   "If the institution of castes is encountered... only in a primitive form in the Ṛgveda, the usage of confiding the difficult tasks in the celebration of the sacrifice according to rites to those who had a special knowledge, of giving a competent person the responsibility of speaking on behalf of those concerned, 5.65.1, has been clearly established."

   An impartial analysis of the Ṛgvedic references has led me to the same conclusion, see my book *La déesse Uṣas. Recherches sur le sacrifice de la parole dans le Ṛgveda* (The Goddess Uṣas. Studies of the sacrifice of words in the Ṛgveda), Paris-Louvain, 1988.

14. *Le discours et le culte dans le Ṛgveda* in *Cahiers de littérature orale,* No. 4, 1978, especially p. 124.
15. See certain remarks on this subject in the study of *Védique* dhénā *avestique* daēnā: examen des critiques de H.P.Schmidt, p. 316, no. 32.
16. One more remark of Renou is worthy of mention (*EVP*, III, p. 35): *Yájamāna / sunvánt* must designate one and the same person who is both officiant and beneficiary in the archaic liturgical type; moreover, *yájamāna* is not necessarily "the one who offers sacrifice for himself". Cf. L. Renou, *La valeur du parfait dans les hymnes védiques,* Paris, 1925, p. 132.
17. Renou has brilliantly and briefly formulated this: "As opposed to Brahmanic variations, Vedic narration is usually interrupted, broken by reflections and parentheses, certain facts are perfectly narrative, others are shown as remarks or allusions, yet others describe a durable state which opposes the on-going processes.... What is more, the narration covers only one portion of the hymn which also includes an introduction and a conclusion that are more or less expanded upon." (L. Renou, *La valeur du parfait dans les hymnes védiques,* pp. 163-164).
18. Dumézil has rightly pointed out that the *árya* group is recognised as soon as another interdependence is established (which is, of course, of a quite different kind but which can easily be related to the one which determines the internal cohesion of a group as compared to another which by competing with it, is similar and has identical aims, cf. p. 237 of Dumézil's work: "does the word *arí* designate only *one part of the outsiders*....those who although outsiders to the social group to which the poet or the sacrificer belong, have the same gods and the same cults?"); this interdependence is based more on the relationships between the "I" of the poet who speaks on behalf of his group and the group itself (which can be associated with the concept of *arí*), see p. 241 of the same book. It can be believed that the tension between the "I" of the poet and the "We" of the patrons reflects the intrinsic conflict between the division and the interdependence of their respectvie functions in the sacrifice.
19. I refer to F.B.J Kuiper's study "The Ancient Aryan Verbal Contest" in *Indo-Iranian Journal,* Vol. IV, 1960, pp. 217-168 ff., although I do not entirely agree with his theory of the cosmogonic value of the Vedic verbal dispute which Kuiper interprets on the model of the Amerindian potlatch.
20. Apart from Dumézil's and Thieme's reflections on internal and external hostilities, see a more recent article which sums up the

CHAPTER 4

The *Signifiant* and the *Signifié* in Vedic Sacrifice

If it seems worthwhile to take up once again the meaning and the use of the term *bándhu* which Renou has already dealt with (*JAs*, 1953, pp. 171-175), it is because some recent observations on the language of the Ṛgveda and on the Vedic religious world are conducive to expanding on Renou's intuitions which are very thought-provoking but are sometimes stated too briefly. From amongst his conclusions, the one to be mainly considered is that *bándhu* has a concrete meaning ("near relation", "spiritual relation", and even "birth", AV 4.1.3) and a more abstract meaning ("link", "connection", "correlative link"). Firstly, it can be shown that these two meanings are interconnected in a way that concerns the most ancient Vedic poet much more than Renou has shown, although it must be acknowledged that I owe most of the results presented here to his research. Further, it can also be shown that the term *bándhu* is not as isolated in Vedic semantics as is generally believed, and that the notion of a connection has very firm roots in the Vedic manner of incorporating reflections on speech into speculation on sacrifice.

The Vedic poet had the task of formulating a personal *bráhman,* that is, formulating his knowledge of connections or equations between the human world and the phenomenal world; the *bráhman* according to Renou's and Silburn's this "typical Aryan" who represents "all the Aryans as a whole" (Dumézil, *Les dieux souverains des Indo-Européens*, p. 240) to whom the spokesman of the group belongs, and correlated, as Oldenberg has found, to the *sūráyaḥ*, "the patrons of the sacrifice". As for *purás dhā*, translated as "ehren" by Thieme, it is fruitful to consult J. Gonda's study *Purohita* in *Selected Studies*, II, pp. 320-337, which does not show that this translation is perfectly correct.

24. See H. Oldenberg, *Textkritische u. exegetische Noten*, Berlin, 1912, p. 63 on the difficulties in the interpretation. Without entering into controversy, let us note that the sequence: *aryáḥ...sūríbhir...nṛ́bhir* "the Aryan (patrons)...with these patrons, the warriors", comparable to the 6.25.7 sequence *nṛ́tamaso aryá...sūráyaḥ* "the patrons possessing the vigour belonging to valorous men ...(we) the (groups) of Aryans". Qualifying officiants and patrons of the sacrifice alternately as Aryans is not surprising, for both indeed belong to the Aryans as a whole.
25. Interpretation according to P. Thieme's *Kleine Schriften*, I, p. 8 instead of that given in Th. Aufrecht's edition of the Ṛgveda *(duchúnā minavāmā)*.
26. For the possibility of understanding *sumná-* as designating a verbal ritual act, cf. M. Durante "Nomi e struttura dell 'inno greco e vedico", in M. Durante, *Sulla preistoria della tradizione poetica greca* II, Rome, 1976, pp. 155-166. It could then be said that the patron of the sacrifice finds in the fire not the favours accorded by the gods, but precisely the poetic work of the officiants which has undergone the effects of the mediating sacrificial fire and of its god Agni who is honoured in this work.
27. According to Renou, *EVP*, XII, p. 4, this refers to the god Agni who is invoked here (see Geldner *Der Ṛgveda* I, p. 29).
28. On the colour of the horse *ṛjrá*, see Geldner, *Vedische Studien*, II, p. 165-166.
29. L. Renou, *EVP* I, Paris, 1955, p. 2; *bhára* would mean the taking of booty in a war: H. Oldenberg, *Kleine Schriften*, I, Wiesbaden, 1967, p. 408, n. 2 and L. Renou, *EVP*, IV, 1958, p. 77 on ṚV 5.48.4 containing the word *bhárahūti* "cry of victory".
30. L. Renou, *EVP*, XV, 1966, p. 165 following H. Oldenberg, *Ṛgveda. Textkritische und exegetische Noten*, Berlin, 1909, p. 300 and J. Wackernagel, A. Debrunner, *Altindische Grammatik*, II, I, Göttingen, 1957, p. 65.
31. On the quasi-suffixal nature of- *iṣṭi*, L. Renou, *Grammaire de la langue védique*, Lyon, 1952, p. 114 (note) and H. Oldenberg, *Ṛgveda. Textkritische und exegetische Noten*, p. 300-301; L. Renou, *EVP*, XV, p. 165.
32. On the distinction between the new and the old in Vedic concep-

tions of poetry, L. Renou, *EVP* I, p. 2 and J. Gonda, *Ein neues Lied* in *Selected Studies*, IV, Leiden, 1975, pp. 144-159.

33. *sấm anyám-anyam arthayanty étave vidúr viṣā̃ṇam paripā̃nam ánti té*, "the officiants prepare to go towards the one and the other (of the patrons of the sacrifice), they know (that they have) before them the unharnessing and the distribution of the drink" (translation according to Renou, *EVP*, V, 1959, p. 27).
34. *yátrā ráthasya bṛható nidhā̃nam vimócanam vājíno dákṣiṇāvat* "There where is (carried out) the bringing to rest of the high chariot and the unharnessing of the steeds thanks to which the dakṣiṇā is won."
35. Cf. the summary of my lecture in "Annuaire Pratique des Hautes Études, Vth Section," t. 89, 1980-1981, pp. 271-278 and my two essays *Identity and Substitution in Vedic Sacrificial Ritual* in *Semiotica*, 47, 1984, pp. 165-179 and *La religion du sacrifice védique et le sort de l'officiant et du guerrier dans l'Inde brahmanique* in *Atti del III Convegno Internazionale di Studi Antropologici Siciliani* (Palermo, 7-9 Dicembre, 1981).
36. The complemetary nature of the human participants in Vedic sacrifice which can even be a symbolic assimilation, is certainly different from the warrior's being used to serve the religious cult in the Zoroastrian reform of the Iranian religion, even if this common point can be noted: the warriors use violence, which was an end in itself, only against miscreants; the religion of Zarathustra changes the too clearly-marked oppositions in the Indo-Iranian religious system, in particular the one pertaining to war aspects (see G. Dumézil, *Naissance d'archanges*, pp. 142-146 and *Idées romaines*, pp. 197-201). But we know that the Zoroastrian reform was able to innovate, precisely thanks to its tendency to unify by changing the old polytheism into a uniform system in which only the fight between the Good and the Bad mattered. If in the religion of the Ṛgveda the warriors serve the sacrifice, by this they obey a need of the religious system by which sacrifice and war are clearly differentiated. In no case does this service take on the appearance of submission, and even less the abolition of roles that, while no doubt independent, are connected.
37. See L. Renou, *Études sur le vocabulaire du Ṛgveda*, Pondicherry, 1958, p. 21 and *Hymnes spéculatifs du Véda*, Paris, 1956, pp. 18 and 229. Geldner rightly sees in ṚV 1.163.8 an allusion to both the procession following the sacrificial horse and the triumphal journey of the horse which conquers enemy kingdoms.
38. L. Renou, *Études védiques, 2. bā̃ndhu, JAs*, 1953, p. 174: "which possess connective forces".
39. L. Renou, *JAs*, 1953, p. 172.
40. L. Renou, *L'Inde fondamentale*, Paris, 1978, pp. 149-153 (on the

connection as an explicative procedure which can be related by correspondence to the *nidāna* of Buddhists).

41. On ṚV 3.60.1 see L. Renou, *JAs*, 1953, p. 172.
42. L. Renou, *Et. sur le voc. du Ṛgveda*, pp. 21-22.
43. It is worth remembering that "the bráhman is nothing else but this form of enigmatic thinking which consists of posing a correlation, a correlative identification, this very one that the Brāhmaṇa designated by the terms *nidāna* or *bandhu* and also *upaniṣad*" (L. Renou, *L 'Inde fondamentale*, p. 88).
44. The correspondence between *acíttam bráhma* and *vā́g vádanty avicetā́nani* was established by D.S. Ruegg, *Contributions à l'histoire de la philosophie linguistique indienne*, Paris, 1959, pp. 15 and 19.
45. L. Renou, *L'Inde fondamentale*, pp. 62-63.
46. *nā́man* "name" is at the core of Vedic speculations.
47. A perceptible tendency especially found in H.P. Schmidt, *Bṛhaspati und Indra*, Wiesbaden, 1968.
48. All these examples have been briefly mentioned by L. Renou, *JAs*, 1953, p. 173, but the explanation given here is mine.
49. See again Ruegg's remarks in *Contributions*, p. 19.
50. The officiant poet is the ideologue of the sacrifice, whereas the warrior is the ideologue of his movements, but not of the razzia (which is the subject of my essay "La religion du sacrifice védique et le sort de l' officiant et du guerrier dans l'Inde brahmanique").
51. See my essay "Védique *dhénā*, avestique *daēnā*: examen des critiques de H.P. Schmidt" in *Lautgeschichte und Etymologie*, Wiesbaden, 1980.
52. B. Lincoln, *Priests, Warriors and Cattle*, University of California Press, 1981, p. 102 and n. 32.
53. See in this volume, *The signifiant and the signifié in Vedic Sacrifice*, pp. 153-166.
54. B. Lincoln, in *Priests, Warriors and Cattle* stresses on the eventuality of this gift, for the warriors would tend to avoid it, which is the cause for their conflict with the officiants belonging to Indo-Iranians (pp. 134-163); to this end, he studies the legend of Vasiṣṭha and Viśvāmitra from the Rāmāyaṇa (pp. 143-149), and finds a parallel in Y 29 (the plaint of the soul of the ox, on which see G. Dumézil, *Dieux souverains des Indo-Européens*, pp. 127-131). It can be deduced from the interpretation of Y. 29 by Dumézil that not only is there no possibility of seeing a conflict between the warriors and the officiants, but Vedic hymns do not give any support to the idea of such a confrontation (even if the names of Vasiṣṭha and Viśvāmitra are evoked in circumstances that have nothing in common with the epic legend despite n. 37, p. 148 of Lincoln's work, with bibliography). Personally I see no possibility

of interpreting ṚV 7.104.2 and 10 as evidence that the Vedic warriors wanted to consume the meat which was supposed to go to the officiants (pp. 154-155: the artificial interpretations of Lincoln are based on a misunderstanding, for the reference is not to the harm done by Viśvāmitra to Vasiṣṭha, but the threat of the thieving enemy: *ripú, stená, stenakṛ́t* are terms which designate the scoundrel and the thief, notwithstanding Lincoln's referring to Geldner and Lommel, p. 154, n. 74).

55. The contrary example of the warrior's ideology leading to the officiant's is studied in the essay "La religion du sacrifice védique et le sort de l'officiant et du guerrier dans l'Inde brahmanique."

56. See an interesting discussion on the symbolic aspect of evidence on a culture or a religion, especially in the conceptualisation of the animal world in ethnology: S. Tornay, *Vie des chiens ou Des excréments comme bouillon de culture* in *Production pastorale et société,* n. 8, 1981, pp. 35-42 and F. Sigaut, *Un tableau des produits animaux et deux hypothèses qui en découlent* in *Production pastorale et société,* n. 7, 1980, pp. 20-36 and also F. Sigaut, *Produits animaux et symbolisme. Une réponse à Serge Tornay* in *Production pastorale et société*, n. 9, 1981. I find it impossible to agree with the latter who says: "All that is based on symbolism in a society must be explained, but explains nothing." On the contrary the greatest attention must be given to concepts by which we can make out how things are symbolised, and the working of symbols in a society; the information given above shows the working of symbols connected to rival ideologies of which one (the warrior's) acquires a meaning and undergoes transformations which it would not acquire and which it would not undergo by itself.

CHAPTER 3

Notes on War and Religion among the Indo-Europeans

Various analyses have been made of the characteristics of the Vedic warrior as opposed to his Indo-European counterpart. These have led me to express my thoughts regarding today's popular theories dealing with the question. It should be said here that these theories are numerous and they call for an evaluation.

I

At the beginning of this volume is a study that seeks to compare the Homeric *skhétlios* to the Vedic warrior. This study has shown that, amongst other things, the behaviour of the Vedic warrior seems to govern or at least determine the basic nature of the warrior. From a general point of view, which of course tends to be simplistic as it differentiates only *stereotypes*, the warrior has a certain propensity for finding himself in conflicting situations. The function attributed to the warrior is itself one of the reasons that prompt him to take a leading part in a conflict or even provoke the conflict. In the hierarchy of functions, the warrior's function of provoking conflicts is comparable to that of a king, and it is just one among the many functions that may be assigned to him. In my view, the main thing is that the Homeric *skhétlios* reflects one of the duties of the Indo-European warrior, one that defines his very essence—that of an individual committed to reach beyond limits, be they moral or spatial.[1]

As in other cases of similarities between various Indo-European fields, meanings are not always expressed in the same manner. The Vedic vocabulary does not have expressions that convey the singular quality of the warrior but whereas the Homeric vocabulary possesses the word *skhétlios* the hymns of the Ṛgveda speak of the warrior's violent resolve to reach beyond the limits and justify the same in their characterisic expositions on sacrifice.

This is seen in the regal characteristics of the warrior but also, and more importantly in the reason for his wanderings between the conceptual zone and the region beyond; he is then forced to integrate himself into the sacrifice.

It is this aspect which led me to conclude that though the purpose of these travels is war, they also serve another essential purpose: the sacrificial work of the officiating poet-priests.

It is because of this feature that the Vedic raids are conceptualised in a manner that conforms to the dual aspect of the warrior role.

However this dual aspect seems to have already existed among the Indo-Europeans. This becomes evident when one sees that in other Indo-European spheres, poet-priests (or their counterparts) and warriors make joint or individual efforts that bring into play their aptitude for violent verbal expression as well as their physical aptitudes without making any clear distincton between the two. That they do not take into account their original roles and that consequently poetic activity and war activity are each expressed in terms of the other is neither a coincidence nor a Vedic particularity. On the other hand, one is given to think that the conjunction of these activities which gives rise to the amalgam of their symbolic expressions and favours the creation of Vedic metaphors such as poet-warrior and "officiating warrior" is a Vedic acception of an Indo-European fact.

The intrinsic raison d'être of Vedic raids thus lies in the need to ensure sacrifice. However a vast typology of the conditions leading to the formation of warrior bands among diverse Indo-European peoples seems, at first glance, to set aside the Vedic religion. This typology of F. Crevatin (the article referred to above) which is at once comparative and anthropologic in nature sets forth three elements in the life of an Indo-European society which has seen the professionalisation of the warrior: (1) the society marginalises a group of youth who are (2) dangerous to society for these two reasons; and (3) these youth are likened to wolves who must be exterminated. It should be noted here that marginalisation seems to be the solution to economic or to be more specific, social problems. Economic problems arise from the scarcity of materials: society gets rid of a group that fulfils its needs through war and plunder practised beyond its frontiers (it is thus that Ulysses is said to have been forced to become the chief of a warrior group; he reveals to Eumaeus the extreme meagreness of his paternal legacy, see Od. 14.192 sqq.). The second problem has to do with the initiaton of youth to the warrior profession: this also gives society the opportunity to restore equilibrium by ridding itself of the potential danger of the "wolves".

Of course the basic elements of Crevatin's typology are tenable; this is because he did not choose to take into consideration the religious aspect. But this is an opportune moment to pose the question: what is the reaction of Vedic religion to the problem of creation of warrior groups, to the creation of the warrior profession?

1. The marginalisation, if at all there is one, is only temporary; the warrior leaves, only to later return to a society that believes in sacrifice, that even defines itself through the need for sacrifice. Thus he is not really marginalised: his wanderings are a part of the sacrificial project which would otherwise be difficult to realise. Thus it is not appropriate

here to talk of marginalisation, rather it is the exteriorisation of the individual who is also called upon to sacrifice in his own way. It is thus that war becomes an integral part of the ritual of sacrifice.

2. The overemphasis on the sacrificial act present in all Vedic activities is also explained by the relative weakness of the economic considerations. Of course the Vedic warrior is exhorted to dispossess the external enemy and contribute the plundered wealth to the sacrifice. But the principal reason for this exhortation does not lie in the material insufficiency of the sacrificers; it is essentially the separation of the conceptual zone of the sacrifice from the exterior, the protection of the institution of sacrifice from the threat of non-sacrificers and finally the rewarding of the officiant. This is explained by the fact that according to the archaic vision of the hymns of the Ṛgveda, Vedic sacrifice is not really a sacrifice of material offerings like soma or other food preparations, rather it is a sacrifice where the main offering is in the form of poems. The interpretation of B. Lincoln which depicts the movement of cattle taken from the **dāsa* and handed over to the officiants who in turn sacrifice it to the gods cannot lay claim to a pan-Indo-European character for one then risks underestimating the contribution of Vedic religious thought.

3. Lycanthropy, which is proved to have existed among the Indo-Europeans[2] takes on a different aspect in the early Vedic hymns. However the word 'lycanthropy' can be used here only with utmost caution while citing this Indo-European representation. It is indeed Indo-European, but with a few reservations. Here a slight clarification is called for: warriors regarded as wolves or who imagine themselves becoming wolves are not the same in the two contexts. In Vedic hymns it is the enemy who is clothed in wolf's skin, never the warrior fighting for the cause of the sacrifice. Gods are called upon to protect their followers from the enemy mentioned at the same time as the thief (2.28.10, 10.127.6) and from a

paṇí who has the desired cows (6.51.14) and is called a wolf. This makes us think of the external enemy who threatens the institution of sacrifice and in fact the hymns say so explicitly: in ṚV 9.79.3 the supplicant implores the soma to protect him from the hostility of *svá* i.e. "one's own, related or allied to oneself" and from the hostility of the wolf (*vṛ́ka*) "the other, the outsider, the stranger".[3] Consequently Indra and Agni are called *avṛká* meaning "one who protects from the enemy".[4]

Thus the Vedic warrior is not the wolf; affinity between the wolf and the combatant is perceived only when the latter is on the wrong side of the sacrificers. Therefore to plunder a person perceived to be a wolf is to act for the success of the sacrifice and for the society conducting the sacrifice.

Therefore as a counterpoint to the results of the comparative study of Crevatin, it is necessary to make a distinction between plundering for others (which protects a way of life based on sacrificial practices) and plundering for oneself which is a means of survival for warrior gangs which have broken away from society.

The religion of the Vedic warriors is undoubtedly the same one which leads them outside the sacrificial world, and they are naturally under the protection of Indra, the warrior god, but the situation is very different from the one known to the Germanic world. Firstly, the Germanic warriors have their own form of worship; secondly, if they are linked to their society of origin, the link is a correlation of opposites—a society which considers itself homogenous rejects all heterogenous elements. Thus the religious aspect of Germanic warriors appears to be an element of social history that is born of the tension between two groups of humans. On the other hand, the religious aspect of the Vedic warriors is an infrastructural element common to the society and the warriors who are fully integrated into it. For such a society, practising the religion of sacrifice and entering into war with its neighbours are two correlated activities and the correlation is based on the fact that the groups of humans concerned are similar or even identical and not in the least different.

II

These conclusions on Vedic religious practices correspond to those put forth by L. Ch. Muellner more than twenty years ago in his study of Greek verbal culture. Based on extensive study of Greek forms and of Vedic and Avestan phrases or expressions, he observed that in Indo-European culture, any discourse addressed to the gods had a secondary but nonetheless essential function: to surpass the rival who seeks, in Vedic terms, to emulate it i.e. to set a high value on his own discourse addressed to the gods.[5] This leads him to another conclusion that the use of such a discourse in war conditions or on the battlefield led to its being used during confrontations; thus the Greek sacred discourse is an offshoot of the Indo-European agonistic discourse.

This proves all the more interesting when seen alongside a study of Greek phraseology that produced similar results.[6] When applied to Homeric situations, a series of Greek phrases convey a clearly understandable background: verbal production in a confrontation between persons, be it hostile or otherwise, and war activity belong to related spheres.

It appears that the evolution of the semantics of a verb such as *árkhō* is comparable to the evolution found in some samples of Vedic religious ideology. The constant superimposition of expressions of such ideology i.e. verbal or combative confrontations, corresponds, in Homeric poems (particularly in the Iliad), to the evolution of the signification of *árkhō:* the verb signifies firstly "to lead, to command" then "to signal" with the characteristic duality "to signal a verbal confrontation" as well as "to signal a combat".

We have here a situation often found in comparative studies, which is additional proof if ever it were needed, that these studies contribute to the reconstruction of a historic reality and not a mirage that is so dear to comparatists: what many Indo-European fields have preserved in the form of phrases and original or reconstructed expressions, others have retained in their thought, ideologies and narrative patrimony.

It is from this point of view that it is important to note that the Homeric expressions *mū́thōn árkhein* and *ē̃rkh' agoreúein* are used to present a succession of agonistic discourses and signify "introduce a verbal sparring match", "to be the first one to talk" and that the vocabulary is often war-like in nature. I observed this fact independently of the analyses of Homeric texts by Muellner and Bader (see pp. 70-77 as well as a more exhaustive discussion in my book *La déesse Uṣas*) but my observations concern both the Vedic language and the religion of the hymns of the Ṛgveda.

Further, the Greek expressions analysed by Bader refer to language occurrences, to the verbal practice; when inserted into an agonistic discourse, they take on a special signification and connote an usage of discourse which is distinct from its pragmatic usage. This discrepancy in the functions of discourse seems characteristic of correspondences between the Veda and Homer. Thus on comparing the constituent acts of Vedic sacrifice and the behaviour of bards in Homer's works,[7] it is possible to conclude that after its integration into the religious system of the Ṛgveda, the Vedic poetic discourse was transformed into sacrificial discourse but it nevertheless corresponded to the poetic discourse of bards, to the pragmatic act of communication.

There are two aspects of this Indo-European fact: on the one hand, the verbal act undergoes changes that can be explained through a historic religious background and this change, as shown by Bader's synchronic analyses, is visible within the Greek tradition itself (Vedic and Irish narratives only confirm this observation). And on the other hand, the historic dimension is revealed by the comparison of a verbal communicative act to religious practice.

III

Given such explicit links between violent verbal competitions and usual war practices, one could wonder to what extent they are not elements that are sufficiently general to be established as inherited ones.

A recent study that completes Bader's own study analyses the co-occurrence of metaphors found in Vedic and Homeric poetry and finds them reproduced in the works of other Greek authors (Alcman, Hesiod, Pindar and Aristophanes).[8] According to this author, the ostensible custom of comparing war practices with speech acts can only be explained by the continuation of the Indo-European tradition. This is borne out by the identity of the metaphors which serve as a basis of comparison: likening a competition between specialised orators to a combat or to horse races is in fact an Indo-European theme.

Dunkel's treatment is quite comprehensive: numerous evidences are added to those present in Bader's study which was primarily concerned with the reconstruction of forms. There are however two points that require clarification.

It is my view that in the matter of reconstitution of Indo-European facts concerning rituals and religion, it would be more adequate and more appropriate to consider that metaphors presenting language acts are more than just metaphors, i.e. more than just figurative descriptions of verbal conflicts. They are designations of an Indo-European concept that is reproduced with a certain degree of authenticity by sacrifice (verbal offerings) of Vedic poets and verbal confrontations of Greek protagonists. It is because of the conceptual reach of these metaphors that we become aware of the distance separating them from all other representation of verbal exchanges, violent or otherwise, exchanges that form the core of any dialogue. For, all things considered, comparison of theses, their juxtaposition, the desire to complete the given information etc. as well as aggression or irony (which is just a mitigated form of aggression) are all present in one form or the other in any dialogue. Dunkel is correct in saying that the opposition of action to discourse being specific to Greek litterature, there is a good reason for analysing physical conflicts (war, games) by opposing them to verbal conflicts (quarrels, debates in the agora, poetry competitions) and not placing verbal conflicts at one of the extremes of the opposition but between the two: it is a medial term, not a marginal one. But it is precisely this approach which respects one of the specificities of Greek sources tending to respect the specific character of this form of Indo-European religion which expresses itself through the concept of stylised and ritualised verbal conflicts.

Dunkel also underlines the close links between war booty and the dakṣiṇā of the officiating poet-priests in the Vedic conceptual system precisely because both have been subsumed under war metaphors (see above p. 110 and p. 125 on the relationship between the booty and the dakṣiṇā). He is right in emphasising the similarity between the gift of fifty cows offered by Hermes to Apollo and the Vedic dakṣiṇā, a reward that crowns the discourse of the poet-priest, just as the gift of cows crowns the song of Hermes. But this extract from Hermes' hymn No. 437 is not as isolated as it may seem. In 436, Apollo hails Hermes with the words "a companion who exerts himself during festivities", *ponéumene daitòs etaîre*. Is this not an allusion to the role of the bard, just as Demodocus amongst the Pheacians who receives a share of the meal as a reward for his song, a share consisting of a piece of flesh from the pig, a domestic animal? This offering made to Demodocus is also related to the dakṣiṇā by its function as well as its materiality: offered through the gesture of Ulysses, it retains its symbolic ties to sacrifice and is a sign of movement of cattle in a situation that reproduces the essential features of the movement of cattle in Indo-European sacrifice.[9]

In 438, Apollo who announces to Hermes that his song was worth fifty cows (I translate *pentēkonta boûn antáksia taûta mémēlas* as "these fifty cows (now) take care of them; they are worth as much as your song") foresees more transactions to follow ("after this we can peacefully divide things"). In fact, we know that the cows are exchanged for the song and the lyre and that Hermes urges Apollo to work towards spreading the fame of Hermes, the inventor of the lyre (h. Hermes 477). The series of transactions is thus actually continuous just as in Vedic sacrifice.

REFERENCES

1. This is also found in F.Crevatin's essay, *Aspetti militari delle società i.e. e società militari* in *Ricerche di antichità indoeuropea*, Trieste, 1979, p. 59.
2. Apart from the works mentioned by Crevatin, see some important syntheses that have numerous valuable typological parallels: V.V. Ivanov, *Drevnebalkanskij i obšÞeindojevropejskij tekst mifa o geroje ubijce psa i jevrazijskije paralleli* in *Slavjanskoje i balkanskoje jazykoznanije*, Moscow, 1977, pp. 181-213 and *K balkano-balto-slavjano-kavkazskim paralleljam* in *Balkanskij lingvističeskij sbornik*, Moscow, 1977, pp. 152-164.
3. The two expressions cited are those of G. Dumézil, *Les dieux souverains des Indo-Européens*, Paris, 1977, pp. 247.
4. See R. Hiersche's study on the subject, *Zu ṚV.7.88.6c und 5b*, *Indo-Iranian Journal*, 8, No. 3, 1965, pp. 165-170. See also E.Campanile, *Meaning and Prehistory of Old Irish Cú Glas* in *JIES*, 7, Nos. 3-4, p. 245 (it is the hostile stranger who is the wolf, not the internal enemy).
5. L. Ch. Muellner, *The Meaning of Homeric* eúkhomai *Through its Formulas*, Innsbruck, 1976, pp. 134-135.
6. F. Bader, *De "protéger" à "razzier" au neolithique indo-européen, phraséologie, étymologies, civilisations*, in *Bull. Société de Ling. de Paris*, 73, 1978, especially pp. 182-195.
7. See my forthcoming essay "Les stratégies de l'aède homerique et le sacrifice du poete officiant védique" and also its summary in *Annuaire de l'École Pratique des Hautes Études, Sciences religieuses*, t. XCI, 1982-1983, pp. 189-192.
8. G. Dunkel, *Fighting Words: Alcman Partheneion* 63 mákhontai in *JIES*, 7, Nos. 3-4, 1979, pp. 249-272.
9. See the summary of my lecture: *Annuaire de l'École Pratique des Hautes Études, Sciences religieuses*, t. XCII, 1983-1984, pp. 175-180.

CHAPTER 4

The *Signifiant* and the *Signifié* in Vedic Sacrifice

If it seems worthwhile to take up once again the meaning and the use of the term *bándhu* which Renou has already dealt with (*JAs*, 1953, pp. 171-175), it is because some recent observations on the language of the Ṛgveda and on the Vedic religious world are conducive to expanding on Renou's intuitions which are very thought-provoking but are sometimes stated too briefly. From amongst his conclusions, the one to be mainly considered is that *bándhu* has a concrete meaning ("near relation", "spiritual relation", and even "birth", AV 4.1.3) and a more abstract meaning ("link", "connection", "correlative link"). Firstly, it can be shown that these two meanings are interconnected in a way that concerns the most ancient Vedic poet much more than Renou has shown, although it must be acknowledged that I owe most of the results presented here to his research. Further, it can also be shown that the term *bándhu* is not as isolated in Vedic semantics as is generally believed, and that the notion of a connection has very firm roots in the Vedic manner of incorporating reflections on speech into speculation on sacrifice.

The Vedic poet had the task of formulating a personal *bráhman*, that is, formulating his knowledge of connections or equations between the human world and the phenomenal world; the *bráhman* according to Renou's and Silburn's definition "is nothing but that form of enigmatic thought which consists of posing a correlation, a correlative identification, the one which the Brāhmaṇa designate by the terms *nidāna* or *bandhu*, or also *upaniṣad*. The "bearer of the *bráhman*", when it is not the *bráhman* (masc.) himself, is the *kaví*, the poet having profound intuition which is far above the level of the usual laudators and narrators".[1] The Vedic hymns are a part of the texts which the literary and religious tradition of India calls Śruti "Revelation"; Śruti, according to L. Renou, is in essence symbolic and is based on "secondary"[2] and indirect semantics. This means more exactly that the hymns are based on a network of correlations, equivalences and identifications or connections among various orders: divine, ritual and human, that is, macrocosmic and microcosmic.[3] To understand the true nature of the hymns, it is therefore necessary to understand this dual fact: the hymns are created by the poets who formulate and resolve the enigmas by using correlations and identifications, and the hymns are themselves full of symbolism and hidden and secondary meanings, and this is in fact due to the attitude of the poet to the words formulated by him.

By creating his *bráhman* the poet specifies a *bándhu*; specifying it is for him a way of displaying his skill in giving form to his knowledge and, in the event, referring to his belonging to a family tradition. Referring once again to Renou, it can be recalled that the poet prides himself on being related to the Aśvin gods. ṚV 3.54.16: *nā́satyā me pitárā bandhupṛ́chā sajātyàm aśvínoś cā́ru nā́ma* "The Nāsatya, when questioned about their family, (call themselves) my relatives; the pleasant name of the Aśvin has the same origin (as mine)."[4] The context is significant: the poet is related to the Aśvin and his own name has the same origin as that of the gods. And, if he goes on to say ṚV 3.54.17 *mahát tád vaḥ kavayaś cā́ru nā́ma yád dha devā bhávatha víśva índre sákhā ṛbhúbhiḥ puruhūta priyébhir imā́ṃ dhíyaṃ sātáye takṣatā naḥ* "Great, O poets, is your pleasant name, while you are all in Indra, O ye gods! Friend of the beloved Ṛbhu, (you are O god). Thus invoked, create (O Indra and the Ṛbhu) for us this poem so that we may win the (poetical) fight!" it must be understood that he means to state the ability of the poet to find the secret and hidden names thanks to his poems which he will use in a poetry competition in which he hopes to win against his rival. This is because searching for and discovering the name signifies, in the hymns, the appropriation of the object which bears the name. The poet has at his disposal secret words (*padā́....gúhyāni* ṚV 10.53.10 and 1.72.6) to which correspond the *pā́dani...gúhā* (ṚV 1.164.45) "the secret, hidden traces" or "the abodes" of the Word, while the latter is described as the cosmic Cow which knows inexpressible things (ṚV 8.100.10 *vā́g vádanty avicetanā́ni*).

The discovery or the conquest of the cow is, for the Vedic poet, a great adventure associated with the discovery and formulation of names by means of his words. The giving of a cow to a poet entrusted by the patron of the sacrifice to officiate and hence offer sacrifice, is the favourable completion of the sacrifice, a completion that consists of obtaining a value corresponding to his sacrificial speech. The value which rewards the poet and which will be given to him at the conclusion of the sacrifice is designated by the term *dákṣiṇā*. In the old Veda, this term is closely associated with the cow and tends to become an independent designation of the cow. Vedic religion freely deals with the association and even the identification of speech to the cow, but rather than thinking that the animal is overestimated because of its economic importance and its role as supplier of milk products offered at the sacrifice, it is interesting to see in this relationship the preoccupations of the officiant poet, preoccupations which seem to be oriented towards the determination of the value of the poetic and sacrificial words. For the determination of this value is expressed by the linking of the words to the cow and by the giving of a cow to the poet by the patron of the sacrifice who must change his situation from warrior to patron of the sacrifice. If this is so, it is because the cows raided by the warrior from a neighbouring enemy and given to the officiant poet as dakṣiṇā, act as a means by which this warrior can be incorporated into the sacrifice from which he would otherwise be excluded and, more precisely, as a means by which he can be associated with the conceptual sphere of the sacrifice. It has been shown elsewhere that the predominant symbolism in the Vedic razzia from the poet's point of view lies in the establishing of a correlative link between the words and the cow.[5] The cows brought by the warrior are, in the conceptual world of the poet, the material for speculation on the poetic words which the poet uses when relating the words to the cow. More than just the source needed to provide milk products for the sacrifice, cows are conceptualised and treated as the value of the sacrificial words. They are therefore necessary for the officiant poet who manipulates words in the sacrifice, and it is indeed the reflection on the words which governs the symbolic conceptualisation of the razzia effected by the patron of the sacrifice.

Thus a correlative link is established not only when the poet creates his *bráhman,* but also when he receives his dakṣiṇā. The *bándhu* or correlative link which is revealed when the *bráhman* is formulated is thus the counterpart of the bond linking the words to the dakṣiṇā, the stake in the poets' competition which stems from another rivalry, the war, which is a war to dispossess the external enemy by the patron of the sacrifice. This analogy is clearly attested in the hymns and in some mythical stories which recall that it is thanks to the *bandhútā* "relationship, close connection, correlation" that the poets destroy the hiding-place of Vala's cows (ṚV 4.4.11 *rujāmi bandhútā vácobhis,* cf. 4.1.15, 4.2.15, 6.39.2.) Vala's story in which is mentioned the theme of destruction of the hiding-place and the setting free of the cows is a story in which are mingled the theme of the warriors and the theme of the power of the poetic sacerdotal words of the Aṅgiras who accompany the warrior god Indra.

But what exactly is the notion of Vedic relationship and how does it fit in with the notion of a correlative link? An answer can be found in Vala's story which deals with the complex nature of this notion.

The Aṅgiras, the officiant poets, set free the auroral cows and declare their relationship to the goddess Dawn (Uṣas). ṚV 4.2.15 and 4.2.16 explain that the Aṅgiras wish to be born of mother Uṣas like their predecessors and would like to emulate their Fathers by setting out to discover the luminous source Dawn. Now, for the Vedic poets, the discovery of the imprisoned cows is above all the discovery of their hidden names (ṚV 4.1.16, cf. H.P. Schmidt, *Bṛhaspati und Indra,* p. 223), or, more exactly, the recognition of the connections and the correlative links between their words and the cow-dakṣiṇā which are similar to the connections and links between the secret words that they know and the name of Dawn often represented by a cow. The dakṣiṇā of the Aṅgiras naturally consists of the auroral cows. We can then understand that the Marut gods momentarily likened to the Aṅgiras, reply to the questions concerning their spiritual relationship by recalling their mother, the cow Pṛśni (ṚV 5.52.16 *prá yé me bandhveṣé gā́m vocanta sūráyaḥ pṛ́śnim vocanta mātáram*). We can also understand, since the recognition of the name is in fact the revelation of the names and forms, that the god of fire Agni is *pṛṣṭabándhuḥ*: ṚV 3.20.3, the poet declares that the names of this god are numerous and that the gods have set in him numerous forms (*ágne bhū́rīṇi táva .. nā́ma yā́ś ca māyā́. . . tvé pūrvīḥ samdadhúḥ pṛṣṭabandho*). Agni is *pṛṣṭabándhuḥ* "the one whose relationship is being asked about" because it is up to the poet to reply to the questions (*pṛch-*"to interrogate") and to establish the connections which reveal the identity and the relationship of the god and which are even given in the hymns in the form of definitions such as 2. *ágne trī́ vā́jinā trī́ ṣadhásthā tisrás te jihvā́...pūrvīḥ* "threefold are thy victory forms, O Agni, threefold thy abodes, threefold thy numerous tongues"; 4. *agnír netā́ bhága iva kṣitīnā́ṃ. . . sá vṛtrahā́ sanáyo* "Agni (is) the leader of the divine populations like Bhaga...he is the ancient breaker of resistances...."

Being anxious to establish the identity of the god and thus reveal the hidden names and forms, the poet does nothing but take up again the task of the original creators of the language, the onomatothetes[6] known in ṚV 10.71.1 who gave names to things. He recalls the problem of the names and forms of the god, then he specifies them. He juxtaposes and identifies the numerous names, forms and dwellings of the god, thus falling in line with the Vedic practice of defining the nature of an object by mentioning its name, its dwelling and its origin by means of correlative identifications [cf. the meaning of the term *padá* "word, name, dwelling"[7] and the clear parallelism of the expressions *dhā- padám* "to find, pose a word", *man- dhā́ma* "discover, invent a form", which recalls the parallelism of *padá/dhā́man* and *nā́man* (name)/*rūpá* (form). Coming back once more to the correspondence between the *padā́...gúhyāni/padā́ni...gúhā* which denotes the correlative link between the poetic words and the traces (or the abodes, the names) of the word, it can be observed that the idea of *bándhu* is already present. It takes on the aspect of equivalence having a correlative value. The poet has at his disposal secret words revealed to him which he puts into correspondence with the names (traces, abodes) of the objects sought, such as the transcendental word identified with the cosmic cow; the traces of the cows; the names and forms corresponding to the mysterious nature of the god etc.

Note that the cow given as dakṣiṇā to the poet as the value of the poetic words has the same origin. The dakṣiṇā, according to Vedic sacrificial ideology, is what crowns the effort of the poet who reveals symbolic connections. It is also that form of riches brought by the warrior who intends to join the poet's sacrifice, and by which the poet is rewarded for his effort in formulating the sacrificial words. It is, from the point of view of the warrior who becomes patron of the sacrifice, his entry permit to the sacrifice; but from the point of view of the officiant poet, it is the justification of the formulated words, the valorisation of these words that the sacrificial ideology relates to a fraction of the riches available to the patron of the sacrifice thanks to the sacrifice and the wars of dispossession. It should be remembered that the preferred and predominant form of dakṣiṇā is a cow and that the words which are effectively formulated during the sacrifice and which establish the symbolic connections, are rewarded by the poets' being given a cow or a herd of cows. It is not surprising that the Vedic hymns exalt this keyword of a mystery as the "hidden footprint (or the name) of the cow" which is known to Agni and revealed to the poet by him (ṚV 4.5.3 *padáṃ ná gór ápagū̄ḷhaṃ vividvā̂n agnír máhyam préd u vocan manīṣā̂m*); the phrase *padáṃ (ná) góḥ* is a succint and metaphorical formulation of the value of the inspired and poetic words, of the words that the poet learns and which earns him a cow at the end of the successful sacrifice.

Thus it is seen that the notions covered by the terms *bándhu* "link, spiritual and correlative link" and *dákṣiṇā* "reward, cow given as reward" represent, each in its own way, the nature of the relationship between the poetic words and their value in the sacrifice. They seem to tell us that the effective and fortunate poetic words which promise the officiant poet a reward as soon as he formulates them by establishing a *bándhu*, have a meaning and a value. The hymns use the words "an illusion without a cow" to describe the words of the poet who is not fit for a poetry competition and who has used uninteresting words which bear no fruit (ṚV 10.71.5 *naínaṃ hinvanty ápi vā̂jineṣu ádhenvā carati māyáyaiṣá vā̂caṃ śuśruvā̂ñ aphalā̂m apuṣpā̂m*); and "stiff and thick in friendship" to describe an unlucky officiant poet (ṚV 10.71.5 *sakhyé sthirápītam*), for success in the sacrifice depends on the solidarity of the congregation of poets (compare with ṚV 10.71.6 *yás tityāja sacivídaṃ sákhāyaṃ ná tásya vācy ápi bhāgó asti* "the one who has abandoned his friend, his colleague in learning, no reward will come unto his words"). The inspired poets who are loyal to Indra will say that they are deprived of *bándhu* compared to Indra who is richly endowed with it: ṚV 8.21.4 *vayáṃ hí tvā bándhumantam abandhávo víprāsa indra yemimá...ā́ gahi..sómapītaye* "We the inspired poets who (have not) *bándhu*, we have captured thee...come then (towards us) to drink the soma." Renou (*JAs*, 1953, p. 174) has assumed that one of the possible meanings refers to the "connective" energies of Indra which are lacking in the human poet. This conclusion can be modified. Indra, warrior-god and model for the patron of the sacrifice, has wealth which the officiant poets hope to obtain. These latter are *abandhávo* "without links" as long as the god has not come to their sacrifice and as long as the relation between the words used to invoke the god and the favour which the god accords them by just coming to the sacrifice has not been established (as mentioned in ṚV 8.21.1 *tvā́m...vā́je havamahe* "we invoke thee in the competition around a prize" and 2. *tvā́m ...avitā́ram vavṛmáhe sákhāya indra* "we have elected thee as our support, we the friends, O Indra"). The association between the willingness of the Aśvin gods to go to the place of sacrifice and the desire of the faithful not to witness these gods held back by their rivals is strengthened by the reference to the affective bond (or the umbilical cord) which has already been put (ṚV 4.44.5cd *mā́ vām anyé ní yaman devayántaḥ sáṃ yád dadé nā́bhiḥ pūrvyā́ vām*: see Renou *EVP*, XVI, p. 36 on *sám-dā-* "to link"). Thus it is not insignificant that the two bonds *bándhu* and *nā́bhi* [the latter meaning "umbilical cord, navel" and perhaps even "kinship" in ṚV 9.79.4: *diví te nā́bhā paramó yá ādadé* which Renou in *EVP*, VII, p. 60 translates as "thou whose supreme relation with the sky is connected (to ours)"] are connected in a certain way: on the one hand, the poets are *abandhávas* compared to Indra *bándhumant*, and this explains why they are deprived of the favour which is the arrival of Indra at their sacrifice; on the other hand, the poets who worship the Aśvin will lay emphasis on the *nābhi*, the affective bond, which indeed seems to be the condition necessary for the realisation of a *bándhu* with the Aśvin. (Is there not, in the term *bándhu*, an echo of its historical relationship with Greek *pentherós* "who contracts a family tie by marriage" and Lithuanian *beñdras* "comrade" from which it derives its meaning "kinship, relationship"?).[8] The notion of affection binding the poets and a god is apparently part of the semantics of the two terms. It is because of the affective bond between him and his devotees that Indra favours them in a manner in keeping with his warrior nature. ṚV 1.132.3 *sá ghā vide ánv índro gavéṣaṇo bandhukṣídbhyo gavéṣaṇaḥ* "Indra is in fact known as he who seeks to fight (to take for himself) the cows for the benefit of the *bandhukṣít*." The devotees are here called *bandhukṣít* "who live in *bándhu*", they are the likely possessors of the connective force *bándhu* which enables them to exercise their aptitude for formulating the symbolic connections. The association of the warrior god and the poets who possess the connective force is all the more natural in the Ṛgveda for, as Renou has already seen (*JAs*, 1953, p. 174), the theme of the combat is superimposed on that of the poets' verbal contest; but it must be noted that this superimposition belongs not only to the hymn being considered. It is dictated by the relationship between war and the poetic sacrifice which are likened to each other because they serve to conquer the cows by different but superimposable means (violence of war in one case, rivalry of the poets in the other). The ability of the poet to establish a *bándhu* by his *bráhman* is easily convertible to his claiming his dakṣiṇā, and this claim is substantially inherent in the poetic sacrifice which is successful.

It can be seen that in AV 2.1.3 and 4.1.3, there is a sort of finalising of the tendency already begun in the Ṛgveda. If *bándhu* contains any reference to the relationship and ties of affection and sometimes to the clientele of a god like Indra (which Renou stated in his analysis of ṚV 1.132.3), the two

Atharvanic texts speak of the person of the poet and his aptitude for formulating a *bándhu:* 2.1.3, the poet is the connection, the father and progenitor and is at the same time the one who knows all the planes of the universe and all beings (*sá naḥ pitā́ janitā́ sá utá bándhur dhā́māni veda bhúvanāni víśvā*) and, because of this, is capable of giving names to the gods (*yó devā́nām nāmadhá éka éva*). According to 4.1.3 he is the living connection of the universe who can interpret all the begettings of the gods (*vidvā́n asyá bándhur víśvā devā́nām jánimā vivakti.*)

In the exegetic Vedic prose, the term *bándhu* designates "the meaning", "the signification" (Minard, *Trois énigmes sur les cent chemins*, I, p. 50-51; Renou, *JAs*, 1953, p. 174); as Minard points out, it has shown evolution and progress; the term denotes successively "explicative identification", "explanation of the deep meaning", and also "symbolic or mystic signification" by moving from "existing link between a sacrificial act and a phrase or a sentence in the sacrifice". Would this be new stages which reveal the efforts to describe the term by Indianists or a real progression that the meaning of the term has undergone? Even while being faithful to Renou's ideas, one can believe that this multiplication of meanings did nothing but specify the Ṛgvedic meaning "real or sacerdotal relationship" (*ibid.*, p. 174).

The mythical content of the Ṛgveda justifies in a large measure the concomitance of the significations taken on by this term. The notion of *bándhu* associated with that of *dákṣiṇā* has already been elaborated in such a way that we can see in it the reflection of a conception of the meaning of the spoken words, which are first and originally the words pronounced in a sacrifice, offered as a sacrificed object. According to this conception, the terms of a discourse are necessarily connected to a value by a tie that is described as parental or affective. In very ancient times, the Vedic hymns seem to have devised a theory which affirms that words have signification only if they are associated with values given to them by mystical methods. The poets implicitly lay emphasis on the ties between the terms of the discourse and their values, and it is futile to try an answer the old question of whether or not these values are symbolic. The words are either effective or not. In the former case, they are connected to a value, in the latter, have no value, and will be unfruitful (*aphalá, apuṣpá*). Thus no distinction is made between meaning and value and the explanation for this is that the intended result of the sacrificial words and the conditions of their being pronounced render useless this distinction which is otherwise essential.

It is interesting to note that a similar practice is the basis of Vedic lexicography of which an example is provided by the *Nighaṇṭu*. We know that this work contains lists of Vedic words arranged in groups, but the allocation of the words to the groups as well as their association within the group, depend on a principle which is difficult to determine. Nevertheless Renou observed that the term *nighaṇṭu* being translated as "secondary accidental (designation)", the words are put together insofar as they can be "designations which are indirect, incidental or figurative of a certain notion", substitutes for one another. More generally, they are explanations of words which have the nature of symbolic glosses. These glosses do not give the synonymous significations of the words, but their values footing on more or less arbitrarily chosen equivalences (even according to their proximity in context in the Vedic hymns), or from alliterations; most of the classifications are based on rapprochements having a particular affinity with the presentation of values selected from the hymns. Again, in Renou's study of the *nighaṇṭu* (p. 215), it is seen that "the correlation of values creates on a larger plane associations of images and combinations between the profane domain and the ritual domain, between the microcosm and the macrocosm, between the human milieu and the divine milieu". A curious example that Renou discusses and which corresponds to the concrete figures of symbolism in the hymns can be cited: the word *gaúḥ* "cow" means the "word", both because it is brought closer to the root *gā-* "to sing" and because, if we follow Renou's conclusions on the principle of correlative references, one can remember the likening of prayers to cows in the hymns. We have seen how this similarity was established, which is certainly one of the "semantic co-ordinations" (Renou), but it is not a simple product of the poets' imagination, for it is in fact a formula which briefly summarises an entire speculative approach which aims to discover the value of poetic speech in the sacrifice. Thus, what is presented as a value justified by one of the correlations in force is taken up once again as a gloss which has the nature of a lexicographical definition. It is worthwhile to remember that a purely lexicographical work of this kind would not be successful if Indian philological tradition had not turned to Vedic sources and Vedic poetry. In his analysis of the *nighaṇṭu*, Renou has clearly shown that the list of words found in them bring out the principle of correlations exploited by Vedic poets. This fact itself is not without consequence as it enables us to suggest that the creation of the terms *bándhu* and *dákṣiṇā*, however firmly they may be fixed in specifically Vedic mythology and ritualism, served a linguistic train of thought which it would be unjust to refer to as just being developed at that time. If the Vedic poet indicated a symbolic *bándhu* by formulating his words, if it is clear from the analysis of the complex relations between the protagonists of the Vedic sacrificial ritual that the formulation of the sacrificial words earned the poet an object of value (the cow given as *dákṣiṇā*), it is because the Vedic doctrine of sacrifice as shown in the hymns is largely based on the acknowledgement of this linking of the formulation of the words to a reward, in reality, the linking of the word to its value and to its effect in the sacrifice. Let us remember that giving the dakṣiṇā is a compulsory action which ends the sacrificial procedure carried out effectively by an officiant poet who has succeeded in his task. By adhering to this theory of the words, one can imagine the preoccupation of modern linguistics which gives its version of the problem of the link between the sign and its value, between the *signifiant* and the *signifié*. Benveniste has redefined certain old principles of the Saussurian approach to the arbitrariness of the sign by stating that there exists a symbiosis between the *signifiant* and the *signifié* which behave like the *incorporant* and the *incorporé*, and that it is necessary to pose the consubstantiality of the *signifiant* and the *signifié* in order to understand the structural unity of the linguistic sign.[10] He has also redefined what is to be understood by value of the sign: it is an element and an attribute of its form, not of its substance.[11] We would not be modernising the views of Vedic authors by noting that their constructions which are discovered through mythology and ritualism are close to the purely theoretical observations of the linguist. At the most, the way in which they have approached them may seem unconventional—the nature of the correlative links established by the formulations which are necessarily reflected on the plane of taking possession of the values that these formulations attract.

REFERENCES

1. *Sur la notion du bráhman, JAs*, 1949, p. 13.
2. *Le destin du Véda dans l'Inde, EVP*, VI, 1960, p. 27.
3. *"Connexion" en védique, "cause" en bouddhique*, in L. Renou, *L'Inde fondamentale*, Paris, 1978, p. 149.
4. L. Renou, *EVP*, V, 1959, pp. 13-14, gives a different translation, if rendered in English, "the commonness-of-birth with the Aśvin is a pleasant name."
5. *Le symbolisme de la razzia d'après les hymnes vediques* in *Études Indo-européennes*, no. 5, pp. 1-17 (The search for booty and meaning in Vedic sacrifice, pp. 120-142 of this volume).
6. I use "onomatothete"and not "nomothete" according to the current usage based on the corrections of Plato's texts in which can be

found, however, an etymological formula (*hó onomathétēs étheto*) and the very archaic expression (*ónoma étheto*) which doubtless comes from an Indo-European source, cf. Ved. *nāman dhā*, Av. *nāman dā* "pose, establish the name" which correspond to Hitt. *laman te* "evoke the name" and to an expression that is reconstructed for the common Slavic **jīme děti* "call by the name, give the name". The comparisons between all these expressions are taken together and commented in V.V. Ivanov's study *Drevneindijskij mif ob ustanovlenii imjon i iego parallel v grečeskoj tradicii (The ancient Indian myth of the position of names and its parallel in Greek tradition)* in *Indija v drevnosti* (Ancient India), Moscow, 1964, pp. 88, 90.

7. L. Renou, *Études sur le vocabulaire du Ṛgveda*, Pondicherry, 1958, pp. 21-22, cf. p. 11.
8. M. Mayrhofer *Kurzg. etym. Wb. des Ai.* 2, p. 408.
9. L. Renou, Sur les nighaṇṭu védiques in *Bulletin de l'École Française d'Extrême-Orient*, 1951, p. 214 (a final gloss of the lists figures in the genetive which Renou interprets as "as substitutes for...").
10. E. Benveniste, *Problèmes de linguistique générale*, Paris, 1966, pp. 51-52.
11. *Ibid.*, p. 54.

CHAPTER 5

The Cooking of Poetic Words and the Creation of Double Meanings in Vedic Poetry

I

The authors of Vedic hymns seem to have concerned themselves with a certain problem which assumes importance as soon as it is viewed in the context of the questions raised by sacrifice in the Ṛgveda. What should be offered to the gods? What is the food of the gods? The second question leading to the first implies the notion of foodstuff, and is better understood if it is compared with the notion of food substances in the formal sense of the term. In fact, the Vedic hymns abundantly deal with the idea of giving vigour to the gods, of favouring their growth by making offerings to them (verbs such as *vṛdh-*, *mah-*, *ukṣ-*, *vakṣ-* are the usual ones which express this most constant desire of the worshippers of the gods).

The institution of sacrifice is presented in the hymns as the place where the problems faced by the theoreticians of the sacrifice, themselves the officiant poets and authors of the hymns, are stated by them. The questions that have been posed earlier become more specific once they are integrated into the totality of the problems and questions. Since men can offer solid as well as liquid food to the gods, and thus a first distinction is made, since all the gods do not take the same kind of food, the question apparently implied in the hymns is in fact the following: how to offer sacrifice to satisfy the gods when their natures do not permit them to consume solid or liquid offerings?

It will be seen that this second distinction between material and non-material offerings merely enhances the first distinction between solid and liquid offerings.

Amongst the offerings made to the gods, there is one that has a special status, that is, the offering of the brew called *soma*. Its prestige arises from the fact that it is the means by which the inspiration or the inspired thought of the poet is strengthened[1] or inversely, from the fact that the poetic words sung by the poet strongly influence the brew. To say that the words of the song are purified by the brew[2] is to say that the words contribute to the preparing (forming, giving a shape) of the *soma*.[3]

The offering of the brew is first and foremost meant for gods such as Indra, and also for the men who are given a high rank by religious tradition, the officiant poets, compared and likened to gods according to the tendency to favour the cosmico-ritual continuity. Thus the poets Āyu follow the old custom, but in a novel way, for by the same gesture they create the sun[4]. This is a way of saying that their ritual work has repercussions on the cosmic plane, although it is tempting to agree with Geldner that the sun here is in fact the soma.

By this comparison, the brew would become something other than what it would be if it were not introduced in a reflection on the essential articulations of the sacrifice. The effect of the brew on a human or divine being is such that he no longer is what he was before consuming it (the famous hymn RV 10.119, in itself a song of praise of the god drunk on soma, gives a series of information on the matter). But not every being is capable of feeling the effects of the brew. In particular, the one who has not undergone a maturing process of cooking, properely *tápas* "warmth".

In ṚV 9.83.1, it is said "Thy filter has been stretched out, O Brahmaṇaspati, being powerful, thou dost completely envelop the limbs (of the one who has drunk thee). The one whose body has not been warmed, (the one who is) raw, does not attain this (effect of the somic brew), only the (well) cooked beings, those who carry (the somic offering or the words) have truly attained it."[5] In this can certainly be seen at first a sort of exaltation of the religious practice which is expressed by the words of the officiant poet, the master of eulogistic discourse. But beyond this first distinction between the officiants who are experts in words and the officiants who remain outside the sphere of words or who manipulate them awkwardly, another distinction can be discovered, the one between soma that can be consumed by terrestrial beings and the soma that these beings cannot consume because they lack the necessary qualification[6]. This is clearly brought out in ṚV 10.85.3-4, "We think we have drunk the soma because (or when) we crush the plant, but the soma known to the brāhmans (the holders-of-the-secret, Renou *EVP*, IX, p. 14, n. 2) is consumed by none. Hidden by those who should protect it, (scil. the gods), guarded by the inhabitants on high (of the sky), O Soma, thou livest by hearing the stones (which are activated to press the stalks of soma, adds Renou, *Hymnes spéculatifs du Veda*, p. 244); no terrestrial being consumes thee" (3. *sómam manyate papivā́n yát sampiṃśánty óṣadhim/ sómam yám brahmā́no vidúr ná tásyāśnāti káścaná;* 4. *āchádvidhānair gupitó bárhataiḥ soma rakṣitáḥ/grā́vṇām íc chṛṇván tiṣṭhasi ná te aśnāti pā́rthivaḥ*). Thus it is seen that the distinction between the soma that can be consumed and the soma that cannot, artificial though it may be, serves to establish a hierarchy among the terrestrial beings and to show that the consumable soma is in fact reserved for its officiants and for the poets who are conversant with the techniques of the words that accompany and sublimate the consumption. This is what is defined as the true consumption (cf. ṚV 2.19.1). If this hierarchical distinction among human beings is compared to the known distinction among the gods (there are gods who consume the soma and those who do not), it can be seen that the two distinctions are similar and are essentially of the same nature. But, and this is important, the rigid division of men into two categories is singular because it is made according to whether or not they are capable of the ascetism required to become an officiant poet who creates and formulates the words in a ritual sacrifice. However, even though the hymns do not say so explicitly, the division of the gods is done according to the affinity that some of them may have for the words. This indicates a specific state of affairs—if a god does not receive material offerings (milk, soma, rice cakes, clarified butter...), his oblatory substance will be words, poetic inspiration, inspired thoughts. The goddess Dawn, Uṣas, is one such and she has the same noted anomalies because she does not consume material offerings. Thus since the whole homage consists of praise in the form of a hymn and a food offering, the homage paid to Uṣas is incomplete and she will attract, exceptionally, a single form of homage i.e., verbal praise. The doctrine of Vedic sacrifice does not stop here. Once the hierarchy among the beings has been established so as to distinguish two more groups in each of the two groups of celestial and terrestrial beings, there is further a kind of justification. The resulting classification is both exclusive and inclusive. It excludes certain beings from the consumption of soma and includes others. It also effects the mutual assimilation of the two constituents of the complete homage—the somic offering and the verbal offering.

Regarding this assimilation, the authors of the hymns have unhesitatingly stated that firstly, the somic offering is effective only if it is accompanied by the sung *bráhman* (ṚV

7.26.1 "the soma, if it is not pressed, does not intoxicate Indra; the pressed juices, if they are not (associated) with *bráhman* (do not intoxicate) this noble (god)"; ṚV 7.26.2 "As far as the hymns are being sung, the soma intoxicates Indra."[7] Secondly, the sung words and the soma are assimilated in the essential step of their production. The brew must be decanted, "clarified", as the hymn itself says (the Vedic verb is *pū-* "clarify, make limpid"), and it is perhaps because of the close association of the words and the brew, so necessary for the success of the sacrifice, that one frequently evokes the clarification, the "cleaning" of the words.[8] ṚV 9.73.3 says, "the poets equipped with the filter gather around the words...only (these) sages have been capable of taking them right in their foundations",[9] where the foundations referred to are probably those of the soma. But ṚV 9.73 is precisely one of these hymns that are centred around the profession of poet and it is not surprising to find in it a large number of more or less explicit references to the words that are constantly paralleled to the somic drink. This is what explains the features common to both, so much so that it is sometimes futile to try and make out whether reference is being made to the soma or to the words, to the work of the poet or the work of the officiant who prepares the drink.[10]

To Renou's and Geldner's brief notes we will add some remarks on the way in which the poetic words and the somic drink are connected in ṚV 9.73. As Geldner has observed, the keyword of the hymn is the verb *saṃ-svar* "resound powerfully"; here it is the waves of the soma which resound (verses 1, 4 and 6), but the most general characteristics of the language of the hymns make it impossible that there is no allusion and even a direct reference to the resounding songs of praise as in ṚV 8.33.2: *svấranti tvā suté náro...ukthínaḥ* "the men who proffer their hymns at the pressing (the soma) make their words ring out in thy direction" or in ṚV 9.85.3: *indo pavase...abhí svaranti bahávo manīṣíṇo* "thou dost clarify thyself, O drop of soma, (while) many inspired poets make (their songs) ring out", in which the uses of *svar-* "to resound, to make resound, to intone" are no doubt induced by the situation. Further, if ṚV 9.73.2 says: *mahiṣā́ aheṣata síndhor ūrmā́v ádhi venā́ avīvipan,* "the (poets-) buffaloes have incited (the soma to flow), the (poets) seers have made (the soma) tremble on the wave of the ocean"[11], ṚV 9.96.7 gives the inverse image of the wave of the words which make the soma tremble (*prā́vīvipad vācá ūrmím*). Renou's interpretation of this is certainly correct ("this "trembling" caused by the poets is indeed the incitation to speak, the holy inspiration" see *Ét. sur le voc. du Ṛgveda*, p. 30), but we would like to make it explicit that the inversion of roles is possible thanks to the concomitance of the two forms of homage compared to each other and even mutual sources of each other. ṚV 8.6.28-29 completes the presentation of the poets who make the soma tremble. Indra is born thanks to the words and he is rightly called *vípra* "eloquent narrator, orator" (*dhiyā́ vípro ajāyata*); in an ecstatic movement he breaks out from the depths of the somic ocean (*vipāná éjati*), "trembling (with intoxication) and inspired at the same time" (Renou, *Ét. sur le voc. du Ṛgveda*, p. 30).

According to this assimilation which must always be taken into consideration, the hymn creates the image of the poetic soma: echoing ṚV 8.6.28 that has been mentioned above, ṚV 9.73.2 says that the song in honour of Indra is produced by the honey flow of the soma brew and that the body of the god is strengthened by it (*mádhor dhā́rābhir janáyanto arkám ít priyā́m índrasya tanvàm avīvṛdhan*). It can be easily understood that this expression serves only to prepare the development of the theme of the soma the poet, for without it, we cannot make out what is expressed in ṚV 9.73.5 ["The (streams of) soma have resounded by lighting up like chanted verses, by causing to burn the lawless"] and in ṚV 9.73.6 ["The (streams of) soma have resounded in the old manner...they, the inventors of the violent (soma); the blind and the deaf have remained at the back, those with evil intentions do not cross (the space) which leads to the path of Truth"].[12]

The reason for this is that since the somic brew gives rise to the song and strength to Indra, it acts like the typical officiant poet whose praises invigorate the gods, and who is exposed to the rivalry of his confreres as well as the hostility of the non-sacrificers who are here referred to as the lawless. The rivals in the competition are called blind and deaf and the non-sacrificing enemies, those with evil intentions (*duṣkṛ́t*—opposite of *sukṛ́t*—"who acts according to the bad law"). It can then be understood that the poet soma is the guardian of the Truth possessing the good inspiring strength (ṚV 9.73.8 *ṛtásya gopā́...sukrátu*), that it has at its core three filters (*ibid., trī́ ṣá pavítrā hṛdy àntár ā́ dadhe*), and that it sees all beings and punishes the wicked (*vidvā́n sá víśvā bhúvanābhí paśyaty ávā́juṣṭān vidhyati karté avratā́n* "he who is endowed with knowledge, he sees from afar all beings, he pushes the undesirable ones, the lawless, into the pit"). It can also be understood that it is this view-point that enables the author of ṚV 9.73 to attribute a tongue of honey to the streams of soma[4] and also to say that the thread of Truth, that is, the thread stretched out by men who come to know the Truth is stretched out in the soma filter and on the tip of the tongue (9. *ṛtásya tántur vítataḥ pavítra ā́ jihvā́yā ágre*).[13] Finally, the preceding explanations clarify why the verse 7 of the hymn announces that "in the filter of hundred streams, stretched (in the somic sacrifice), the poets who hold the meanings clarify their words": the soma is as much the object offered in the sacrifice as the place where the words and the source of the words are elaborated.

By bringing together the liqueur and the words and making them one, Vedic religious thought deliberately puts together the object offered and the means of rendering the sacrificial words effective; when all is said and done, throughout the hymn 9.73 whose main points have been presented here, nothing lets you forget that it is the somic liqueur that is spoken of. The method of identifying an offering and a means of rendering efficient the concomitant words is, moreover, widely used in the Ṛgveda.

To this example of analysis of ṚV 9.73 which certainly does not exhaust the treatment of the problem in the hymn, can be added the parallel case of Agni, the god of fire offered to Vedic godheads. In ṚV 3.26.7-9 the god pronounces an *ātmastuti*, an eulogy of himself ["I am Agni, the melted-butter is my look...triple song...offering (this is what) I am"], then he clarifies the song with his three filters and recognises in his heart a poetic thought; and in the last line, he is given the capacity to understand the inspired words and the state "of the father of things which must be said".[14] This does not affect his being called "the rustling of the fire "(*meḷí*), which reminds one that the author of the hymn has not lost sight of the physical nature of the fire, even while making its god comparable to a human poet, but superior to him because he possesses the qualities of a poet to the highest degree.

Now that we have seen the motives which justify the identity of the somic offering and the offering of words, and that the technique of identification is not restricted to the case of the brew, we can ask an essential question: by affirming this identity, the theoreticians of Vedic sacrifice were doubtless trying to find a solution to a certain problem. What is this problem and how does the proposed solution correspond to it?

By asking this question one is obliged to re-examine certain related facts which will be also clarified, and which enable one to glimpse the nature of the paradoxes that one seeks to understand. Thus, when the authors of the hymns lay stress on the resemblance between the soma and the mental offering, and accentuate the idea of *pavítra*, of "filter" which serves to perfect the two, they deliberately do not define the border between the material purification and the purification in the spiritual task.[15]

This imprecision in semantics does not arise just from the

style of the poetic language of the hymns. The language of the hymns is no doubt a language serving the ritual and its evocative description. It originates from a prescientific theoretical speculation which has rigorous principles referred to as "vorwissenschaftliche Wissenschaft" by H. Oldenberg. What must be primarily observed is that the comparison of the decanted and clarified somic liqueur to the oblation by words is but one of the many identifications practised in the hymns in order to create an esoteric language in which "the values are transmuted in such a way that the sacrificial things evoke effortlessly a larger order of phenomena" (L. Renou, *EVP*, XI, p. 9). This language aims at both terrestrial and cosmic phenomena, so much so that, according to Renou, "behind this modest arrangement for pressing (the soma), it is the arrangement *ordo rerum* which is at play"(*ibid.*, p. 10). Let us take a closer look.[16]

When the somic brew is prepared by the officiant one is given to understand that this terrestrial soma is the same as the divine soma which creates the world and holds supraterrestrial knowledge. Thus by denying the exclusively human and terrestrial origin of the brew concocted by the sacrificers and by recognising its identity to the god Soma —the divinised soma, the divine archetype of the brew, the authors state a basic correlation, the one between matter of human origin and an element belonging to the world of the gods or, to be exact, the correlation between an entity which has its abode in the high skies of Ṛta, of Truth (see H. Lüders, *Varuṇa*, II, pp. 599 ff.). The place given to language is very important here. The soma prepared for the gods is imbibed on the path of Ṛta and it is through the language that it receives its name (ṚV 6.44.8 *ṛtásya pāthí vedhā́ apāyi śriyé mánāṃsi devā́so akran/dádhāno nā́ma mahó vácobhir vápur dṛśáye venyó vy ȧ̀vaḥ* "It is on the path of Ṛta that (the soma) is drunk, this master of the rite; the gods directed their thoughts to its beauty; it receives its powerful name thanks to the (poetic) words; it is lovely to behold, it has unveiled its splendour so that one may see it.").[17]

Now, the theme of correlation between the terrestrial soma and the divine soma is one of the most constant Vedic themes. This correlation has the value of an identity, it indicates a *link* between the two somas. ṚV 9.10.8 is significant in this respect. "It (the soma) has put our umbilical cord into its umbilical cord, just as the (human) eye (is put) into the sun; the descent of the sage has thus been milked" (*nā́bhā nā́bhiṃ na ā́ dade cákṣuś cit sū́rye sácā kavér ápatyam ā́ duhe*). Considering the meaning covered in the Ṛgveda by the notions of umbilical cord, relationship and descent, for they mean to establish correlative links and have the value of an identity, the lines quoted above must indicate the affinity between the poets referred to as "us" and the divine soma, or, as suggested by Renou, (*EVP*, IX, p. 10, n. 1), between the divine relationship and the human relationship of the poets. ṚV 9.73.1 (an extract from the hymn referred to earlier) repeats this idea of relationships between the soma and the divine Soma. While the soma is pressed by stones, "the relationships (celestial and terrestrial of the soma) have resounded together, they have met in the abode of the Truth" (*sám asvarann ṛtásya yónā sám aranta nā́bhayaḥ*). The concern of the officiant poets who are sacrificers as much as philosophers of the ritual language (used in the ritual which seeks to formulate the speculative conceptions of the universe grasped by the language) is therefore to prove the relationship between the soma pressed here on earth and the soma which dwells up there in the skies, by reaffirming this relationship many times, and consequently to prove the affinity between the poets and their words and the divine Soma.[18]

It must be remembered in order to understand the bearing of this theme, that one of the major concerns of the Vedic poets was the formulation of connections between all kinds of phenomena, between the microcosm and the macrocosm, between the ritual and the mythical world, between the human order and the divine world (according to Renou, *L'Inde fondamentale*, p. 149 ff.). The word *nā́bhi* "umbilical cord" gives concrete expression to this concern which is shown both by the practice of Vedic sacrifice and also by the speculation inspired by it. The theme which is often seen in the soma hymns, that of the pressed soma rising to the sky to rejoin its divine kin is another expression of the same idea.[19]

It is not without importance that the affirmation of the affinity and the relationship between the two somas comes from an indirect and symbolic language whose imprecision (see earlier) is due to the double and transmutable values and which favours the use of enigmas and paradoxes created by combining and correlating images which evoke correspondences between various planes, including the plane of human deeds and the plane of cosmic events.[20] This language is therefore remarkably apt for the theme of the relationship between the two somas. But it refers implicitly to the earlier-mentioned theme of the distinction between consumable and non-consumable soma. We have seen that this distinction stands for the one between the two groups of gods. We have also seen that the gods who consume the soma are related, or, to put it in the Vedic way, are put into an explicative correlation with men matured by the practice of *tápas* who have access to the soma and to words.

It would seem significant that the *similarity* of the somic offering and the verbal offering is accompanied by the *distinction* between the soma that can and the soma that cannot be consumed by men, and the *distinction* between the gods who consume the soma and those who consume eulogistic words.

There are three series of distinctions (mature men who have undergone the *tápas*/men who think they can consume the soma but cannot do so as they have not known the *tápas*; the gods who receive the soma/the gods who receive eulogistic words; the terrestrial soma/the divine soma) having interesting common characteristics which can explain the Vedic speculation regarding the similarity of the somic and verbal offering. Here are the correspondences that can be observed between the various ways these distinctions are effected.

We have already seen the first distinction—the true consumers of soma, the officiants, are distinguished from the false consumers, whereas we know that there are gods who consume soma and those who do not. Next comes the division of the officiants into officiants of the soma and those who manipulate and offer poetic words. Further, although there exist (at least, in theory) the officiants who prepare other material offerings, the Vedic religious system does not give them the same importance (Was it because the officiants of material offerings were not specialised enough? This is what one can believe, given the absence of conceptual value attached both to other specialists and a certain kind of material offering. In fact, to complete the picture, we must include in the list of distinctions that between material and non-material offerings, of which the former is further divided into solid and liquid offerings whereas the latter consists of only words. To put it in another way, the solid offerings, just like the false soma consumers are outside the set of religious values).[21]

The division of the officiants into two groups is rendered complicated by the distinction between the terrestrial and the divine soma. For when they institute this distinction, the hymns do not envisage the specialisation of the functions of the somic officiants. This must have created a feeling of contradiction that they wished to avoid. Instead of imagining that certain officiants were assigned to the preparation of the soma for the gods and others for the preparation of soma for men, they simply declared that the soma and the offering of words were comparable and even identical. We can believe that this is what contributed to the development of the terrestrial soma equated to the divine soma and transmuted into divine soma. We are dealing with two operations of religious thought which are related but profoundly distinct.

When the hymns repeatedly emphasise that the somic offering is successful and effective only if accompanied by words, when we are told that the thoughts and the words are similar to the soma in that they are decanted and clarifed just like the liqueur, and when the same power is attributed to the words as well as the somic offerings, (especially the power of making the gods grow in stature), a *conversion* is effected. One offering is first compared to the other, then substituted for the other.

Moreover, the reversibility is absolute and is perhaps explained by the liquid nature of both words and soma, which appears in circumstances when the nature of the words in the sacrifice is described.[22]

But when it is stated that the terrestrial soma is identical to the celestal soma, a mystical *equation* is established which tries to explain different kinds of phenomena by comparing them. By establishing this equation (or connection) a complex explanation is put forward which involves not just the somic offering.

Going beyond and rupturing the framework of the somic brew is no doubt a consequence of the conversion of the brew into words, so much so that it would distinctly appear that conversion and equation are closely connected. Lüders has this apt observation on this subject: "....they like to present the gestures made by the officiants for the terrestrial soma as if they were applied to the celestial soma" (Lüders, *Varuṇa*, I, p. 205, cf. Renou, *EVP*, IX, p. 101-11). This means that the utterances regarding the soma prepared down on earth are, at the same time (and this is an important detail), the utterances which reveal the nature of the celestial soma. This also means that the somic officiants are presented *like* officiant poets (and this is in perfect accordance with the indifference which consists of not distinguishing among the officiants their allocation to one of the somas).

Thus ṚV 9.79.4 attests the relationship, that is, the mystical connection between the terrestrial soma and the celestial soma by using the notion of the navel or umbilical cord. It claims that the branches of the soma plant grow on the summit ("on the back") of the earth and seems to describe the preparation of the terrestrial brew on the hide of bulls, but states nevertheless that it is handled by the officiant poets "holders of the meaning" [*diví te nā́bhā paramó yá ādadé pṛthivyā́s te ruruhuḥ sā́navi kṣípaḥ / ádrayas tvā bapsati gór ádhi tvacy àpsú tvā hástair duduhur manīṣíṇaḥ* "In the skies is thy supreme (navel) which is joined to (our navel), on the back of the earth do thy branches grow. The pressing stones crush thee on the hide of a bull; in the water (stirring) with their hands, the officiant poets have milked thee."] Thus ṚV 9.92.2 seems to first speak of the soma brew ["it went forth (the soma) which embraces men with its look, *áchā nṛcákṣā asarat*], but attributes the quality of poet to the soma (*pavítre nā́ma dádhānaḥ kavír asya yónau*" poet, it takes his (true) name in the filter, the sage (he takes it) (during) its course (or: at the end of its course)".[23] It can therefore be suggested that the following scheme was operative in the system of thought in the Ṛgveda:

Celestial soma
(the god soma) [⇒ words of divine origin]
↑ ↑
Terrestrial soma ⇒ words of praise
(somic offering) verbal offering
Key ⇒ conversion
↑ connection

Thus there is parity between the somic and verbal offerings which can be mutually converted, and there is an explicative connection between terrestrial offerings and their celestial counterparts. It will be noticed that, if one follows the logic of connections that Vedic thought establishes between elements of various kinds (microcosm-macrocosm;

Schematic representation illustrating the distinction between men, gods and offerings

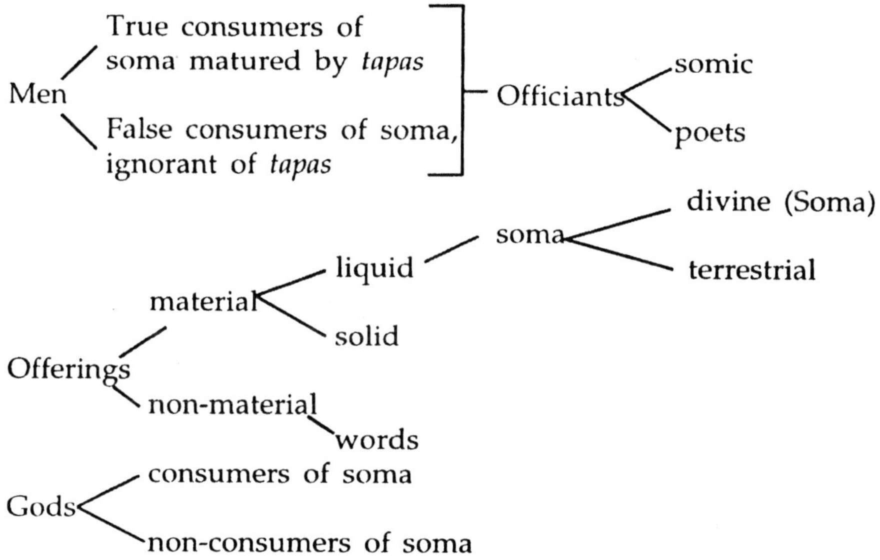

rite-myth etc.) the divine words correspond to the terrestrial words. But it must be said of this correspondence that it has its place in the series of connections based on the conversion effected between the soma offered to the gods and the verbal offering and also on the correlation between the terrestrial and celestial soma. Not that the words of divine origin are not mentioned in the Ṛgveda; on the contrary, the celestial origin of human words is specifically evoked in the hymns. What is worthy of interest is the possibility of deducing the reason for the celestial origin of the words thanks to information regarding the somic offering and its connection to the verbal offering. If it can be deduced that the words of divine origin are homologated to the poetic words of the officiant, we do not claim that an analogous conversion of the celestial soma into words must have been envisaged by the authors of the hymns. But it is undeniable that a large number of verses exalt the god soma and present him as the all-knowing (ṚV 9.27.3 *viśvavíd*), the first inspired poet (ṚV 9.91.1

manótā prathamó manīṣī́ "inventor of poetic thought, the first of those who hold the meaning", see Renou, *EVP*, IX, p. 40, who thinks of the brew soma rather than the god Soma), the creator of songs who understands the inspired words (ṚV 9.96.22 *sā́ma kṛṇván sāmanyò vipaścít*), or an inspired one and a poet who knows how to address the gods (ṚV 9.107.7 *ṛ́ṣir vípro... tvám kavír abhavas*) to give but a few examples. These hymns seek to highlight the qualities of the god which place him on the same plane as other gods. We know that, generally speaking, the Vedic gods dispense human speech, as well as inspire and reactivate it.

If this schema explains the interdependence of the somic offering and the two kinds of Vedic speech, it is essential to follow the details of the images of the connection which Vedic authors establish between the two kinds of soma. We shall see that the rich mythology of soma is inspired by this principal feature of connections brought about by their presentation *in statu nascendi*, their dynamic character translated as the comparison of connected terms.[24] We shall also see that the narrative elements constituted around this connection rejoin the Vedic speculations which make use of enigmas and paradoxes having the value of explanations formulated in a cryptic language and which pertain to the object to which the authors give importance—the words in the sacrifice. Here, more that anywhere else is seen the importance of the notions of voyages, journeys and movement which try to reduce the interval separating the phenomena that one tries to explain by stressing on the correlative link which joins them. It is in order to denote this progress of the terrestrial soma that the hymns evoke the *yójanās* "the distances traversed" by the soma, the distances which separate the terrestrial zone of the soma from its celestial counterpart (see, for example, ṚV 9.102.3 *mimīte asya yójanā ví sukrátuḥ* "(the soma) has embraced, while travelling its *yójanās*, the one endowed with good intelligence". It cannot be ignored that *yójana* also means "harness" (ṚV 1.88.5, 8.72.6, 10.94.7), which makes one think of the *yóga* of the soma, of the "harness" of the soma, since this is the primary meaning of the term *yóga* in the hymns. It means indeed the practice of symbolic connections to which the Vedic poets were given—the harness is the means of making the journey, thus covering the distance to establish an explicative connection.[25]

Even if there must have been several reasons for attributing the faculty of quick movement to the somic liqueur which is decanted and passed through the sieve, the comparing of the soma to a horse (which, according to Bergaigne *Religion védique* I, p. 222, "in mythology is the main symbol of movement"), is probably due to the need felt by its mythology to create images which denote the rushing of the terrestrial soma towards its celestial double. This explains why the movements of the soma are often described as rapid movements which have a goal.[26] The horse-soma leaps forth (*sṛj-*, ṚV 9.46.1, 9.66.10), leaps forth and runs (*sṛj-*, *dhāv-*, ṚV 9.87.7; *sṛj-*, *tak-*, ṚV 9.16.1), it leaps forth like a race-horse towards a barrier [ṚV 9.36.1: *ásarji ráthyo yathā pavítre camvòḥ sutáḥ / kā́rṣman vājī́ ny àkramīt* "It is released, the horse of the chariot so that it may (enter) the filter, the two vessels, the pressed (juice), the steed has gone forth to the barrier", cf. ṚV 9.74.8] in which are evoked the bowl which collects the soma as also the barrier towards which the soma-steed runs. The vessels in which the soma is poured out are no doubt identical to the heaven and the earth. We are always faced with the dual reference simultaneously to the treatment of the terrestrial soma and to its cosmic journey. The succint descriptions in the hymns refer to the steed-soma guided by its reins (ṚV 9.87.1, 10.36.8), taken in hand and guided (ṚV 9.24.3) and harnessed like a draught animal between the two shafts (ṚV 10.101.10) and drawing a chariot (ṚV 9.21.4). It is probably by proliferating along the lines of this identification that ṚV 9.45.4 compares the soma passing through the sieve to the steed which goes out of its shaft during its run (*áty ū pavítram akramīd vājī́ dhúraṃ ná yā́mani*), that ṚV

9.83.5 says that the sieve of the soma is its chariot (*rā́jā pavítraratha* "king who has the sieve for a car") and that in keeping with the common tendency to substitute the thing which is used for the object being described by the comparison, the soma is said to be harnessed like a chariot (ṚV 9.88.2), or, more exactly, like a chariot rushing forth towards the riches that it must gain (ṚV 9.90.1, 9.92.1, cf. 9.10.1, 9.67.17, 9.69.9, 9.38.1, 9.111.3). This last-mentioned characteristic is particularly important since the hymns attribute to the words of praise the ability to gain riches, whereas by attributing it to the soma and at the same time highlighting its steed-like quality, they seek to make an even closer comparison to the words spoken for the gods.

Alongside with the image of the steed and the chariot, the representation of soma in the form of an eagle or a falcon also tries to denote a rapid movement, especially skywards and reaching the heavens. The eagle-soma flies towards the firmament, the songs of the poets have a nostalgic desire for it, nevertheless the authors immediately say that the poetic thoughts cherish (or: lick) the golden bird which sits on the earth (ṚV 9.85.11 *nā́ke suparṇám upapaptivā́ṃsaṃ gíro venā́nām akṛpanta pūrvīḥ/śíśuṃ rihanti matáyaḥ pánipnataṃ hiraṇyáyaṃ śakunáṃ kṣā́mani sthā́m*).

The ambiguity of the terrestrial soma which is the celestial soma in becoming is but another expression of the connection between the two somas. ṚV 9.86.1 speaks of the somic brews precipitated by the thoughts of the poets, compares these brews to fast steeds and finally says that the drops of soma are the celestial eagles which sit around the vessel in which the soma is prepared (*prá ta āśávaḥ...dhījávo mádā arṣanti raghujā́.../ divyā́ḥ suparṇā́...pári kóśam āsate*). It is seen that whatever may be the primary image by which an initial basic identity of the varieties of soma is established, the lines quoted above do not omit to mention the connection that this identity expresses. But all of them (and they are only samples of which many manifestations can be seen) exploit the paradoxical images of a bird or a steed evoked in order to denote a movement, endowed with attributes which translate this movement and yet deprived of it since they are immobilised on the earth or around the cosmic vessel.

It is possible that one of the myths which is centred around the soma, the one about its ascent towards heaven is only a repetition of the motif of the connection between the two somas. In fact, most of the time, it is rather about the ascent of the terrestrial soma than the descent of the celestial soma (as H. Lüders noted this in his *Varuṇa* I, pp. 207-213). The reason is obviously that the myth of the ascent of the soma incorporates the motifs which are characteristic of the concepts of soma that have just been discerned. The soma goes towards the gods and is then presented in the form of a steed (ṚV 9.5.4 and 9.98.7, cf. 9.71.8); when it goes to meet the gods, it is *gātuvíd* "the one who knows the way" (ṚV 3.62.13); its meeting with the gods has often been mentioned as *niṣkṛtá*: ṚV 9.78.1, 9.86.7, 9.107.22); it is therefore not without importance that ṚV 9.71.2 should interpret this meeting as a meeting with the Father, probably the god Parjanya, for we know that recalling the parental ties is very much the Vedic way of referring to an explicative connection); it is the same when the allusion made to the equation between the somas and the gods states the ability of the soma to be more effective than friends. Friendship, like kinship, is over-determined as it is loaded with references to a correlative link. (ṚV 9.45.2). It can be considered that when ṚV 9.12.8 says that the soma always attains the pleasant abodes of heaven and that its ascent results from the efforts of the inspired poet (*abhí priyā́ divás padā́ sómo hinvānó arṣati/ víprasya dhā́rayā kavíḥ*), reference is also made to the link between the terrestrial soma identified with the poet and the celestial regions which are friendly with it. The representations known in Vedic religious thought are also followed. First, the abode (*padá*) is another denomination of the name, often kept secret, of the thing that must be discovered so that it can be mastered; secondly, the notion of a friendly nature is no doubt close to that of kinship. The soma which reaches the regions of heaven is thus the soma which completes a journey to join the celestial soma.

Finally, and this is an essential detail, once the correlation between the two somas is established, the terrestrial soma that has become the celestial soma must celebrate the gods (ṚV 9.84.1 *urukṣitaú gṛṇīhi daívyaṃ jánam*). No better confirmation can be found of the schema given above in which it was anticipated that the correlating of the terrestrial soma and the celestial soma is followed by the conversion of the celestial soma into divine speech, while this speech is correlated to the human words offered to the gods.

There is yet another Vedic theme which though probably elaborated outside the mythology of soma is connected to this mythology by a motif that is found in the somic cycle. This is the theme of opening and discovery. In its most general formulation it is the discovery of the *bráhman*, then of its understanding and its enunciation. Now, *bráhman* means "the equation, the form of thought which consists of posing a correlation, an explicative identification" (L. Renou, *L'Inde fondamentale*, p. 88). Given this apparently most archaic significance of the notion of *bráhman*, this theme is undeniably evoked in ṚV 9.96.10 and 11. These two verses say that the primordial soma is protection against agressive speech, and that when clarified it procures the happy outcome of the *bráhman* (96.10: *sá purvyó...abhiśastipā́...vidád gātúm bráhmaṇe pūyámānaḥ*) and that it must open the barriers; verse 6 of the same hymn reminds you that the soma prepares the path for the poets and this refers in the most immediate way to the constant preoccupation of the Vedic poets—the suppression of obstacles that stand in the way of the discovery of the *bráhman*, as well as its enunciation. The operations of clarification of the terrestrial soma, conceived on the model of the journey and ascent, and which try to relate the terrestrial soma to the celestial soma, thus have the same end as the search for the best way of enunciating the *bráhman* by the poets. When the operators clarify the soma to obtain the liqueur which will be offered to the gods, they seek the means of propitiating the gods and at the same time they seek the means of rendering the sacrificial words more effective. But when the clarification of the soma is associated with the search for the *bráhman*, Vedic religious thought repeats the theme whose study is central to the mythology of soma. It is obviously the theme of identification of the somic offering and the offering of words.

II

What was the most general impact of the identification of a brew to speech, both being treated in the doctrine of sacrifice? This is a question that must be asked. Since the ambiguity inherent in the presentation of the brew in Vedic hymns is not only almost never resolved, but on the contrary is exalted and exploited by religious thought, it can be concluded that the theoreticians of Vedic speculation wavered when it came to the nature of the sacrificial offering. In other words, by stressing on the affinity between the brew and the words, on their essential convertibility and by testing, on the level of the semantics of their style the limits of their poetic language in which the primary and secondary values merge with each other[27], the Vedic authors pose the problem that was enunciated at the beginning of this chapter (What should be offered to the gods? What is the food of the gods?), but they pose it by joining it to a more precise question: "What promises the success of a sacrifice, a material oblation or a spiritual offering? This detail which transforms the problem is of course related to the initial large division of the gods into two categories: the gods who consume material offerings and the gods who consume non-material offerings.

The apparent reply to these questions is that only maintaining the link between the two kinds of offerings and understanding the convertible nature of these offerings guarantees the effectiveness of the sacrifice. But we have seen in what a convoluted way religious thought arrived at affirming the link between these two offerings: since it was not possible to economise on the macrocosmic level without the risk of being incomplete, this thought had to envisage the connection between the terrestrial soma and the celestial soma and necessarily include the theme of the connection in the reflections on speech in the sacrifice. Thanks to the works of Renou on the language of Vedic hymns, we know that these reflections and the usage of language have resulted in the creation of a poetic language having several keys, a language in which double meaning is not a possibility but a fundamental feature. It would seem that we can maintain that Vedic speculation on somic sacrifice and its relation to verbal sacrifice has strongly contributed to the elaboration of the semantics of Vedic language.

Not that this is the only case in which a religious problem has been treated in such a manner as to first provoke the superimposition of the two offerings, then the interpenetration of linguistic values of expressions which denote them (moreover, it is not certain that things happened thus, for the values which are properly linguistic had already merged with each other so much so that what they evoked of the "objective" world only followed the ambivalent and even polyvalent train of thought which was translated by the poetic language of the hymns, albeit with a certain amount of approximation).[28]

But it is seen that studying the problem of different kinds of offerings which the authors of the hymns tried to solve or at least pose, has a very special value for the conception of Vedic poetic language which can be discerned from this very poetry. For the curiosity of the poets concerns the usage of language in sacrifice when they are dealing with the somic offering. Since the whole sacrifice, a kind of ideal, consists of the offering of soma and the propitiation of the gods by means of words, it was inevitable that the study of the problem of sacrifice should be treated in terms of the relation between these components of the whole sacrifice. This is where the mechanism of double values in language comes in, the language which is both the means and the material for verbal sacrifice and also the words which accompany the food oblations. Of these the somic oblation is special because it can be related to the words by conversion. This is the operation which, in the cycle of the hymns to soma, has loaded the words with double meanings. The second operation of giving an explicative correlation to the two somas has only served to increase the potentiality of the double meanings and to expand the multiple semantics of the language.

The method is, for the rest, the same that Vedic poetry uses to create double meanings. It can be described as drawing a parallel between two terms. They are given a relation without omitting to voice their diversity. This is why the Sanskrit treatises on poetry refer to the famous verse of the Ṛgveda (ṚV 1.164.20): *dvā́ suparṇā́ sayújā sákhāyā samānáṃ vṛkṣám pári ṣasvajāte/ táyor anyáḥ píppalaṃ svādv átty ánaśnann anyó abhí cākaṣīti* "Two eagles, joined to each other, two friends, embraced the same tree. One of them eats a delicious fig, the other looks at it intently, without eating."[29] Whatever may be the significance of the verse (the tree is the nocturnal sky, the eagles are the stars, the "sweet fig" is the light, according to P. Thieme, see Renou, *EVP*, XVI, p. 90-91), what is important for our discussion is that there are *two* eagles, that they are said to be joined or associated with each other (*sayújā*, a word based on the verb *yuj-* thus meaning more exactly "bring near to one another, the one matching the other (to reveal their nature), similar, the one explained by the other", for such is the end of Vedic *yóga*.[30] It is also significant that the second part of the verse advocates the difference that separates the eagles which are nevertheless bound by affective ties of friendship (*sákhi* "friend", like other terms which denote kinship or affection, is associated with the Vedic theme of explicative connections).[31]

A religious problem specific to the somic cult is thus understood by using a poetic method quite common in the Ṛgveda, but the originality of the solution to the problem of the whole sacrifice does not consist only of affirming the convertibility of the somic offering and the speech. It is not by chance that the speculative procedure itself which involved a food offering and the gift of words to the gods adopted the technique of treating the phenomena that Vedic thought tried hard to explain. This is the technique of enunciating correlative links, for the object of the procedure—the offered words—called for it. Here we once again see the usual organisation which in the Ṛgveda has an impact that goes beyond the simple usage of language since it serves to present entirely religious data. The deliberate confounding of the *object* and of the *means* of succeeding in seizing or describing the object (such is the example, interesting in many respects, of the tongue as an anatomical organ and also the activity of language often designated by the word *jihvā́* "tongue, anatomical organ"). We have seen earlier this kind of union between the soma offered and the soma as a means of rendering effective the offering of words.

The double meaning is as if prepared by the train of thought which at first only takes up purely religious questions. But it is not in the nature of this thought which is deliberately oriented towards the formulation of correlative links to compulsorily impose its procedure on language; it could be otherwise. The only restraint that is exercised (and this is explained precisely by the tendency to confound things which are hardly compatible) arises from the fact that the sacrificial offerings are mixed and composite, that along with the soma, words are offered, and that to describe the working of the sacrifice it was imperative to pay attention to the words. Thus, although I do not mean to say that this is the unique source of the double meaning, the description of the somic sacrifice has demanded the inclusion of words among the objects to be presented.

Considering that the gods whom they wanted to feed were of two categories, the Vedic authors must have been indecisive when it came to the correspondences between the nature of the gods and their food. The subtlety, it must be said again, and the extreme originality of the solution to the paradox created, lay then in posing the equivalence of the two offerings (it is however also true that this does not concern all the gods, for there remain those for whom a single kind of offering was reserved). Thus recourse was made to the old traditional bases of Vedic speculation in which the play of correlations and associations counted.[32]

But this could not happen otherwise than by bringing in and using the mechanism of correlations ["which, wrote Renou, in the mind of a poet, joined the ritual world to the cosmos within a faultless network"[33]]. This mechanism is perceptible at a precise moment thus confirming Renou's observation quoted above, i.e., when one poses the link between the terrestrial soma and the celestial soma, a link that is the necessary corollary of equating the offerings.

III

The "cooked words", the phrase that I used for briefly designating the similarity of the somic offering and the offering in the form of words, arises from a religious concept based on a widespread principle (according to a recent study by R. Lazzeroni): the substitution of the act of speech for the object that this speech must present to the recipient of the offering.[34] R. Lazzeroni also reminds us that cultural anthropology has taught that an essential characteristic of the sacrificial object is precisely its ability to be replaced with another object which often takes the name of the first object.[35]

The principle of ritual substitutions is no doubt known elsewhere than in the Indian world, but it is uncontestable that it is in Indo-Iranian that the relation between the words and the food offering has given a special aspect to the very notion of the growth of the honoured gods. Among the verbs which designate this notion, *mah-* "to magnify, pay hommage" and *vṛdh-* "to cause to grow" are used side by side in the hymns. ṚV 10.43.7 says *vṛdh- máhas* "make the greatness (of Indra) grow"; in ṚV 5.31.4, the poets magnify Indra by their songs (*mah- arkaíḥ*) and make him grow (*vṛdh-*).[36]

Now, in another study, Lazzeroni has established in a convincing way that the Vedic adjective *ūrdhvá* does not mean "straight" as it was commonly translated, buc rather "fed, grown, strengthened". Not only is the adjective related by diachronic derivation to the verb *vṛdh-*, but its meaning is dependent on their contiguous use in the Ṛgveda hymns, so that being *ūrdhvá* is a state which follows the act of *vṛdh-*.[37]

It is probably also the meaning of the Avestan *ərədwa* that can be posed as related to the Vedic *ūrdhvá* (that is supposing that **u̯ṛdhu̯o* < **ṛdhu̯o*). The Fravaši of Yt. 13.76 "were in full strength" (*ərəδwå hištənta*) during the creation of works by the Good and the Bad Spirit.[38]

The conclusions of R. Lazzeroni lead us to accept that the verbs *vṛdh-* and *mah-* have a concrete and physical meaning "strengthen (in) the body, "fatten, nourish". Thus they have acquired meaning in the context of a conceptual system in which prayer and material offerings have equally served to feed the gods.[39]

REFERENCES

1. ṚV 9.21.7 *etá u tyé avīvaśan kā́ṣṭhām vājíno akrata/satā́ḥ prā́sāviṣur matím* "these (juices of soma) have, we know, mooed; the (steeds) seeking to win the prize of victory have crossed the quarry; they have in the same way stimulated the (poetic) thought."
2. ṚV 9.2.7: *gíras ta inda ójasā marmṛjyánte apasyúvaḥ/yā́bhir mádāya śumbhase* "the songs of praise (which) are meant (for thee), O juice of soma, are powerfully cleansed thanks to the strength

(which is theirs), (they who) activate themselves, with which thou dost embellish thyself for intoxication ".

3. ṚV 9.97.22 *tákṣad...mánaso vénato vā́k* "the word (born) of the mind of the (poet) seer fashioned (the soma)".
4. ṚV 9.23.2 *ánu pratnā́sa āyávaḥ padám̐ návīyo akramuḥ rucé jananta sū́ryam* "The ancient Āyu have followed (the traces of the past), they have (found) a new name, they have created the sun so that it may shine". This seems to be the meaning of this verse but Renou has translated it differently (*EVP*, VIII, p. 15), although has himself commented it in such a way that my translation seems correct. The Āyu are "the privileged humans, eminent beneficiaries of the somic cult"; they imitate their ancestors; a beneficiary of the somic cult not only can consume the brew but also gains from his offering to the gods, which means that he obtains the prize of victory in poetry thanks to the soma (9.23.6 *índo vājaṃ siṣāsasi* "O drop of soma, thou seekest to win the prize of victory"), whereas the officiant poets use their knowledge to find or even invent the new name(s), both guarantee and result of their sacrificial and poetic activity (ref. to H. Lüders, *Varuṇa* II, pp. 521-528). In 9.23.2 as in the other verses of this hymn, the somic offerings are deliberately paralleled to the efforts of the officiant poets, the prototype of which is the Aṅgiras confronting Vala.
5. ṚV 9.83.1 *pavítraṃ te vítatam brahmanas pate prabhúr gā́trāṇi páry eṣi viśvátaḥ/átaptatanūr ná tád āmó aśnute śṛtāsa íd váhantas tát sám āśata*
6. The successful discourse is compared to a well-woven piece of work, a bad speech to threadbare rags (ṚV 10.71.9 *imé yé nārvā́ñ ná paráś caranti ná brāhmaṇā́so ná sutékarāsaḥ/tá eté vā́cam abhipádya pāpáyā siri̇̄s tántram tanvate áprajajñayaḥ* "They go neither forwards nor backwards who are not brahmins or (officiants) who are busy preparing the soma; they make use of words, but in an improper way, ignorant they weave the thread (of the words and, at the same time, of the soma), (but the result of it is) only rags." This is how ṚV 9.83.2 explains the link between the words and the soma by introducing the image of the thread. First it says that the filter that clarifies the soma stretches to the sky (*pavítram vítatam divás padé*), then that the threads of the filter are spread out into the distance (*asya tántavo vy àsthiran*), and finally that the fast steeds of the soma climb to the skies thanks to or by their thought, as well as help the clarifier of the soma (*ávanty asya pavitā́ram āśávo divás pṛṣṭhám ádhi tiṣṭhanti cétasā*). In the hymns, the fast steeds endowed with thought are the officiant poets co-operating with the somic officiants; the stretching of the threads in a somic operation is changed into the creation of words by the poets. This is just one example of a metaphor that combines the production

of the liqueur and the elaboration of the poetic discourse.

7. ṚV 7.26.1ab *ná sóma índram ásuto mamāda nā́brahmāno maghávanaṃ sutā́saḥ* and ṚV 7.26.2a *ukthá-ukthe sóma índram mamāda.*
8. See especially L. Renou, *Études védiques et pāṇinéennes,* I, p. 26 and XVI, p. 16.
9. ṚV 9.73.3 *pavítravantaḥ pári vā́cam āsate...dhī́ra íc chekur dharúṇeṣu ārábham.*
10. Cf. L. Renou, *Études védiques et pāṇinéennes,* X, p. 16 and K.F. Geldner, *Der Rigveda* III, p. 66 on the principal theme of the hymn, poetic art, which determines both the insistance of the poet on the effectiveness of his work and the fact that it subsumes the somic brew in the guise of the words in the sacrifice.
11. L. Renou, *Études védiques et pāṇinéennes,* IX, pp. 22-23 and *Études sur le vocabulaire du Ṛgveda,* 1st series, Pondicherry, 1958, p. 30 (in which can be found the study of the verb *vip-* "to tremble, vibrate", used in Vedic for physical movement as well as to denote the working of thought, of speech, in short, of language and of the men who produce the discourse).
12. ṚV 9.73.5 *ā́ yé samāsvarann ṛcā́ śócantaḥ saṃdáhanto avratā́n;* ṚV 9.73.6 *pratnā́n mā́nād adhy āyé samásvaran...rabhásasya mántavaḥ/ ápanākṣāso badhir ahāsata ṛtásya pánthām na táranti duṣkṛ́taḥ.*
13. In this context it can be remembered that Vedic authors attempt a deliberate confounding of the tongue (organ) and the language (produced by the organ) see Renou, *Études védiques et pāṇinéennes,* XIV, p. 81 (on ṚV 10.53.3 and 11).
14. ṚV 3.26.7 *agnír asmi...ghṛtám me cákṣur...arkás tridhā́tū...havír asminā́ma;* 3.26.8 *tribhíḥ pavítrair ápupod dhy àrkám hṛdā́ matíṃ...ánu prajānán;* 3.26.9 *vipaścítam pitáraṃ váktvānām/meḷim...rodasī piprtam* [the accusatives in the last line are justified by the invocation of the Two Worlds: "him who understands the inspired words, father of things that must be said, this rustling (of the fire), save it, O Two Worlds!"].
15. Cf. L. Renou, *Études védiques et pāṇinéennes,* I, p. 25. In this respect, what is significant is the difference between the uses of the verbal roots *mṛj-* and *pū-*. Both mean "to clean, clarify", but the former refers to the entire treatment to which the soma is subjected during the preparation of the brew, while the other is applied more to the clarification of the thought and the language, see L. Renou, *Études védiques et pāṇinéennes,* IX, p. 93.
16. See the apt remarks of R. Ambrosini, *Dal X libro del Ṛgveda,* Pisa, 1981, p. 3.
17. On this verse, see H. Lüders *Varuṇa,* I, p. 468 and L. Renou, *Études sur le vocabulaire du Ṛgveda,* p. 10. 'The path of Ṛta' is most probably an expression to denote the songs celebrating the gods. In the Ṛgveda, the name is not only the name but is also the

essence of the being and the very reality of the thing it designates" (L. Renou, *ibid.*, p. 11); the notion of name also has a close connection to that of abode and traces (*padá*), which is interesting here because of the Vedic theme of the abode of the soma in the places of Ṛta. See H. Lüders, *Varuṇa*, II, 559-602.

18. See L. Renou, *Études védiques* 3. *Quelques termes du Ṛgveda. b. bándhu* in *Journal asiatique*, 1953, pp. 171-175 and the chapter *The signifiant and the signifié in Vedic sacrifice*, pp. 153-166.
19. See, among other references, ṚV 9.19.3 *vṛ́ṣā punānā́ āyúṣu...háriḥ sán yónim ā́sadat* "(the soma), the bull that clarifies itself among the Āyu...in the form of a chestnut horse has settled in its (supreme) abode"; ṚV 9.99.7 *sá mṛjyate sukármabhir devó devébhyaḥ sutáḥ/vidé yád āsu saṃdadír mahī́r apó ví gahate* "(the soma) is cleaned by the clever sacrificers, the god pressed for the gods, it finds itself with these (waters), it joins (them), it plunges into the vast waters" (as to *saṃdadí* "which joins", compare with ṚV 9.10.8 *ā́ dade*, ṚV 9.79.4: *ādadé*, ṚV 4.44.5 *sam...dadé*, ṚV 1.139.1 *samdā́yi*, see L. Renou, *Études védiques et pāṇinéennes*, IX, p. 112; what is referred to is the navel "as a point of attachment between the heaven and the earth"); ṚV 9.95.3 *prá manīṣā́ īrate sómam ácha/namasyántīr úpa ca yánti sáṃ cā́ ca viśanty uśatī́r uśántam* "the poetic thoughts rush forward towards the soma, paying homage to it, they approach it and join (it), they willingly enter it, which is willing".
20. L. Renou, *L'enigme*, in *L'Inde fondamentale*, pp. 13-14.
21. See especially A. Bergaigne, *La religion védique d'après les hymnes du Ṛgveda*, t. I, 2nd edition, Paris, 1963, pp. 261ff. A schema can also be put forward in which the correspondences and the lacunae are represented diagrammatically (see p. 181).
22. See especially L. Renou, *Les pouvoirs de la parole dans les hymnes védiques* in *L'Inde fondamentale*, p. 56 and *Les pouvoirs de la parole dans le Ṛgveda* in *Études védiques et pāṇinéennes* I, pp. 23-24.
23. It is preferable, at least in this context, to give to the word *yóni* its primary meaning of "path, route" which evolves to the meaning of "abode" (see, on this subject, L. Renou, *L'acception première du mot sanskrit* yóni, *Bulletin de la Société de Linguistique de Paris*, 41, 1940, pp. 18-24).
24. For more details see the chapters *Primitive Vedic Yoga* and *From Vedic Speculation to Poetic and Religious Indo-European Themes*, pp. 199-222 and pp. 223-250.
25. Recent research by T. Burrow ("Sanskrit mā-" *to approach, meet, join; (trans.* "to bring to"), *Bulletin of the School of Oriental and African Studies*, XLIV, 1981, pp. 85-104) corrects the traditional ideas on the verb *mā-*.
26. In Bergaigne's *La religion védique*, I, p. 221-225, is found a general

view on the representation of soma as steed and horse. What follows is only an attempt to review the results obtained by Bergaigne and to find the motivations of symbolism that he really presents in a perspective which remains deeply anchored in his interpretation of the Ṛgveda from which I have distanced myself here.

27. L. Renou, *Les traits linguistiques généraux de la poésie du Véda* in *L'Inde fondamentale*, pp. 36-37; cf. my essay *Védique* dhénā, *avestique* daēnā: *examen des critiques de H.P. Schmidt*" in *Lautgeschichte und Etymologie*, Wiesbaden, 1980, pp. 293-316.
28. We shall retain the very perspicacious remarks of L. Renou on ambivalence in Vedic poetry according to which the case of the hymns to soma are distinguished by the ambivalence residing in the thoughts of the authors without affecting the language; there probably were projections of plans, translation of plans for the rites for the preparation of the somic brew on the celestial plane.(L. Renou, *EVP*, IX, p. 12). He however speaks of it differently in his essay *Les traits linguistiques généraux de la poésie du Véda*, p. 36: the thought circulates simultaneously on two or three different planes, the double meaning is an organic element of this poetry, it is the consequence of the religious mentality which dominated poetic invention.
29. Quoted by L. Renou, *Le destin du Véda dans l'Inde* in *Études védiques et pāṇinéennes*, VI, p. 25 and n. 1; translated in N. Stchoupak and L. Renou, *La Kāvyamīmāṃsā de Rājaśekhara (Cahiers de la société asiatique*, VIII), Paris, 1946, pp. 30-31. It is in this work that Renou rightly says that the Two Birds symbolise the double meaning when this verse is repeated by Rājaśekhara who wishes to illustrate the argument that it is poetry that enables the Veda to be understood.
30. See below the chapter *Primitive Vedic Yóga.*
31. See my *Terminology of Parental and of Friendly Relations in Indo-European and Vedic* in *Three Studies in Vedic and Indo-European Religion and Linguistics*, Poona, 1990, pp. 21-34.
32. On this subject see L. Renou, *Les débuts de la spéculation indienne* in *L'Inde fondamentale*, p. 148.
33. L. Renou, *Les traits linguistiques généraux de la poésie du Veda*, p. 43.
34. R. Lazzeroni, *Oggetto materiale e atto verbale nella cultura vedica* in *Problemi di lingua e cultura nel campo indoeuropeo*, a cura di E. Campanile, Pisa, 1983, pp. 47-52. In Roman religious practice, it is indeed the association of the word and the gesture of the offerer which renders the sacrifice valuable and effective, but without the words, the offering would not be considered a sacrifice. See E. Risch, *Zur altlateinischen Gebetsspache* in *Incontri linguistici*, 5, 1979, p. 45.

35. R. Lazzeroni, *ibid.*, p. 51, with reference to ṚV 1.114.9 and 10.127.8 in which the hymns have a metaphorical relation to cows. Very rightly Lazzeroni shows that these metonymies are ritual rather than simple poetic images and that they have their place in the conceptual systems of substitutions. In this volume, I have had many occasions to dwell upon the meaning of the link between the cow and poetry in the Ṛgveda. As for ritual substitution, see my "Identity and Substitution in Vedic Sacrificial Ritual: Essay on a case of Figurative Disguisement of the Formal Scheme" in *Semiotica*, 47, 1984, pp. 165-179.
36. R. Lazzeroni, pp. 48-49. On the verbs *mah-* and *vṛdh-* in the lexicon of sacrifice, see J. Haudry, *L'emploi des cas en védique*, Lyon, 1977, pp. 228-230.
37. R. Lazzeroni, *Sscr.* Ūrdhvá: *per una etimologia statica* in *Studi e Saggi linguistici*, XXI, 1981, pp. 22-26.
38. R. Lazzeroni, *ibid.*, pp. 35-36 gives his arguments for this meaning of the Avestan adjective. The translation "were in full strength" is by H. Lommel, *Die Yašt's des Awesta*, Göttingen-Leipzig, 1927, p. 121 ("in voller Kraft standen?").
39. R. Lazzeroni, *Oggette materiale e atto verbale nella cultura vedica*, p. 50.

CHAPTER 6

Primitive Vedic Yoga

The purpose of this essay is to re-examine the meaning of the term *yóga* and to give it its proper place in the system of Vedic speculative and religious thought. The pages that Renou devoted to the study of the occurrences of this word in the Ṛ(g) V(eda) and the A(tharva) V(eda) are still authoritative and serve as a guide, but it must be specified that one can try to go further, particularly to research the ultimate motivations for the meanings of the term.

We know that Vedic *yóga* is a derivative of the verbal root *yuj-* ("to harness, put under the yoke, unite, join, assemble, to pair, to match; to start off, put something into action (the car, the plough, more generally, the vehicle"); in the middle voice, "harness oneself (to the car), prepare oneself for combat" (these are the most frequent meanings in the Vedic hymns, for more details, see H. Grassmann, *Wörterbuch z. Rigveda*, col. 1115). It is instructive to see the modifications that the initial meaning "to harness" must have undergone, for it would seem that all the other meanings developed from it, and particularly to observe how these modifications have helped the rich speculation of Vedic authors about speech. It is also not without interest that the very idea of harness is not unmotivated within this speculation, and indeed obtains its justification there.

Although it can easily be seen that the usages of the term *yóga* and its derivatives from *yuj-* are not, in most cases, with respect to a personal experience (it is rather the harnessing of the car of the gods who are surprised at the time of their departure or the harnessing of draught animals such as the ass or the horse), Vedic usage quickly moves to the person of the officiant poet. This usage is seen in the evocation of the sacrifice seized in its movement. Thus is evoked the *yóga* of Agni, his harnessed teams, that is, his movements between the sacrificial site and the sky [ṚV 2.8.1 *vājáyann iva nū́ ráthān yógā́ñ agnér úpa stuhi* "Like the one who seeks (to obtain) a prize-of-victory (and exalts by praise) the cars (in a racing contest), sing the praises of the harnessing of Agni!]." Now, the journey of a god during the sacrifice is all the more susceptible to being the object of praise and the exhortation of the singer, as it is included in the liturgical acts that are directed, tendered, ordered (Renou, p. 179), just as the praise itself is directed and tendered, and also the soma or the sacrificial spoon offered to the gods, and as the sacrifice and the offering are tendered (ṚV 6.11.5 *agnā́v áyāmi srúg ghṛtávatī suvṛktíḥ* "the oblatory spoon is tendered to Agni, filled with butter, as well as the well-composed hymn"; ṚV 7.54.5 : *eṣá stómo varuṇa mitra túbhyam sómaḥ...ná vāyáve 'yāmi* "This praise, O Varuṇa, O Mitra, like the soma to Vāyu, is tendered to thee;" ṚV 10.130.1 *yó yajñó...tántubhis tatá* "This sacrifice is tendered by the strings." We then come to the idea of thought that is directed and tendered, thought that is in itself an offering and a sacrifice, and that is also harnessed. Thus the thoughts of the officiant poets are *áśvayogāḥ* "drawn by horses" (ṚV 1.186.6 *ā́...índraḥ...na ihá gamyāḥ* and ṚV 1.186.7 *utá na īm matáyó 'śváyogāḥ śíśuṃ ná gā́vas táruṇam rihanti* "May Indra come to us here itself" and "our poetic-thoughts drawn by horses lick (Indra) like their new-born young one."

Finally is conceived the mental harness, the harnessed prayer ṚV 5.81.1 *yuñjáte mána utá yuñjate dhíyo víprāḥ* "the inspired poets harness their mind, harness their poetic thoughts"; ṚV 7.27.1 *índraṃ náro nemádhitā havante yát pā́ryā yunájate dhíyas tā́ḥ* "the men (the warriors) invoke Indra during a combat (in which they face adversaries), so that he may harness the powerful poetic thoughts"; etc. (other than Renou's observations in the quoted article, see his *EVP*, XV, p. 47). Renou concludes that "to harness one's mind or thought" means "to direct" them, "to maintain" them, that is, imprint on them both "vigour and discipline", it is also, he adds, "the meaning of the numerous expressions with *mánoyuj, brahmayúj* and analogues which condense the secret of the "directed" inspiration characteristic of the poet of the Veda" (article quoted, pp. 177-178). But it seems possible to imagine a somewhat different interpretation based on the elements of the edifice of Vedic thought which Renou's conclusions do not eliminate straightaway.[1]

Why do Vedic hymns exploit the idea of harnessing thought and inspiration? The origin of these images can be traced and the images not accepted as a fruit of the poetic imagination which arbitrarily chooses one simile or the other. The success of sacrifice, says ṚV 1.18.7, depends on the help of a god, Sadasaspati, "master of the (ritual) spot" who is in all probability the double of Brahmaṇaspati or Bṛhaspati, "master of the bráhman, of the formulated prayer" because he favours the harnessing of poetic thoughts (*yásmād ṛté ná sidhyati yajñó vipaścítaś caná sá dhī́nām yógam invati* "He, without whom the sacrifice cannot be accomplished, even if it is done by an enlightened man, he favours the harnessing of the poetic thoughts"). Like the sacrifice, the poetic discourse and words are frequently compared and even identified with the harnessed cars; the hymns make abundant use of the images created around the harness. "If we are told of harness, ...it is often with reference to a discourse".[2] Very well, but once again, why is the comparison between the harness and discourse constantly repeated? Why are the fashioned poem and the constructed car compared? [note that a number of studies among those which have been mentioned omit the reference to ṚV 10.39.14 *etáṃ vāṃ stómam aśvināv akarmā́takṣāma bhṛ́gavo ná rátham* "We have fashioned for you the song of praise for you, O Aśvin, we have constructed it like the

Bhṛgu (have constructed) the car"]. Why does a hymn (ṚV 2.31) which exalts the poet's car end with an evocation of the poem visibly likened to a car? These same questions can be asked when observing that the car of the Aśvin filled with accumulated and distributed gifts is compared to a man endowed with speech which he will use to compose poems [ṚV 1.112.2 *yuvór dānā́ya subhárā asaścáto rátham ā́ tasthur vacasáṃ ná mántave* "Towards your car came the inexhaustible riches (they that are) a pleasant help for (serving as) gifts, as (the thought) goes towards (the man) endowed with speech so that he may create (with his thoughts)"; cf. a prayer to the Aśvin ṚV 1.46.7 *ā́ no nāvā́ matīnā́m yātám pārā́ya gántave yuñjā́thām aśvinā rátham* "Come with the ship of our thoughts to effect the crossing! Associate yourself with the car which is (our poem), O Aśvin!"].

It is uncontestable that there are clear traces of one and the same concept of speech that traverses a space and which does so in order to join its extremities and create a link between them. There is, as we know, FL, the same trait in the role of the officiant poet in archaic Vedic ritual sacrifice entrusted to pose correlations and explicative identifications by establishing correlative links between various kinds of phenomena, especially between the microcosm and the macrocosm, between the ritual world and the mythical world, between the human and divine order (L. Renou has often stressed on this aspect of the Vedic poets' activity).[3] The formulation of a correlative link, in addition to being part of the officiant poet's professional activity, subjected as he is to the constraints of sacrificial procedure by which he is obliged to respond to the incitation of the patron of the sacrifice to offer sacrifice, also has one more constraint: formulating a correlative link having cognitive significance, showing the correlative connections and equations among the phenomena is compelling oneself to create a way of reducing the space separating these phenomena, of effecting a movement in this space. This brings us back to the notion of "expedition", "departure" and "journey" that Renou found in the concept of *yóga* (pp. 177-178). In fact, this notion occupies a special place in the range of meanings of the term *yóga*. If we accept what Renou says, despite some grammatical difficulties,[4] that the poet of ṚV 7.67.1 calls the gods Aśvin with the car that awoke them (*práti vām rátham...jarádhyai yó vām..ájīgar* "I call you with the car that awoke you," according to Renou, *EVP*, I, p. 15, but another translation is possible:"I would like to invoke the car of you two. . ."), we can also accept that the help requested from the Aśvin for the poetic thoughts (ṚV 7.67.6) is connected to what is said in ṚV 7.67.8 *ékasmin yóge...samāné pári vāṃ saptá sraváto rátho gāt* "With one and the same harness, your car (can we take it to be "the car of poetic thought addressed to the Aśvin"?) has gone around the Seven Rivers." We can conceive that the car of poetic thought directed towards the Aśvin has completed a reconnaissance and intelligence expedition around the seven rivers in order to define their phenomenon. This same kind of expedition must be implicit in ṚV 10.39.12: when the poet addresses the same Aśvin "Come here with the (car) faster than the thought (the mind), the car that the Ṛhbu have constructed for you, O Aśvin, it is during (the course) of (this) harnessed team that the Daughter (of the sky) (the Dawn) was born" (*ā́ téna yātam mánaso jávīyasā ráthaṃ yáṃ vām ṛbhávaś cakrúr aśvinā/ yásya yóge duhitā́ jā́yate diváḥ*). This is the explanation of the birth of the Dawn as imagined by the poet; the conventions of Vedic speculation necessitate the image of the car explicitly compared to thought, while we know that the poets deliberately mix them up, or, to be exact, that they need the image of the car because they have to express the idea of travel, of *yóga*.

We can therefore understand why the hymns often associate the path and the *bráhman* (the enigmatic thought that poses a correlation, a correlative identification according to the definition given by Renou and Silburn[5]): the poet is supposed to open up a path to the *bráhman*, he seeks an opening and asks the gods for it, for the opened-up path will favour the journey, the route needed for establishing a connection. ṚV 4.4.6 *sá te jānāti sumatíṃ yaviṣṭha yá ī́vate bráhmaṇe gātúm aírat* "The one who has created a path for the *bráhman* like the one (which follows), he knows your favour, O strongest of gods;"[6] the phrase that comes after this sentence is therefore very probably both the *bráhman* itself and the fruit of its enunciation [*víśvāny asmai sudínāni rāyó...ví dúro abhí dyaut* "may all days be good days for him, may riches (belong to it)! Open the door to it by shining!"], for to succeed in one's personal *bráhman* and to succeed in making a path for it promises the poet all kinds of riches[7] and favours amongst which is naturally the access to a door, a door which must be understood as the point at which the successful journey ends.

It is no doubt because the thought, the words and the hymn of praise as their most complete expression are intended to find a way that can join the terms of an explicative connection, that the praise itself is presented as *práyukti* "harnessing (of the mind)", "impulse" (ṚV 1.153.2 *prástutir vām...práyuktir áyāmi mitrávaruṇā suvṛktíḥ* "the praise was offered to you, O Mitra-Varuṇa, it is the harnessing (of our thought), it is a (beautiful) hymn (recited)"]. It is perhaps because he uses the same concept of a path to be taken that the poet calls himself a steed that knows its destination and gives the same intellectual quality to the shaft of his car (or to his car): ṚV 5.46.1 *háyo ná vidvā́ñ ayuji svayám dhurí tā́m vahāmi pratáraṇīm avasyúvam/nā́syā vaśmi vimúcam nā́vṛ́tam púnar vidvā́n patháḥ puraetá ṛjú neṣati* "Like a steed, I who know, I have harnessed myself to the shaft (of the car) of my own free will. I draw it (this shaft) which goes powerfully forward, which ensures the favours (of the gods). I do not want it to be unharnessed, nor to turn back. May it, knowing the way, leading the way, take me straight on!" At the end of the journey, the *bráhman* of the poet finds itself rewarded by the god of whom he has sung the praises, or by the patron of the sacrifice, and this reward is given in the form of a cow (frequent form of the dakṣiṇā that has finally become symbolic of it), but he says that it is divinity that made it possible for him to discover the cow. [ṚV 10.112.8 *suvedanā́m akṛnor brahmáṇe gā́m,* "thou hast acted in such a way (O Indra) that the cow was easy for the *bráhman* to find", which can be compared to what Oldenberg suggested in *Ṛgveda, Textkritische u. exegetische Noten,* p. 334 on ṚV 5.29.3 *tád dhí havyám mánuṣe gā́ ávindad* "for this oblation has found cattle for men"].

The explanations given by Renou and Silburn about the denouement that the divinities had to find for the *bráhman* give over a large part to the idea of an issue which must be understood as the metaphorical expression of the posing and solving of a ritual equation (or connection);[8] but it is also true that the notion of a path leading to the discovery of the issue has been given the same attention in the hymns, and that too in its proper and durative aspect. The concrete, the tangible and the abstract in the form of figurative expressions intermingle; the poet and his words make their way towards the solution of the formulated paradoxes. Now, the formulation as well the elucidation of these are presented in their duration, which gives rise to the idea of the harnessed team making its way on a route, and its ultimate success crowned with the gift of a dakṣiṇā. If the hymns say that the offerings to the gods, whether they be words (*bráhman*) or the oblation, terminate in the giving of a material reward, this is again the concept of a correlative link that is being exploited.When the *yóga* is accentuated, what is brought into play is its scope; when one's attention is turned towards the winning of the dakṣiṇā, one looks at the value that I have tried to explain in the context of the linguistic concepts of the Vedic authors as the concrete expression of the meaning of the words that proclaim the correlations. It is not surprising that the words should also be *correlated* to their value[9].

The war aspect of *yóga* is also connected to the departure, the journey, the expedition (cf. Renou, *JAs.*, 1953, p. 78): ṚV 5.43.5 *ásāvi te jujuṣāṇā́ya sómaḥ...hárī ráthe sudhúrā yóge...índra priyā́ kṛṇuhi* "the soma has been pressed for thee (thou) that dost rejoice...O Indra, act so that the two chestnut horses be harnessed to the car, the beloved (horse) suitable for being harnessed, so that the expedition (may be undertaken)"(see also *EVP*, V, p. 24); ṚV 4.24.4 *kratūyánti kṣitáyo yóga ugrāśuṣāṇā́so mithó árṇasātau/sáṃ yád víśó 'vavṛtranta yudhmā́ ā́d ín néma indrayante abhī́ke* "The peoples are thinking of war, O powerful (god), they are excited confronting each other (in order to wage) war around the (riches that move like) water. When the warring tribes faced each other, a few of them turned immediately towards Indra." It is possible that the verb *yuj-* in itself is connected to the meaning of *yóga* in the war context: ṚV 6.25.3 *índra jāmáya utá yé 'jāmayo 'rvācīnā́so vanúṣo yuyujré* "The jealous (enemies), O Indra, the relatives and the non-relatives have harnessed themselves (to the spirit of war against us)." What is easily understood here is the warlike nuance of Vedic expeditions undertaken with the pre-sentiment of adverse parties facing each other, and including the razzias which we know were conceptualised by Vedic authors in such a way that in them they saw the means for warriors to capture the cattle converted into the value of poetic and sacrificial words, which value was then given to the officiant poets as dakṣiṇā.[10]

If this seems to be the primitive meaning of the term *yóga,* it can easily be comprehended how the semantic nuance of a determining constraint for its content in later Sanskrit literature was brought about. The imperative nature of the connective practices of the Vedic officiant poets is also brought out as soon as one considers their place and their function in the sacrificial cult. This cult had a strict distribution of socio-religious roles—the officiant poet, the patron of the sacrifice and the godheads who necessarily respond to the call of men. The Vedic sacrifice is the setting into motion of these tripartite roles wherein everything is organised in such a way that the first interaction between two roles is necessarily followed by the interaction between two other roles [we thus have at first a series of interactions (1) officiant poets-gods; (2) gods-patrons of the sacrfice; and (3) patrons of the sacrifice-officiant poets, then the series is repeated beginning with the role of the officiant poet]. The effectiveness of the sacrifice is possible only if the interactions are continuous and renewed.[11] The officiant poets who exercise *yogyā́*, the practices of "harnessing (thoughts and words)" correspond to the constraint of the effectiveness of the sacrifice which is threatened with failure in case the alternance or the solidarity of the socio-religious roles is not maintained. Is this not the distant source of the value of "magic constraint" taken on later by the term as opined Renou (*JAs*, 1953, p. 180), and of this "renunciation of obscure freedom, of instinctive essence, of the individual", of the "submission of the individual to an absolute order (Veda)", as Eliade so rightly expressed it?[12]

It would be tempting to re-evaluate the nature of the *yogyā́* that Renou interprets as "training" or "exercises which are the object of poetic meets" (p. 180, n. 1). In fact it would be precisely these strictly sacrificial activities of the officiant poets that are noticeably tinged with rivalry and competition which are an integral and essential part of his spiritual work (actually this is the term Renou uses to explain the *yogyā́*, see *EVP*, XVI, 1967, pp. 49-50).

In fact in ṚV 7.70.4 the gods Aśvin are invited to find pleasure in the grasses and the waters (of the somic sacrifice) when they come towards the "harnesses of the poet seers" (*caniṣṭám devā óṣadhīṣv apsú yád yogyā́ aśnávaithe ṛ́ṣīṇāṃ*); harnesses are explained in the same hymn as *bráhmāṇi*, the enunciations of the *bráhman* that the present poet seers address to the Aśvin following the example of the poets of past ages [ṚV 7.70.5 *śuśruvā́ṃsā cid aśvinā purū́ṇy abhí bráhmāṇi cakṣāthe ṛ́ṣīṇām... asmé vām astu sumatíś cániṣṭhā* "You have, O Aśvin, heard indeed a good number of (pious and praising songs), be generous to those of the poet seers (now)...May be ours (the expression) of the pious thought destined to you!", while ṚV 7.70.6 specifies the ambience of violence around the offerings in the form of oblations and of words that the poet Vasiṣṭha is anxious to get accepted by the Aśvin: *yó vāṃ yajñó nāsatyā havíṣman kṛtábrahmā samaryò bhávāti úpa prá yātaṃ váraṃ ā́ vásiṣṭham imā́ bráhmāṇy ṛcyante yuvā́bhyam,* "Whatever be the sacrifice offered to you, O Nāsatya, (may it be) an oblation or may the words (suitable) for combat be pronounced, come according to your desire towards Vasiṣṭha, these words (these *bráhman*) are sung for the two of you."

It is then quite normal to find the association between the *yogyā́* and the images of the poetic discourse which compare it to the harness in ṚV 10.53.7 and 11. The first of these verses describes a harness[13] which can only be a special vehicle hardly similar to the cars of the Ṛgveda. It has eight seats, pointed out Edgerton, while the common car has only one, with the exception of the cars of the Aśvin and of the god Soma which have three.[14] Since it is the officiants who are asked to prepare it (and in any case they are associated with the soma), it is legitimate to suppose that what is harnessed is not the car, but the poem, all the more so because the hymn brings together the cutting and splitting of wood and sharpening of tools by which the poets fashion their words (we can easily concur with Edgerton who observes that the only reason for making poets into builders is to bring out the resemblance between the car and the poetical work), for this, see 9. *tváṣṭā...śiśīte nūnám paráśuṃ svāyasáṃ yéna vṛścā́d étaśo bráhmaṇas pátiḥ* "Tvaṣṭar...hone now the axe made of good metal with which the Master of the Word, the colourfully-dressed (god) will split (the wood)" and 10. *sató nūnáṃ kavayaḥ sáṃ śiśīta vā́śībhir yā́bhir...tákṣatha/vidvā́ṃsaḥ padā́ gúhyāni kartana yéna devā́so amṛtatvám ānaśúḥ* "Now, all ye poets, hone regularly all the axes by which you fashion (the words). Ye who know make the secret words thanks to which the gods have attained immortality" (Renou, *EVP*, XIV, p. 17). The last verse of the hymn significantly follows the exhortation to the poets to create a secret discourse; for it formulates a veritable Vedic enigma which can be said to be unsolvable[15] but it is constructed as a series of paradoxical connections [ṚV 10.53.11 *gárbhe yóṣām ádadhur vatsám āsány apīcyèna mánasotá jihvā́yā* "(the officiant poets) have placed the young woman in the womb, the calf in the mouth (of the cow) (for they show themselves) by their secret spirit and (their abstruse) language".[16] Once the connections are formulated, it ends with a maxim for the use of the poets who have to face competition: *sá viśvā́hā sumánā yogyā́ abhī́ siṣāsánir vanate kārá íj jítim* "He who always has a courageous spirit, who desires victory in the competitions (for the poets), always wins the true combat." It can be said that the true combat [or, according to Renou's translation (*EVP*, XIV, p. 17) "the decisive moment"] refers once more to the *yogyā́*, these poetic practices whereby the subject harnesses himself in order to follow a path at the same time as he reveals the explicative connections of which the elements are also "harnessed" to one another. Just as the sacrificial thought is itself tendered and directed, so also the poet is harnessed and the objects to which his thoughts are directed are connected when the poet takes care to enumerate them one by one. Such transfers of an idea which acquires an obvious importance in Vedic sacrifice could not be dissociated from inversions in the speculative procedure of which we have just seen some examples. It is probably this tendency that came into play when the author of ṚV 10.114.9 asks: "Which sage knows the harness of (poetic) metre? Who has understood in an adequate manner the inspired (ritual) word? (*káś chándasāṃ yógam ā́ veda dhī́raḥ kó dhíṣṇyām práti vā́cam papāda*), and when he continues by making a reference to Indra's horse [*hárī índrasya ní cikāya káḥ svit* "who then has truly understood (the true nature) of the two Indra's chestnut horses?"], which must be taken as the poets' mounts given as connective correspondence to the harnessed metres. Moreover, the entire hymn ends by giving up allusions and by speaking directly of the harnessed poets standing on the shafts of the car and undertaking the reconnaissance journey around the limits of the earth (ṚV 10.114.10: *bhū́myā ántam páry éke caranti ráthasya dhūrṣú yuktā́so asthuḥ*).

Thus the Vedic term *yóga* stands for an essential part of the sacrifice in the Ṛgveda. It is, according to Geldner (*Der Ṛig-Veda in Auswahl*, II, p. 235) an "Intätigkeitsetzen," a setting into action (of stones which press the soma, for example, ṚV 10.35.9), which has, however, a very definite aim: to harness, to put together, to conjugate the things between which correspondence is to be established, which are to be qualified as identical or close on the speculative plane. The Vedic sacrifice about which the authors of the hymns have long reflected is in fact a powerful explicative device, a set of gestures and intentions which condense a whole speculative experience. Thus there can be no misunderstanding the highly specific nature of the objects that are said to be "harnessed" in the hymns. They are vehicles, all kinds of animals, in short, all that is capable of effecting a journey and, as we have seen, the words of poetic discourse, the thoughts directed to the gods, and also quite naturally the homage to the god Agni (ṚV 1.65.1) and the sacred work (ṚV 1.151.4 *ṛtám ā́ ghoṣatho bṛhát...gā́m ná dhury úpa yuñjathe apáḥ* "You, Varuṇa and Mitra, strongly speak out the Truth, you harness the (sacred) work as (one harnesses) the cow to the yoke"). The authors have visibly not hesitated to give a broad meaning not only to the harnessed objects but also to the action of harnessing, for it is difficult not to see in ṚV 10.101 (the hymn exhorting the officiants to the sacrifice), that when speaking of ploughs and yokes (3a. *yunákta sī́ra ví yugā́ tanudhvam*, 4. *sī́rā yuñjanti kaváyo yugā́ ví tanvate pṛ́thak* "harness the ploughs, strain the yokes!" and "the officiant poets harness the ploughs, they strain the yokes one by one"), the accent is very evidently on the actions rather than the objects, and that, without finding a means to interpret these objects, the intention of the lines quoted above bring out the so to speak abstract nature of the actions of harnessing and tendering (the play of the roots used contributes to this: *tan- yugā́* "strain the yokes" somewhat explains *yuj- sī́rā* "harness the ploughs).[17] However, possibly precisely because of the attention drawn to the action itself, what is "conjugated" during the action has a definite importance. We shall take into account the fairly frequent turns which evoke the harnessing by words and by thoughts (this is the meaning of the words *brahmayúj, vacoyúj, manoyúj and ṛtayúj* and of the phrases *bráhmaṇā yuj-, sūkténa, vácasā yuj-, mánasā yuj-* (for this, see Lüders, *Varuṇa*, pp. 450-454), which is not surprising considering the association between the mount, the vehicle and the words, but calls for an observation. The hymns deliberately confound the object and the instrument of harness, as they do not seek to distinguish between the subject and the object of the action of harnessing when speaking of the poet.[18]

The inevitable conclusion is that the action of harnessing had to be imagined as an independent act, with a specific yet abstract significance even if the objects that are involved are most often of a concrete nature. This really means that, given this abstract value of the verb *yuj-*, its uses can be reasonably oriented to emphasise that aspect of *yóga* which is expressed by the connective practices of the Vedic poets. In fact, imputing to words and thoughts the ability to serve as a means of harnessing or to harness themselves in order to effect a connection, is giving prominence to the very operation of connection and stressing on the explicative value of the link established between the various connected elements, or, to be more exact, the elements joined to one another by being compared. It is not by accident that the hymn ṚV 10.101 having poetic inspiration as general reference (as Renou observed in *Hymnes spéculatifs*, p. 250), should speak of the act of harnessing ploughs and yokes that the poets handle. The implements are the means of transport by which the poetic thoughts can travel, so also the poetic thoughts that they must tender (10.101.2: *dhíya ā́ tanudhvam*) and the vessel that will cross the seas [same line: *nā́vam aritrapáraṇīṃ kṛṇudhvam* "make a vessel that crosses (the seas) using oars," cf. the end of verse 2 *prā́ñcaṃ yajñám prá ṇayatā* "lead the sacrifice forward!" Verses 2 and 3 (see above) explain each other and especially make clear the intentions of the hymn to present the modes of sacrifice specific to the various officiants amongst which this special mode of sacrifice finds its place—tendering the thoughts for oneself, building a vehicle, also for oneself, for the verbs *tan-* and *kṛ-* are in the middle voice (as also the verbs *budh-* "to awaken" and *idh-* "to light up" in the first verse as well as the verb *kṛ-* in the beginning of the second verse: *mandrā́ kṛṇudhvaṃ dhíyaḥ* "render (your)(poetic) thoughts pleasant!"]. The first two verses prepare what is said in the third and fourth in a different way. The latter incite the officiant poets to traverse the path of poetic creation and of the sacrifice, to advance on the path to the sacrifice. The vocabulary of these verses is both sufficiently direct and allusive.

As Renou has observed (see note 17 above), the entire hymn must be read like a presentation of poetic inspiration, while the terms used in it take us to another plane. The two verses that refer to the harnessing of ploughs and yokes have sufficiently clear indications that can make us understand that it is indeed poetic activity that is referred to. In 3, after the incitation to harness the ploughing implements, faith in the power of the word is expressed (*girā́ ca śruṣṭíḥ sábharā ásan no nédīya ít sṛṇyàḥ pakvám éyāt* "if the generous hearing (given to our word) carries the same weight as the word (itself), the ripe fruit will come nearer the sickles";[19] in 4, as we have seen earlier, it is the officiant poets who are expected to harness the same implements. Thus, harnessing the words or by the words, harnessing an object to the words and relating an object to the poet who pronounces the words, all these acts, expressed by the verb *yuj-* or its derivatives, translate the role of words in the sacrifice.

When it is said that Indra desiring the (re)conquest of the cows is *ṛtayúg* "harnessed to the *ṛtá*, the (enunciated) Truth", there can be found one of the explanations of the nature of this god in the explanation added in ṚV 6.39.2a to this expression (*ṛtadhītibhir ṛtayúg yujānáḥ* "harnessed to the *ṛtá*, he is harnessed to those who think by the *ṛtá*). He admittedly is not identical to the words, but he is made to correspond to the act of its enunciation, he is put in juxtaposition to it, as to the Aṅgiras designated here by *ṛtadhītibhir* with whom he becomes one so that he can destroy the hiding-place of the cows belonging to the Paṇi. Like the Aṅgiras, officiant poets in his service, he can be called the one who was victorious over the Paṇi by using words (ṚV 6.39.2d *paṇī̐r vácobhir abhí yodhad índraḥ*), whereas we know that he fought essentially with typically war weapons. It is because he confided the sacrifice to the words of the Aṅgiras, a sacrifice that takes on the appearance of arms and destroys the hiding-place, that it is said of him that he travels with the horses harnessed to the words of the *ṛtá* (ṚV 6.39.4 *ayám īyata ṛtayúgbhir áśvaiḥ*); it is not impossible that this sentence should owe its origin more to the association of Indra with the effects of the *ṛtá* than with the horses in the literal sense; anyhow, it can be maintained that the horses of the *ṛtá* are more a figure of style by which the horses stand for the speed of the sacrificial words than animals in the concrete sense.

There is a fleeting memory of the god Indra correlated to the animals that carry the formidable words in the invocation to Indra mentioned earlier (ṚV 7.27.1 *índraṃ náro nemádhitā havante yát pā́ryā yunájate dhíyas tā́ḥ*), this god is appealed to so that he can activate the (or his) harnessable poetic thoughts, so that he may be present through the thoughts that are harnessed like horses, when men are in the midst of the fight against their adversaries (*náro nemádhitā*).

It is this interpretation of the object linked to the words and of the words themselves that is spoken of in ṚV 9.7.3 *prá yujó vācó agríyo vṛ́ṣāva cakradad* and ṚV 1.46.8 *dhiyā́ yuyujra índavaḥ*. In the first verse, "the bull (that) has lowed, the one that walks ahead, preceding the word, its ally (which it has joined)" is the somic drink offered to the gods, but owing to the vicissitudes of Vedic sacrifice, the drink and the word, the two main offerings, are conceptualised in such a way that they cannot be distinguished from each other. As "ally"(noun-root *yuj-* "associate, ally, companion"), the drink tends to be identified with the word or at least share with it certain essential traits which the above-mentioned line expresses by using the notion of ally, of being correlated in such a way as to become one with this word.[20] The second verse ("the drops of soma are harnessed to the poetic thought") seems to accentuate the movement imprinted on the soma related to thought, but in fact it only continues what is said in 1.46.7 (the preceding line) in which appear the ship of thoughts which has to effect the crossing[21] and the incitation to the Aśvin to rejoin this vehicle (*ā́ no nāvā́ matīnā́m yātám pārā́ya gántave yunjā́thām aśvinā rátham*). This sentence can be translated differently from Geldner's interpetation: "come with the ship of our thoughts to effect the crossing, associate yourself with the car (which is our poem), O Aśvin!" (Instead of "kommt auf dem Schiff, um ans andere Ufer zu gelangen, schirret euren Wagen an, ihr Aśvin!": the invoked gods are thus subjected to the same operation of alliance with the thoughts and the poem as the soma of line 8, to the extent of being given a trait common to thought as well as the poem, that of moving forward on a route).

It is quite probable that even outside the harnessing by or with the words, the verb *yuj-* has retained a nuance referring to an act whose aim is to show a resemblance, or even the identity that is established at the time of its enunciation. ṚV 5.80.3 gives this definition of the goddess Uṣas: *eṣā́ gṓbhir aruṇébhir yujānā́* "She is the one who is associated with the pink cows," which is to be understood as a presentation of the identification of the goddess Dawn with the cows. We know however that the links between this goddess and the cows are very complex, for the goddess is not really similar in all ways to the cows whatever the hymns may often say about this, but she is indeed momentarily associated with them in the conception of Vedic poets who seek to study these links for speculative purposes.[22]

But it is the use of *sváyukta, sváyukti and svayúj* which throws light on the value of *yuj-*. These terms most often translated as "harnessing oneself of one's own accord, of one's own volition" should, in fact, designate the result of the act of identification to a *svá*. ṚV 1.168.4 specifies the nature of the gods Marut: *áva sváyukta divá ā́ vṛ́thā yayur* "harnessed of their own accord, (the Maruts) have arrived from heaven of their own volition", and adds: *ámārtyāḥ káśayā codata tmánā* "set yourselves in motion of your own accord, O immortal (gods) by inciting yourselves with the whip!" [cf. ṚV 1.168.2 *yé svajā́ḥ svátavasa*" they who have taken-birth themselves, who (find) their strength in themselves" and ṚV 5.52.8 *té...naraḥ prá...yujata tmánā* "these noblemen harness themselves of their own accord".] The value of the spontaneous harnessing in *sváyukta,* though justified by the image of the Marut, seems to lessen as soon as we see the use of the phrase *yuj- tmánā*[23] in which the verb tends to lose its transitive sense because of the quasi-pronoun *tmánā*, but it is clearly shown in ṚV 1.50.9 that this value has already been significantly weakened *áyukta saptá śundhyúvaḥ sū́ro ráthasya naptyàḥ/tā́bhir yāti sváyuktibhiḥ* "(the Sun) has harnessed the seven splendid daughters of the car of the sun; it goes, (started off) by these (daughters) who harness themselves". *Sváyukti* is visibly superfluous, unless it signifies, especially because it is preceded by *yuj-* used transitively, that it should be understood that the daughters of the car of the sun have a relation of identity to the *svá* which here is the sun taking the form of a car. Does the word *sváyukti* refer to the literal harness of the Sun-god (as suggested by Roth see apud Geldner and ṚV 1.50.9), or to the figurative harness of the daughters of the car of the sun? It can be considered that the term *naptī́-* "daughter" indicates not so much a natural relation as a connecting term that indicates a relationship which serves as identification or correlation,[24] just as a large number of similar Vedic terms do. It is therefore a sort of gloss of the term *sváyukti*. The use of this term which seems at first sight to derive its meaning only from mythological context, has in all evidence contributed to the creation of the adverb *sváyuktyā* (in fact, the instrumental form of *sváyukti*) and *sváyuktitas*, both of which mean "naturally, which is understood by itself", that is, "joined or identical to itself in a natural way".

One is also led to believe that the use of certain nominal formations of the verb *yuj* tends to delexicalise them. ṚV 7.70.2 certainly has at first a concrete meaning *átāpi gharmó...yó...étagvā cin ná suyújā yujānáḥ* "the offering has been heated...(it) has been harnessed as (one harnesses) two steeds easy to harness". An offering is sent on its way which is supposed to cross the seas and the water courses (*yó vāṃ samudrā́n sarítaḥ píparti*), it is juxtaposed with the steeds as if it was also easy to harness. The offering is *like* that which enables the crossings (the *ṛtá*, the *bráhman*, the *gā́thā*, says Lüders, *Varuṇa*, p. 452, n. 4). It is an aspect of style rather than grammar, more so because Renou observes that in this sentence, the particles *cin ná* do not have their strictly comparative function and that *cid* takes the meaning of "like". On the other hand, Lüders feels that the steeds and the offering are co-ordinated[25] and agreeing with him, we could say connected. Although the terms derived from *yuj-* retain their literal sense, they overdetermine the conjunctive and even assimilative value of the double particle *cin ná*, a value that only *cid* has in the examples quoted by Renou, *Grammaire de la langue védique*, p. 381: ṚV 1.41.9 *catúraś cid dádamānād bibhīyā́d ā́ nídhātoḥ* "He who holds in his hand the four, be he feared until the moment he throws (his dice)":[26] *cid* has a bearing on *nídhātoḥ* and functions like *iva* (Renou) which, on freely paraphrasing, gives "may we fear the one who can (thanks to his art of throwing dice) be likened to the best player"; 2.33.12 *kumārā́ś cit pitáram vándamānam* "like a boy bowing before his father"; 3.31.12 *pitré cid cakruḥ sádanaṃ sám asmai* "they have made for him a seat as (if he were their) father"; 3.53.22 *paraśúṃ cid ví tapati* "he burns (the enemy) as (one heats) an axe". And, on the border between the lexical value and the value of a formal tool of comparison, there is a use found in a series of three derivatives of *yuj-* in a sentence that is difficult to interpret: ṚV 8.41.6 *vrajé gā́vo na saṃyujé aśvā́ñ ayukṣata* "like cows in the enclosure, (the officiant poets in competition against one another) have commonly harnessed the horses so that they can join them".[27] In this can be seen the permanent longing of the poets to liken themselves to steeds, but it is expressed by searching for an alliance which one would like to see transformed into an identity.

Once the possibilities of the derivatives of *yuj-* are understood in this way, there is immediately room for amending the translation, if not the interpretation of the phrases *matáyó 'śvayogāḥ* (ṚV 1.186.7, see above), *rátha...háriyoga* (ṚV 1.56.1). This is because there is a second level of reading which is not less important than the first, for the Vedic authors felt that the harnessed poetic thoughts or the car are familiar representations in which horses are brought in, as well as saying that the poetic thoughts or the car harnessed to horses are *like* horses from a certain point of view. Therefore the final member in the compound words with *yóga-* intends to express this procedure of identification or explicative equation. Lüders hesitatingly suggested that "it would be difficult to say what must be the 'songs harnessed to the horses' " (*Varuṇa*, p. 452). We can elucidate that. The implied simile is accompanied by an explicit identification when the image of the poet-steed appears, see above and particularly

ṚV 3.38.1 in which the poet calls himself a steed, winning a victory trophy and fitted with a suitable yoke (*abhí táṣṭeva dīdhayā manīṣā́m átyo ná vājī́ sudhúro* "Like the carpenter, I imagined this poem, like a steed winning its trophy, fitted with a fine yoke"). It is perhaps because it is said that the winds harness themselves (ṚV 10.78.2 *vā́tāso ná svayújaḥ*) and because Indra nevertheless uses the horses of the Wind-god [ṚV 10.22.5 *tyā́ cid vā́tasyā́śvā́gāḥ...tmánā váhadhyai* "thou hast come to drive thyself even these two speeds of (the god) Vāta"], that is ventured this otherwise inexplicable figure of the poet by which it is said that he brings home the word, as he would a young woman, while the word has joined the poet of its own accord (ṚV 5.44.8 *yādṛ́śmin dhā́yi tám apasyáyā vidad yá u svayáṃ váhate*). To be able to compare the word to a woman who is led home (cf. also ṚV 5.37.3 and 10.27.11), it was necessary to have the permanent image, so to speak, of the poet who travels thanks to the harness, whereby the verb *vah-* "to drive" is used, often in conjunction with the verb *yuj-*.

It can be seen that this use of *yuj-* and its derivatives has remarkably maintained the balance between a concrete meaning in which the notion of harness can be distinguished, and a more abstract, if not more exact meaning which turns the verb as well as its derivatives towards the expression of a connection which can take place only between that which has common traits or can be given one of these traits once the connection has been established. It cannot be doubted that it is indeed the semantic developement which was decisive in the formation of a number of words, both in Vedic and in later Sanskrit, which have the dominating principle of an association of pairs, of matched couples, probably couples of equals, and in any case of couples with each individual partner corresponding to the other. One such example is the Vedic *yújya*, having a complex meaning, nevertheless revolving around the idea of commensurability, then around the idea of resemblance which is caused by the first. This is as much "the alliance" itself (ṚV 4.25.2) as the state that results from the alliance of likes, whether they are animate beings or inanimate objects for which the equality of rank or nature is established (if wealth is allotted, it must be *yújya,* of a corresponding rank: ṚV 7.36.7; the person who states the birth of a great god will be by his renown superior to someone who is *yújya,* the equal of the gods: ṚV 1.156.2; the god Agni goes forth with flames, his ilk, *yujyébhiḥ,* ṚV 1.145.4; the gods rejoice in the offering of milk which is their *yújya,* their ilk, ṚV 6.52.10). If, on the one hand, the Ṛgveda speaks of *yugá,* n. "yoke, harness of animals put under a common yoke" and also "generation" and "age, temporal sequence", we can better understand these meanings by comparing them to *ayujá* "without companions" or even *ayugū* "only daughter, who has neither brothers nor sisters" (Gobhila Gṛ. Sū. 3.5.4), *yugmá, yugmát, yugmán* "peer, like"(on the morphology of these, see Wackernagel-Debrunner, *Altind. Gr.* II, 2, p. 750) in contrast to *ayujinī, ayugma* "unequal, odd, which is not straight", *ayogya,* "improper good-for-nothing", *ayogatva* "quality of being inapt for something". This is because the notion of generation and, by extension, of age, must have been constituted from the notion of grouping in pairs, of associating individuals by virtue of their common age.

REFERENCES

1. L. Renou, *Études védiques,* 3. *Quelques termes du Ṛgveda, d. yóga, Journal asiatique,* 1953, pp. 177-180.
2. L. Renou, *Études védiques et pāṇinéennes,* I, 1955, p. 15.
3. This comparison, the source of one of the most consistent Vedic metaphors, has been studied in an essay that is already old, but whose important conclusions have been more or less forgotten. This is F. Edgerton, *The Metaphor of the Car in Ṛigvedic Ritual* in *American Journal of Philology,* 40, 1919, pp. 175-189. The opinion of the author is that if, as a first stage, the comparison of the car to the hymn is facilitated because both are constructed (the action

is *takṣ-*), it corresponds in fact to the major preoccupation and essential goal of Vedic liturgy, to set right a dangerous situation which has to be overcome or, in Vedic terms, "traversed, crossed" (the verbs *tar-* and *par-*), which applies to any obstacle, whether material or spiritual, all the more because the figurative representation denoting difficulties and dangers in the Ṛgveda is that of a water-course. See also L. Renou, *Études védiques et pāṇinéennes*, I, 1955, p. 15 and M. Durante, *Epea pteroenta. Die Rede als 'Weg' in griechischen und vedischen Bildern* in R. Schmitt, *Indogermanische Dichtersprache*, Darmstadt, 1968, p. 252; M. Durante, *Sulla preistoria della tradizione poetica greca*, II, Roma, 1976, p. 130; V.V. Ivanov, *Estetičeskoje nasledije drevnej i srednevekovoj Indii* in *Literatura i kultura drevnej i srednevekovoj Indii*, Moscow, 1979, p. 13.

4. See the discussion: J. Haudry, *L'emploi des cas en védique*, Lyon, 1977, p. 337.
5. Sur la notion de *bráhman*, *Journal asiatique*, 1949, p. 13.
6. The translation of *yaviṣṭha* as "the strongest" or "the most (greatly) endowed with vital force" is preferable to the one traditionally given as "the youngest" (Geldner, Renou...); the comparative arguments in respect of semantic and morphological aspects which obtain the function of this adjective from the old sources of Indo-European poetic language are given by C. Watkins, *Latin* iouiste *et le vocabulaire religieux indo-européen* in *Mélanges linguistiques offerts à Émile Benveniste*, Paris, 1975, pp. 527-534.
7. On the *bráhman* and the path: L. Renou, *Études védiques et pāṇinéennes*, XVI, p. 83.
8. *JAs*, 1949, pp. 13-14.
9. See the chapter " The *signifiant* and the *signifié* in Vedic sacrifice" in this volume.
10. See "The quest for booty and meaning in Vedic sacrifice" in this volume.
11. A more detailed argumentation is given in my essay *La dakṣiṇā dans le Ṛgveda et le transfert de mérite dans le bouddhisme* in *Indological and Buddhist Studies. Volume in Honour of Professor J.W. de Jong on his Sixtieth Birthday*, Canberra, 1982, pp. 393-414.
12. M. Eliade, *Yoga*, Paris-Bucharest, 1936, p. 104.
13. ṚV 10.53.7 *akṣānáho nahyatanotá somyā íṣkṛṇudhvaṃ raśanā́ ótá piṃśata/aṣṭā́vandhuraṃ vahatābhíto rátham* "Attach the joints of the axle, O somic (officiants), lay out the cords (that conduct the discourse) and decorate (this) car having eight places, bring it here...."
14. F. Edgerton, *The Metaphor of the Car in Vedic Ritual*, p. 178.
15. See H. Oldenberg, *Ṛgveda, Textkritische u. exegetische Noten*, 1912, p. 256.
16. K.F. Geldner noted the paradoxical nature of this sentence (*Der*

Ṛig-Veda, III, p. 217) and has pointed out others in which the comprehension seems to proceed by inversion of the normal relations between various things: the son remembers the birth of his parents, the wife leads the husband thanks to her eloquence (ṚV 10.32.3), the son is born before his parents (ṚV 10.31.10), the bull, the form of the male god Agni, gives milk (4.3.10). Vedic paradoxes often arise from the supposition that relationships are reciprocal and this is naturally conducive to inversions, and as a particular case, to the transformation of the object on which an action is done into the subject of the action (see further). See the interesting remarks about the paradox of the son begetting the father (who is a father only because he has a son) and the gods who beget fire and are begotten by fire, in R. Ambrosini's *Il primo inno del Ṛg-Veda et l'apparente ambiguità della poesia* in *Linguistica e letteratura*, V, 1, Pisa, p. 16, 19. Note the deliberate confounding in ṚV 10.53.11 of the organ, the tongue, and the language (for more on this, see Renou, *Études védiques et pāṇinéennes*, XIV, pp. 81-82).

17. See L. Renou, *Hymnes spéculatifs du Véda*, 1956, pp. 209 and 250 on the innermost secret of the hymn concerning poetical technique, and J. Gonda, *The Vision of the Vedic Poets*, 1963, pp. 114.
18. W. Wüst, *Von indogermanischer Dichtersprache*, München, 1969, pp. 57-58, prefers to distinguish three stages in the formation of metaphors resulting from the slidings of meanings mentioned above. According to him, there is (1) the act of harnessing by words, the objects being animals, vehicles, the somic brew. At this level, what takes place in daily routine is hardly by-passed by the reference to a means of harnessing, the words; (2) a higher stage: the gods (or the men) harness the words; (3) coming back to the ordinary, it is the poet who knows and masters the harnessing of the poetic metre. I feel that this is misunderstanding the intentions of the Vedic authors who, by moving from the subject to the object, probably meant the deep relationships which unite the two, and which they continually reveal in their reflection on the words.
19. Further, in line 3, after the words reproduced above, "harness the cars, strain the yokes!" there is *kṛté yónau vapatehá bī́jam* "in the furrow (thus) made, sow the seeds!" which also calls for a comment: *yóni* "(traced) path", according to Renou, *Études védiques et pāṇinéennes*, XVI, p. 157, is a word formed from the verb *yu-* "to set in motion". This main value has, in the language of the Ṛgveda, undergone many varied interpretations such as, "to attribute, to give, to impart", and even "to unite", so much so that the notion of path is that of a traversed path (see Renou, *L'acception première du mot sanskrit* yóni in *Bulletin de la Société de Linguistique*, 40, 2, 1939, pp. 18-24). Even if it is difficult to explain what is implied

by the image of the grains, as far as the poetic words are concerned, the reference to the path of the poets is indeed in the right context: it is the path they take in order to accomplish their *yóga*, their work of union.

20. See once again "The *signifiant* and the *signifié* in Vedic sacrifice": the term *bándhu-* which indicates the correlative link and the parental relationship translates the specific Vedic way of understanding particularly close relationships between the objects or the elements involved, just like the notion of ally. In a like manner, the Vedic *priyá* signifies together affectivity and the notion referring to the quality belonging to the object of affection, see the discussion in M. Scheller's *Vedisch* priyá *und die Wortsippe* frei, freien, Freund, Göttingen, 1959.
21. For this reading of *pārā̂ya gántave* see J. Haudry, *L'emploi des cas en védique,* p. 106, n. 2.3.1.2(2).
22. This theme has been developed in my book: *La deesse Uṣas. Recherches sur le sacrifice de la parole dans le Ṛgveda,* Paris-Louvain, 1988.
23. On the relationships between *svá,* possessive adjective having reflexive value, and *tmán* which functions as a reflexive substantive, see L. Renou, *Études védiques et pāṇinéennes,* XIII, p. 124.
24. L. Renou, *Études védiques,* 3. *Quelques termes du Ṛgveda, b. bándhu,* in *Journal asiatique,* 1953, pp. 171-175 studies precisely the meaning taken by a series of these terms.
25. L. Renou, *Études védiques et pāṇinéennes,* XVI, p. 49 and XV, p. 160; *Grammaire de la langue védique,* p. 381, H. Lüders, *Varuṇa,* p. 452, n. 4.
26. For this translation see L. Renou's suggestions, *Études védiques et pāṇinéennes,* V, p. 110 and especially VII, p. 99.
27. Renou's translation, *Études védiques et pāṇinéennes,* V, p. 73 is somewhat different. Cf. his explanations: *Études védiques et pāṇinéennes,* VII, p. 30.

CHAPTER 7

From Vedic Speculation to Indo-European Poetic and Religious Themes

1. Introduction

The preceding chapter presents arguments in favour of the concrete meaning of the verb *yuj-* "to harness". This meaning was soon followed by another, equally visible in the hymns, i.e., "to match (like elements or elements that will become alike after the operation)", "to pair".

Far from being only Vedic, these concrete meanings of the verb and its derivatives are perpetuated in the known poetic figures and religious themes in various areas inhabited by the ancient Indo-Europeans. It seems uncontestable that the figures and themes studied above originate from an Indo-European heritage in which the idea of harness is a throwback to the most ancient representations. Certain correspondences that we shall see have already been commented by experts; it will therefore be sufficient to recall them and place them in a new reasoning. Others that have been located have not been given an interpretation which appears more than plausible.

2. Fresh Views on a Greco-Vedic Correspondence

Greco-Vedic correspondences pertaining to the theme of

harness give importance to the concept of the words surging forward like a steed, like a car making its way. M. Durante has indeed shown that even if Greek authors made use of images of the winged arrow or the car of the poet, their intention was not to stress on the speed of the words but rather the ability of the poetic discourse to reach its goal and make its way.[1] What has been less observed till now, and what must also be common to the two poetic traditions, although Durante has mentioned it very briefly,[2] is that the harnessing is implied by the reins of the discourse guided by the inspired poet, and the representation of the poet as a steed, and moreover the image of the car transporting the Greek poet (especially used by Pindar and Parmenides) or the car which in Vedic poetry serves as the metaphor of the hymn. This can be seen in some Greek and Vedic passages that are quoted in these cases, but with reference to other contexts. ṚV 1.84.16: *kó adyá yuṅkte dhurí gā́ ṛtásya śímīvato bhāmíno durhṛṇayū́n / asánniṣūn hṛtsváso mayobhū́n* "Who harnesses today to the yoke the oxen of the ṛta, (they) who devote themselves to the (sacrificial) work, irritable, who go into a dangerous rage, who have arrows in their mouth, who strike at the (very) heart, who perform miracles?"[3] The harnessed oxen (or the cows) must be either the poetic songs or the officiants themselves. This can be seen not only through Vedic parallels (as shown by Geldner and Wüst), but also through verses 14-15 of the same hymn which deal with that fragment of Vedic religion concerning research and discovery, a theme that has a definite importance in the Ṛgveda. Verse 14 tells of the head of the horse whose bone (see also verse 13) will help in finding the hidden soma (a summary of related legends is made by Geldner in *Der Ṛig-Veda*, I, p. 108); 15 repeats the motif of the discovery of the cows, another but more central theme of Vedic sacrificial ideology which gives most prominence to the officiant poets who discover, find and even invent the secret names of the cows, thanks to their knowledge of secret words.[4]

Amongst the thematic correspondences between Pindar's odes and Vedic hymns can be mentioned the one between the harnessed words or songs (Nem. I.7, Isthm I.6)[5] but attention has not been paid to the apparently isolated use of the theme of harness in Ol. VI.22-27 (the poet incites the driver to harness the mules in order to go on the paths leading to the genealogy of the Iamides, while the doors of the hymns open before these mules).[6] It is however easy not only to recognise the counterpart of the Vedic motif of going on a path leading to a discovery due to poetic inspiration, but also to compare certain details in the treatment of the poetic journey, such as the harness with a specific goal, which will lend more weight to Greco-Vedic parallels in the field of the terminology of poetic creation.

Nevertheless we shall not lose sight of the fact that these correspondences do not repeat the poetic formulary of the two traditions, that they are limited to the repetition of common themes. Although there are traces of an old formulary, probably ruined and which can be partially reconstituted thanks precisely to these common themes, we must note that what corresponds to the strictly religious impact of the theme of Vedic harness is a Greek poetic theme, even though it is noticeably altered if not used in another perspective. If, in the Ṛgveda, the act of harnessing the words, or by the words, refers to a journey over a distance and the enunciation of connections, Pindar, who has no ready-made formulae to follow, tries to make his statements consistent by giving them other motivations. For example, it is said in Isthm I.6 that the words are harnessed so that the poet may successfully complete his composition *[amphoterân toi kharítōn sùn theoîs zeúksō télos]*.[7] In the sixth Olympic ode, Pindar introduces a mediator (the charioteer) between the poet and the harness, and even if it can be supposed that the motif of the doors of the hymns is authentically archaic, it is no longer the poet who does the harnessing.

We know, however, that Pindar gives importance to the

charioteers by the side of the poet who sings the praises of a hero. This is doubtless a theme that is common to Pindar's poetry and Indo-Iranian poetry—we know to what extent the drivers of the cars and their roles as counsellors to the warriors are characteristic of the latter.

3. Correspondences between the Ṛgveda and the Avesta

This same problem of partial correspondences which are offset by thematic correspondences is found when comparing the Vedic hymns to the Avestan Gāthās. On the one hand, we know a formal correspondence pertaining to our theme:[8] Y. 30.10 *asišta yaojantē* "the fast (steeds) will be harnessed" and Y. 44.4 *yaogət̰ āsū* "(who) has harnessed the pair of fast (steeds)" correspond to ṚV 3.35.4 *(bráhmaṇā te brahmayújā) yunajmi (hárī). . . āśū* "I harness by (using) a *bráhman*, two fast (steeds) for thee, (steeds) that are (thus) harnessed by a *bráhman*." But it is instructive to see the themes served by this correspondence, themes which though they appear only in filigree can nonetheless be found.

Y. 30.10 deals with the defeat of falsehood by the fast steeds harnessed to the abode of the Good Thought (*adā zī avā drūjō [avō] bvaitī skəndo spayaθrahyā at̰ asištā yaojantē ā husitōiš vaŋhəuš manaŋho*)[9] thanks to Ahura Mazdā and the Ahuras; thanks to them too the existence (the world) will be renewed, as is said in Y. 30.9 (*at̰cā tōi vaēm h'yāmā yōi īm fərašəm kərənaon ahūm mazdåscā ahuråŋhō ā. mōyastrā baranā ašācā*, "Therefore may we be those who shall make this world healed! O Ahura Mazdā and Ahuras ye other lords, be present to me with support and truth").[10] S. Insler has indeed found[11] that it was possible to compare the steeds making their departure to the abode of Good Thought to the Vedic mares of Sūrya (the Sun) in ṚV 7.60.3 *áyukta saptá harítaḥ sadhásthād yā́ īṃ vahanti sū́ryam ghṛtā́cīḥ* "He has harnessed the seven bay mares departing from the place of their common abode, (they) who are shining with melted butter, draw the Sun," but it would seem that the context is less ordinary than one may think. To the defeat of falsehood and the call for support and truth of Ahura Mazdā corresponds in Ṛ̣V 7.60 not only the mares departing from a common place but also the Sun declaring that men are absolved from sins and the desire of men to be friendly linked to the Sun seeing what is right and what is crooked in mortals and stating the truth to Mitra and Varuṇa (ṚV 7.60.1 *yád adyá sūrya brávó 'nāgā udyán mitrā́ya váruṇāya satyám* and 2. *ṛjú márteṣu vṛjinā́ ca páśyan*). Even more generally, other correspondences between Y.30 and ṚV 7.60 ensure that the figure of the steeds surging forward to safeguard the truth and to destroy the false are not present merely by chance either in the Avesta or in the Ṛgveda. Firstly, of the two texts, one is meant for Mitra and Varuṇa, the holders of Truth and the avengers of Untruth (ṚV 7.60.12 *iyáṃ deva puróhitir yuvábhyām yajñéṣu mitrāvaruṇāv akāri* "this call for help, O ye (two) gods is achieved for you two amongst (other) sacrifices, O Mitra-Varuṇa"; 7.60.5 *imé cetā́ro ánṛtasya... santi imá ṛtásya vāvṛdhur duroṇé* "They are the avengers of Untruth;. . . they grew up in the house of Truth"), the other announces from the very first line the importance attached by Zarathustra to the devotion to Ahura Mazdā based on the cause of Truth (*ašāyāčā* "for Truth", restitution of Hoffman and Insler, p. 162), which is in opposition in every line to the dangers of succumbing to the bad choice of falsehood and deceit.[12]

Further, apart from this substantial resemblance, the two texts have more precise similarities. These pertain to the fate of the devotees and the miscreants, the reward and the punishments which await them respectively depending on their attitudes. If Y. 30.9 says that the support and Truth of Ahura Mazdā will cause "one (even) to be convinced even while his understanding is wrong" [*hyaṭ haθrā manå bvaṭ yaθrā cistiš aŋhat maēθā*[13]], ṚV 7.60.6 gives a similar expression *imé mitró váruṇo dūḷábhāso 'cetásam cic citayanti* "These (two) gods

Mitra and Varuṇa, difficult to deceive, will give understanding to the very person who is without understanding;" ṚV 7. 60.7 continues *cikitvā́ṃso acetásaṃ nayanti* "(the gods) who have understood guide the one who has no understanding". Y. 30.8 anticipates the moment when the sinners are chastised, when Good Thought triumphs and the deceit is given into the hands of Truth (*yadā aēšam kaēnā jamaitī aēnaθham. . . vohū manaθhā vōi. vīdaitē . . yōi āšāi dadən zastayō drujim*), while ṚV 7. 60.8 makes the faithful swear that they will not commit any misdeed which could anger the gods (*mā́ karma devahéḷanaṃ*), cf. also 7.60.10 *yuṣmád bhiyā́ vṛṣaṇo réjamānā. . . mṛḷátā naḥ* "We who tremble with fear before you, O ye bulls, have pity for us!" and Y. 30.10 which speaks of the fast steeds leaving from the abode of Good Thought, adds that they take part in a contest in which the prize is good fame (*yōi zazəntī vaθhāu sravahī*[14]); parallel to this, the last line of ṚV 7.60.11 continues saying that the officiant poets whose sacrifice consists of songs in praise of the gods are involved in a ritual fight around a prize-of-victory [*yó bráhmaṇe sumatím āyájāte vā́jasya sātaú paramásya rāyáḥ* "The one who will offer sacrifice (to obtain) the benevolence (of the gods) for his *bráhman* (when he is engaged) in the struggle (for winning) a prize of victory, the greatest of wealth"]; the poets are accompanied in the contest by the patrons of the sacrifice, warriors by profession who also enter the fray, but in their own way, by competing with an *arí*, a patron of a neighbouring sacrifice whose fury they try to overcome (11c *śī́kṣanta manyúm maghávāno aryás*). ṚV 7.60 and Y. 30 thus have an Indo-European appearance—the theme common to the two texts, that of the true opposed to the false, is developed in a similar way, by using rigid contrasts in the behaviour of men to which corresponds the behaviour of the gods who mete out reward or punishment as the case may be. This is not surprising for gods like Varuṇa and Mitra, as the two gods are the most Indo-Iranian of the Vedic divinities.

A turn common to the Ṛgveda and the Avesta can also be mentioned: ṚV 7.56.23 *ugráḥ. . . árvā* "fearsome (god),. . . steed" and Y. 50.7 (*yaojā*). . . *aurvatō*. . . *ugrəng* "I harness . . . the steeds. . . very strong."[15] As in the case of the preceding correspondence which is based on an Indo-European phrase **i̯eug- ōk'ú-* (Y. 30.10 and ṚV 3.35.4), in this case too the respective contexts of the Vedic and Avestan expressions have not been considered heretofore.[16] They are however significant. ṚV 7.56.23 exalts the god Indra who acts in concert with the Marut; he is the steed which is victorious in the fights (*marúdbhir ugráḥ pṛ́tanāsu sā́ḷhā marúdbhir ít sánitā vā́jam árvā*), but if it is said that he wins the prize-of-victory, the link established between the prize of victory of an officiant poet, the gods Marut and Indra is expressed subtly. The Marut saw to it that a large number of songs of praise were composed for them, since the time of the Fathers [*bhū́ri cakra marutaḥ pítryāṇy ukthā́ni yā́ vaḥ śasyánte purā́ cit* "numerous are the paternal songs of praise, O Marut, that you have (caused to) create, they have been recited to you since a long time"]. It is by a comparison to ṚV 6.33.2 *tvā́ṃ víprebhir ví paṇī́m̐r aśā́yas tvóta ít sánitā vā́jam árvā* "Thou (acting in concert) with the inspired poets, hast (O Indra) destroyed the Paṇi. Helped by the steed wins the *vā́ja*", that we see what is the role given to the songs.

We are dealing with a complex metaphor. The officiant poets have contributed to the defeat of the Paṇi by Indra, just like the Aṅgiras who abet Indra in this mythical feat, they have beaten the Paṇi by their songs, which is why the quality of officiant poet is transferred to Indra who is frequently treated as a poet precisely because of this transfer[17]. Poets, steeds and warriors are the subject of comparisons which produce metaphors throughout the hymns, so much so that the phrase *sánitā vā́jam árvā* which is loaded with several references summarises the complex aspect of Indra, who is at first the winner of the booty, but is also a steed, which cannot but lead to the poet whose competitor's nature calls for the evocation of the ambience of the car races.

There is very little doubt that Y. 50.7 completes the set of Vedic images. If the text says *aṭ ve yaojā zəvištyəng aurvatō . . . ašā ugrəng vohū manaŋha yāiš azāθā* "I harness for you the fastest steeds, very strong with the Truth and Good thought, with which ye will race (in a contest)," the series of metaphors, their very intention, is identical to those of the Ṛgveda. Zarathustra announces to Ahura Mazdā that he is sending a harnessed team, specifying that it is capable of ensuring his glory [if this is how *aurvatō. . . vahmahyā yūšmākahyā* is to be understood "the steeds (going with the victories) of your glory"][18] and winning a contest (against the forces of evil?). Whatever be the solution accepted for this interpretation of the metaphor of the steeds [is it the metaphor for the faithful as suggested by Insler,[19] or is it more correct to see only the steeds likened to the Vedic horses which lead the gods to the men, according to Thieme?], it is possible that what is referred to is the thoughts of the prophet, fast *like* the steeds, a known metaphor of the Ṛgveda which mentions the steeds of Agni who is qualified as oblator and the best of the sacrificers (ṚV 4.2.1 *yó mártyeṣu. . . hótā yájiṣṭho* " Who amongst the mortals. . . the oblator and the best of the sacrificers," 2. *antár. . . īyase yuyujāná. . . vŕ̥ṣaṇaḥ* "thou dost move around. . . having harnessed the male (steeds), 3. *átyā. . ṛtásya manye mánasā jáviṣṭhā* "(these) steeds. . . of the *ṛtá* that I consider faster than thought" and ṚV 6.9.5 *jyótir. . . máno jáviṣṭham patáyatsv antáḥ* "(Agni) who is the light, the thought that is the fastest amongst the (things) that fly.)" Y. 50.6 confirms and justifies the use of the metaphor of the harness. Zarathustra says he is the prophet allied to Truth and asks Ahura Mazdā to be the charioteer of his tongue and his will and to guide him on the right path (*yə maθra . . . urvaθō ašā. . . zaraθuštrō dātā xratəuš hizvō raiθīm stōi mahyā rāzəng. . . sāhīṭ*).

Thus it cannot be eliminated that the Av. *yaog-* is also oriented towards an appreciably more abstract meaning, like the Vedic verb *yuj-*. Further proof is this correspondence between Y. 44.4 and certain passages of the Ṛgveda which is somewhat unexpected, but in any case has apparently never been noticed. Y. 44 is a long series of questions asked by Zarathustra about order, especially the religious and cosmic order. In verse 4, although the reply is given explicitly by Zarathustra himself in verse 7 (in which Ahura Mazdā is said to be "the creator of all things, *vīspanam dātā*), one of the questions pertains to the nature of the wind and to the clouds: *kə vātāi dvanmaibyascā yaogəṭ āsū* "Who has harnessed the pairs of fast (steeds) to the wind and the clouds?" The parallel passages of the Ṛgveda do not repeat the question in the same form but they shed light on it otherwise by bringing into the reply both the agent of the act of harnessing and the reason for this act—the steeds of the Wind-god are harnessed by Indra (ṚV 10.22.4 *yujānó áśvā vā́tasya dhúnī devásya vajrivaḥ* "when thou dost harness the two rustling steeds of the Wind-god, O (thou) that carriest the thunder"), the Wind has Indra for a charioteer (ṚV 4.46.2 and 4.48.2), Indra travels with the steeds of the Wind-god (ṚV 1.51.10 and 1.121.12 etc.). But what leads me to think that Zarathustra's questions are meant for a god like Indra is that the harness of the steeds of the Wind-god is part of a legend in which it serves the god Indra.

This legend, subject of some of the Ṛgveda verses, narrates how Indra, accompanied by his ally Kutsa (ṚV 5.29. 9), prepares to kill Śuṣṇa (ṚV 10,22.7 *śúṣṇaṃ yád dhann ámānuṣam*) and on the way to his destination, he visits the dwelling of the sage Kāvya Uśanas (ṚV 5.29.9 and 10.22.1, 6). The sage then accords him two favours. On his advice, the Wind-god lends Indra his steeds but here the versions vary; in one, Indra comes to obtain the horses [ṚV 10.22.5 *tváṃ tyā́ cid vā́tasyā́śvāgā ṛjrā́ tmánā váhadhyai* "thou hast come to drive thyself even these two white steeds of (the god) Vāta"), whereas ṚV 5.29.9 says: *uśánā yát sahasyaìr áyātam gṛhám indra jūjuvānébhir áśvaiḥ* "When you arrived, O Indra (and Kutsa) to Uśanas, to his dwelling, with (your) powerful and fast steeds. . ."]. Then, and this moment is decisive, it is indeed Kāvya Uśanas who forges Indra's weapon for him and gives it to him and this is precisely why the references of the two lines describing the preparations are invaluable, for they say clearly that Indra comes with the steeds of the Wind and that the weapon made for Indra has a direct link to the separation of the two worlds: ṚV 1.51.10 *tákṣad yát ta uśánā sáhasā sáho ví ródasī . . . bādhate śávaḥ ā́ tvā vā́tasya nṛmaṇo manoyúja ā́ . . . avahann abhí śrávaḥ* "When Uśanas made for thee (the thunderbolt), (this) power with his power, his strength pushes-back-by-separating them the two Worlds; the steeds of the Wind harnessed by thought, O virile (god), have brought thee here for thy (greatest) renown." ṚV 1.121.12 *indra. . . tiṣṭha vā́tasya suyújo váhiṣṭhān. . . kāvyá uśánā. . . vṛtrahánaṃ pā́ryaṃ tatakṣa vájram* "Mount, O Indra, the well-harnessed (steeds) of the Wind, the best of mounts; Kāvya Uśanas has forged the thunderbolt that destroys all resistance and that enables thee to go to the end." Here we can comprehend the value of their gestures: Indra's which is specifically cosmogonic[20], and Kāvya Uśanas' which shows that he only makes possible the creation of the Vedic world by eliminating the obstructions of space, and also the Wind-god's gesture of lending his steeds to Indra.

By juxtaposing Y. 44.4 and the Vedic passages on the steeds of the Wind, we can see the reason for a metaphor which a priori can only appear to be an outcome of pure poetry. In fact, in the Avestan text the question on the wind and the clouds is preceded by another one *(kasnā dərətā zamcā adə nabåscā avapastōiš* "who holds up the earth from below and the clouds (thus preventing) them from falling?").[21] This is therefore another indication of the specifically cosmogonic nature of Y. 44, if one is needed at all. But in the Ṛgveda, the god Indra bestrides the steeds of the Wind, while the long-haired ascetics have the winds for their mounts (ṚV 10.136.3). Is the figure of the steeds not introduced in order to say that the Wind, the winds which transport Indra during his cosmogonic journey are as rapid as race-horses? Just as Zarathustra evokes the fast steeds harnessed to the wind and the clouds to say that these are *like* steeds. Vedic poetry naturally puts together the wind and the clouds which are activated by the same god Indra (ṚV 4.17.12 *yó asya śúṣmam muhukaír íyarti vā́to ná jūtá stanáyadbhir abhraíḥ* "he who who sets off his (combative) fury with war cries, as the rustling winds and clouds that have been pushed" cf. ṚV 1.116.1 *stómān iyarmy abhríyeva vā́taḥ* "I push forward my songs of praise, like the wind (pushes) the clouds").

Let this demonstration for the justification of a modest poetic figure in the Avesta and the Ṛgveda not seem to be excessive—any correspondences between the two texts capable of throwing light on the origin of the thought that is expressed by metaphors which turn out to be identical, confirm the existence in the past of the Indo-Iranian religious tradition. The correspondence that has just been presented and studied is moreover interesting in yet another respect: what the Avestan text offers as readymade figures is shown to be in formation by the comparison with Vedic hymns, and if Y. 44.4 formulates questions, the Ṛgveda gives replies. Is it not true that this is possible only if the basis is a tradition of common thought?[22]

This tradition is most probably very archaic in the sense that it is observed by means of texts belonging to two ancient traditions in which we know there are a number of contact points, but each of which has its own existence and its own milieu. It is striking to see that in the field in which we are interested, i.e., the figures of harness which determine the metaphors, these traditions have continued to evolve in parallel directions, as can be seen from the following example.

4. Skr. *yukti* and Av. *yaoxsti*

This deals with a term which remains fairly obscure, i.e.,

Av. *yaoxšti*. Evidently formed from the root *yaog-*, it means "perception" (for example, Yt. 10.35 *hazaθra. yaoxštī* "(Mithra) having a thousand (faculties) of perception" and Yt. 10.82 *yeθhe hazaθrəm yaoxštinam fradaθat ahurō mazdå* "(Mithra) to whom Ahura Mazdā has given a thousand faculties of perception", and here again *yaoxštibyō* "with (these faculties) of perception"; Yt. 10.107 *miθrasčit. . . hazaθra. yaoxštiš vispəm vaēnaiti* "while Mithra having thousand (faculties) of perception sees each one").[23] What explanation can be given for this evolution of the semantics of *yaog-* "to harness, to attach" (see earlier n. 10 with reference to Y. 49.9 and 46.11)? Can we agree with Bartholomae who modified the meaning of the verb to "make familiar with something, to habituate to" and even to "make something participate"?[24] It is certainly possible to imagine that the meaning evolved as suggested by Bartholomae, but it must be realised that the translation of Y. 49.9 *hyaṭ daēnå vahištē yūjən mīzdē ašā yuxtā* as "those who are linked to the Truth have *made* their visions *participate* in the best prize given as reward" (Bartholomae: "teilhaftig machen") misses out on what exactly the metaphor of the harness must express: the direct and concrete link between a subject and an object (cf. Insler's translation, greatly preferable "those who are yoked with truth have yoked their conceptions on the best prize"). Once again, religious and speculative tradition of India enables the perception of what were the stages of semantic changes of **i̯eug-* in Indo-Iranian. Based on a concrete and manifestly technical meaning expressed in Vedic hymns by the phrase *ṛtásya yóga* and the compound *ṛtáyukti*[25] and similar ones describing the harness, or to be more precise, the union and identification of the subject that harnesses and the object that is harnessed, or, alternatively, of two harnessed objects, it is normal that this tradition should call for the uses of the verb *yuj-* that have resulted in the creation of a speculative theory in the Ṛgveda itself, a theory that could be valid only if it merged with a theory of sacrifice.

It is in this perspective that we must evaluate the

philosophical terms on the one hand, and on the other, the Sanskrit grammatical terms which are constituted from *yuj-* Amongst these, there are *yukti* "clause, sentence" that the grammarian explains as *niyatavāc* "having its words fixed".[26] As a philosophical term, *yukti* serves to explain a method of cognitive examination. This consists of "considering the concurrent causes" thus defined somewhat ambiguously by Caraka in *Sūtrasthāna* (IX.17-27): firstly, it is said that "the production of grain from the conjunction of water, ploughing, seeds and the season is a *yukti*; also, the production of embryos by the conjunction of six components. . . " (*jalakarṣaṇabījartusaṃyogāt sasyasambhavaḥ yuktiḥ ṣaḍdhātusaṃyogād garbhāṇām sambhavas tathā*); then, and this is when the word *yukti* takes on its meaning as a philosophical term, "the knowledge that sees things as produced by the conjunction of a multiplicity of causes, must be recognised as *yukti*" (*buddhiḥ paśyati yā bhāvān bahukāraṇayogajān yuktiḥ. . . sā jñeyā*).[27] Obviously Caraka goes from stating a phenomenon (the conjunction) to the reflection on this phenomenon by denoting them with the same word. The determined facts and the way of knowing them are understood using the same method, the very one which could be found in Vedic practice in which the transitive act of an active agent (to harness, to yoke, to join); the reflexive act of the agent (to harness himself) and the causative act (to cause to harness) cannot be clearly distinguished. Thus the correspondence between Av. *yaoxšti* and Skr. *yukti* does not seem fortuitous, but rather indicates a fact of survival of an old meaning.

Nevertheless, even while noting the possible similarity between the Avestan word and the Sanskrit term, a similarity which is due as much to the primitive meaning of **i̯eug-* as to the semantic developments of its derivatives which satisfy the specific requirements of both the traditions (the religious one in the Avesta, in which the god Mithra is a keeper and therefore obliged by his duties to observe, to keep under attentive and perceptive surveillance, and the philosophico-religious one of Brāhmaṇic India in which the medical theory of a Caraka was inspired by the philosophy of Nyāya), it cannot be forgotten that what separates the Sanskrit term from the initial idea of harnessing is more serious than what distinguishes it from the meaning taken by the Avestan word. But it must be noted that this is less due to the difference between an archaic religion and a philosophy, however rationalist it may be, than due to the relationship between the two strictly religious traditions which have adopted a mode of expression close to the concrete. In short, Av. *yaoxšti* has a more tangible link to **i̯eug-* than the Skr. *yukti* which, moreover becomes a speculative term because of a deliberate negligence of the distinction that there is between the observation of a harness (the series of conjunctive causes) and the perception that is explained as "harness" of a subject to the observed object.

5. Balto-Slavic Data

If the Vedic verb *yuj-* had the central meaning "to harness, to match (paired elements or elements that become alike after the operation), to pair", the meaning of the Indo-European **i̯eug-/*i̯ug-* becomes clearer when seen in the light of their Vedic reflections. A new observation on the chronology of the Baltic and Slavic reflections of the Indo-European verbs **i̯eu* and *i̯eu-g/*i̯ug-* will provide a basis. Since there is no equivalent of **i̯eu̯g-* in the Slavic verbal system (But it is represented in Av. *yaog* "to tie, to harness"), nor, in particular, an equivalent of the infix nasal form **i̯u-ne-g/i̯u-n-g* known in the verbs (Sanskrit *yunákti*, Gr. *zeúgnūmi*, Lat. *i̯ungo)*, it was believed till recently that the Slavic retained only the base **i̯eu* (Common Slavic **junŭ*, **jutiti*) as opposed to Lithuanian *jùngti* "to harness, to associate, to include". Now, according to a fresh point of view, although all the difficulties are not eliminated, Sanskrit, Avestan, Greek and Latin verbs are secondary formations of the I.E. **i̯ugom*, n. "yoke", based on **i̯eug-/*i̯ug-* for it appears that both the meaning and the formation of these verbs relates them in a decisive way to the noun meaning "yoke, harness". It follows that **i̯eug-/*i̯ug-* had a concrete meaning "to place under the yoke",[28] a meaning that the Vedic verb has retained and widely exploited.

6. Hittite *iuga*

A new explanation can be given for comparing Sanskrit *yugá* and the Hittite *iuga* "aged one year, (animal) of the year". In Hittite sources, it is first an adjective from which Benveniste thought of establishing a substantive *iuga* "space of one year" which would be exactly comparable to the Sanskrit word.[29] But the fact of a really attested adjective reveals its entire meaning when we see how *yuj-* and its derivatives functioned in Vedic and post-Vedic texts. As the second member of compounds, their main semantic feature is the one that refers to harness, to the linking that brings about identity and resemblance. It is enough to reconsider in comparative terms the Vedic compounds with numerals as the first member, such as *caturyúj* (ṚV 8.6.48), *cáturyuga* (ṚV 2.18.1), *ṣaḍyogá* (AV 8.9.16), *aṣṭāyogá* [AV 6.91.1 *imáṃ yávam aṣṭayogaíḥ ṣaḍyogébhir acarkṛṣuḥ* "They have ploughed this barley with harnessed teams of eight (and) six (animals)"]. All these compounds denote teams of four, six and eight animals, and *triyugá* alone has *yugá-* meaning "generation" (ṚV 10.97. 1). What is more, we must remember that this only refers to human generations, the ages with respect to men, and not the cosmic ages (Renou, *Études védiques et pāṇinéennes*, XVI, p. 50 and 120) and that *yóga* means the harnessed team or the distance covered by a harnessed team (ṚV 1. 34.9, 7.67.8 with Renou's note in *EVP*, XVI, p. 47). It is a fact that *yugá* meaning cosmic age, is a post-Vedic innovation whose beginnings alone are seen in the Ṛgveda (see again Renou, *EVP*, XIII, p. 134 and XVI, p. 155), and this supports the hypothesis stated above on the formation of the Vedic notion of generation (see p. 219). So if the Vedic compounds conserve the notion of team and the distance covered by the team, and if the archaic semantics of the derivatives of I.E. *i̯eug/ *i̯ug are found in them, the motivation for the Hittite i̯uga cannot be understood by comparing it to *yugá* "cosmic age", but on the other hand, can be explained by the old meaning of the Vedic word[30].

In fact, Hittite *iuga* appears twice in a text, once in a non-compound state and once in composition with a noun of number: KBo 6.6.1.40-42 *ták-ku ša-a-ú-i-te-eš-za Ú-UL ANŠU KUR. RA. MAH ták-ku i-ú-ga-aš Ú-UL. ANŠU. KUR. RA. MAH ták-ku da-a-i-ú-ga-aš a-pa-aš ANŠU. KUR. RA. MAH* "If it is still a suckling, it is not a (true) stallion, if it is one-year old, then it is not a (true) stallion, if it is two years old, then it is a (true) stallion." The translation of *iuga* and *dāiuga* as "aged one year" and "aged two years" is however very artificial. The authors who first quoted this passage[31] translated these as "one-year old" and "two-years old" respectively but we can easily see that their explanations of the Indo-European semantic development which result in a temporal meaning of the Hitt. *iuga* call for a quite different translation: *iuga* is rather a horse that has been placed under the yoke for a single period of time extending from one spring to the next, *dāiuga*, a horse that has been subjected to two such periods of harnessing, and Skr. *yugá* means a series of years "yoked" to each other. But since the value of this Sanskrit word is not ancient, while the simple and compound Hittite terms date back to the extremely archaic Hittite[32] and further since the reference to time measurement in the Sanskrit term is more recent, it is more accurate to intepret the Hitt. *dāiuga* as "(young horse that has known) two harnessings" and the Hitt. *iuga* as "(young horse that has known) one harnessing". Benveniste has explained, by taking up K. Brugmann's examples, that the word *iuga* does not contain any reference to a numeral which is thus implied. Between *iuga* and *dāiuga,* we have to recognise the Indo-European relationship of the Latin type *annículus/bīmus, trīmus* (when speaking of young animals aged one, two or three years).[33] However tempting it may be to think that the Sanskrit and Hittite words take on a temporal value, and to attribute this value to I.E. **iugóm*, it would seem wiser to keep to the value of "harness, yoke" which is definitely more ancient and as such must be postulated as common.[34]

7. Old Persian *yāuma(i)niš*

Sometime the reflection of the Vedic gesture "harness or yoke the mind"[35] was found in the Old Persian expression *yāuma(i)niš*. In addition to all the arguments that can be put forward against the interpretation of the first member of this compound as a derivative of the I.E. **i̯eu̯-* "link, associate",[36] the considerations on the Vedic verb *yu-* evoked by J. Duchesne-Guillemin to justify its meaning of "harness" must be rectified on two more points.

First, the uses of the verb *yu-* which indeed primarily means "attach, fix", prove that the act of attaching is, in its case, quite different from the act of harnessing denoted by the verb *yuj-*. This is more of an act considered in all its materialness, without any attempt to establish an affinity to its subject or its object. Used without a preverb, it will mean "to attach, give something to someone" (ṚV 6.39.1 *íṣo yuvasva gṛṇaté* "give the enjoyments to the one who praises!"), in the middle voice, "to attach oneself, to appropriate for oneself" (ṚV 6.60.2 *apó gā́ agne yuvase nityútvān* "the waters, the cow, thou dost appropriate them for thyself, O Agni, thou that hast harnesses"). In ṚV 8.26.20 *yu-* and *yuj-* are barely synonymous: *yukṣvā́ hí tvā́ṃ rathasáhā yuvā́sva póṣyā* "harness then the two (steeds) that can draw the car (O Vāyu), attach (them), these well-fed (steeds)!", (but see Renou's remark *EVP*, XVI, p. 63 on the isolated nature of this use of *yu-*). With certain preverbs, *yu-* somewhat undergoes a change in meaning. The most interesting case is that of the preverb *ni-* meaning "within", "down below", in the name of harness *niyút*. Thus we have the following modifications: ṚV 8.19.33

vípo ná dyumnā́ ní yuve jánānām "I take on the prestige of the (other) people as (their) vibrating prayers" (according to Renou, *EVP*, XIII, p. 65); RV 10.42.5 *yó. . . śátrūn. . . ní. . . yuváti hánti vṛtrám* "he who acts in such a way that the enemies surrender to him, he slays Vṛtra". We see, however, that the meanings revolve around the idea of "giving oneself" which the verb in its non-compound state has already (Renou, *EVP*, XIII, p. 127: "*yu* finally ends—like so many verbs—in 'to give', perhaps by interposing *ni-yu*, the idea of a gift implying objects that are harnessed in order to give the dakṣiṇā").[37]

As for *niyút*, the meaning of this word owes less to the idea of harness than to the idea of gift, a gift of the Wind-god (Vāyu) to be exact. According to a relevant observation by Renou, *EVP*, XV, p. 109, the gifts of Vāyu are "harnessed" as those of the Ṛbhu are fashioned (*takṣ-*) or those of Agni and Uṣas bear light. Think of the steeds of the Wind-god whose teams serve to transport the gifts. The word *niyút* has probably retained the values of the verb *ni-yu-* (but with the idea of harness less evident than that of giving a gift) to a larger extent than the values imprinted by its contextual association with Vāyu's teams. It is proved by the fact that the preverb *ni-* indicates direction (irrespective of the yoked team making its way) and that, according to a remark by Debrunner (Wackernagel-Debrunner, *Altindische Gr.*, II, 2, p. 45), the action nouns in *-t* formed from root nouns can retain this meaning in composition. Hence *niyút* "offer, gift", but also "series", by the superimposition, frequently used in Vedic, of the two values of the root nouns functioning sometimes as action nouns and sometimes as agent nouns.[38]

The second point follows from the first. It is therefore impossible to draw a parallel between the Vedic sentences with *yu-* and *yuj-*. Although ṚV 1.138.1 has *yu-* beside *mánas*, the idea of harness does not figure in it: *víśvasya yó mána āyuyuvé makhó devá āyuyuvé makháḥ* "He, (he the god Pūṣan) has (vigorously) drawn to himself the spirit of each one, the god (who is like) a warrior-patron, he has drawn to himself (he the god who is like) a warrior-patron.".[39] As Renou has pointed out several times, it is a violent act with the purpose of establishing contact between the god and the sacrificer (or between the patron of the sacrifice and the sacrificer), see Renou, *EVP*, XV, p. 141 and IX, p. 88: "draw to oneself". As to the verb *yuj-*, it takes its entire meaning from the idea of harness with the implications that we have seen, so much so that the two verbs do not overlap. Does AV 2.2.3 present an exception *(tám tvā yomi bráhmaṇā divya deva)*? It is tempting to translate, in spite of the parallel Ṛgvedic uses of the turn *yuj- bráhmaṇā* as "I draw thee, (towards myself) with the *bráhman*, O god, O divine (being)." It would seem obvious that the two verbs express ideas that are close to each other, but fundamentally distinct. This distinction probably dates back to the Indo-European, assuming a denominative verb *yuj-* and rejecting the derivation of *yuj-* from **i̯eu̯-* (Ved. *yu-*) by enlarging the radical.[40]

8. Once again ṚV 10.102 and the Roman *iuges auspicium*

Dumézil's analysis of the rule of Roman augurs regarding the *iuges auspicium* that he has tried to explain by a comparison with ṚV 10.102 shows again the richness of the Indo-European symbolism of the harness.[41]

There is a plethora of interpretations of ṚV 10.102, of which Dumézil's is interesting because it is comparative.

There is however a difference between the situation conceived at Rome and the situation that can be imagined from the Vedic hymn. The charioteer Mudgala's bull is yoked and having gorged itself on grass and water, it drops its excrement in the middle of the race; it is thus provoked *ut stercus faceret*. The *iumentum* " the harnessed beast" of the Roman ceremony involuntarily relieves itself on the way. This difference is such that it can interfere with any attempt at comparison.[42]

Yet what Dumézil calls the "mystic value of the fact of

being yoked" (p. 281) which is seen in the two references remains important.

For, as Dumézil rightly points out, the animals do this deed which is unlucky for the augurs, but fortunate and desirable for Mudgala, only when they are yoked (p. 288). It is significant that expressions formed from the root *yuj-* fill the hymn 10.102, even though the imagination of the author works not on the harnessed team made up of two animals, but on the purpose of the act of harnessing and joining the single animal and the vehicle. There is something strange in Mudgala's equipage which normally should have had a pair of race-horses and not a single bull.

I therefore feel that it would be possible to complete Dumézil's comparative analysis by drawing attention to the same linguistic facts as he did, but by approaching them in the following way. Indeed he discerns (p. 288) a series of uses of *yuj-* and its derivatives as well as paraphrases that describe the act of harnessing . We see that this act concerns on the one hand the attaching of the animal to the car that it draws (verse 6 *yuktá* "the harnessed bull", cf. 6c *dúdher yuktásya drávataḥ sahā́nasā* "of the powerful harnessed (bull) running with the car", 7 *úpāyunag vā́ṃsagam* " he (Mudgala) has harnessed the bull", 10 *yáṃ yuñjanti*"(those) who harness it"). On the other hand, this act has a bearing on the attaching of the animal to the wooden club used by Mudgala to fix the yoke of the animal. This club is called *vṛṣabhásya yúj* "the companion of the yoked bull" [9], cf. *varatrā́yāṃ dā́rv ānáhyamānaḥ* "(the charioteer) who has attached the wood to the strap" [8] and particularly the end of verse 12 *vṛ́ṣā yád ājím vṛ́ṣaṇā síṣāsasi codāyan vádhriṇā yujā́* "(thou, Indra) the bull that art desirous of winning the race with the bull, by inciting (it) with (its) companion, this castrated bull" (Indra is now the charioteer, and as such is identified with the harnessed bull; the club, the instrument of the success of the equipage is more or less also identified with the same harnessed bull). From this, I conclude that the verb *yuj-* and its derivatives retain their Vedic meaning of "to pair, to put together elements or elements destined by the same to become similar". The wooden club, the charioteer (Indra or Mudgala) are thus linked to the draught animal in such a way that they identify themselves with it in order to attain the main goal. i.e., to take possession of the race-course, exactly what the animal does with its *niṣpádaḥ* "waste, excrements" (verse 6).

It is then easy to note that this interpretation of the vocabulary of ṚV 10.102 corresponds to the manifestation of the symbolism of the Roman yoke as suggested by Dumézil (p. 281). "What the yoke adds to the animal is, in short, man. The yoked animal serves its master, is his instrument and an extension of him. It is the master who benefits, not only from its work, but also from its entire conduct, which ceases to be indifferent and becomes significant in relation to man." The I.E. verb **i̯eug-/*i̯ug-* must have indeed lost its concrete connotation in the name of the Roman ritual, *i̯uge-(s) auspicium;* that the *linguistic* Vedic data throw light on Roman *religious* data can but be more greatly appreciated.

9. Conclusions

The observations on the Vedic verb *yuj-* which favours poetic figures, and the observations on the comparable Avestan figures and on some Indo-European linguistic facts that are clarified by them, can create the impression that we have restricted ourselves to presenting Vedic and Indo-European facts without taking into account the problem that cannot however be avoided: do these facts of language, of poetical language and in almost all the cited cases, of religious language, attest the values of the language or the representations known through texts that are religious or ritual in nature? It must be acknowledged that this question is difficult to resolve. It is certain that the I.E. root **i̯eug-* only means "to harness, to yoke" in the technical sense, but it is nonetheless certain that the correspondences in Indo-

European vocabulary often have a bearing on a very precise semantic area, that of the word related to a harness, even though the ways by which this is done vary from one Indo-European area to another. We have seen that the word can be replaced (by the poet or the car), and this is easy to understand; we have also seen the circumlocutions in the poetry of Pindar which adapts in its own way the link between the word and the harness, as well as the singularity of the correspondences between the Vedic hymns and the Avestan Gāthās neither of which totally reproduces the Indo-European tradition. When this semantic area is not involved, the usage of the terms derived from **i̯eug-* is however coherent in at least three Indo-European languages, in Sanskrit, in Vedic, in Hittite and in the Roman world in which the notion of harness is subjected to a restriction which results in the creation of an identification. It is possible that the same procedure is also put into practice in Avestan. But it is dangerous to postulate that we are thereby taking cognisance of common Indo-European linguistic data. At the most, there are figures common to Vedic, Greek and Avestan and, with more perceptible modifications, to Hittite. This thematic heritage that is common to several Indo-European traditions does not however preclude that the verb **i̯eug-* has served to form nouns that first and foremost translate the notion of harness and cognate notions, and not the notion of just any link.[43]

REFERENCES

1. M. Durante, *Epea pteroenta. Die Rede als 'Weg' in griechischen und vedischen Bildern* in R. Schmitt, *Indogermanische Dichtersprache*, Darmstadt, 1968, pp. 248-250; *Sulla preistoria della tradizione poetica greca*, Roma, 1976, pp. 125-127.
2. M. Durante, *Epea pteroenta*, p. 251; *Sulla preistoria*, p. 129.
3. Quoted by W. Wüst, *Von indogermanischer Dichtersprache*, München, 1969, pp. 55-56, but in order to show the formation of the metaphor

of the word piercing like an arrow.

4. For further details see the essay "The *signifiant* and the *signifié* in Vedic poetry" (pp. 153-166 of this volume).
5. W. Wüst, *Von indogermanischer Dichtersprache*, pp. 57-58, 66-67.
6. M. Durante, *Epea pteroenta. Die Rede als 'Weg' in griechischen und vedischen Bildern*, p. 254-255, *Sulla preistoria*, pp. 131-133.
7. W. Wüst, *Von indogermanischer Dichtersprache*, pp. 57-58, p. 66.
8. B. Schlerath, *Awesta-Wörterbuch, Vorarbeiten*, I, Wiesbaden, 1968, p. 152.
9. This version of the text is the one given by S. Insler, *The Gāthās of Zarathustra*, Téhéran-Liège, 1975.
10. S. Insler, pp. 172-173. It is correct to draw attention to Y. 46.11 which denounces the Karapans and the Kavis who have yoked men to bad deeds in order to destroy the world and humankind (*yūjən karapanō kāvayascā akāiš šyaoθanāiš ahūm mərəngədidyai māšim*) and who are in contrast to men who yoked their thoughts to truth as they yoked themselves to the truth (Y. 49.9 *hyat daēnå. . . yūjən. . . . ašā yuxtā*): see S. Insler, pp. 172 and 300; H. Humbach, *Die Gāthās des Zarathustra*, II, p. 71. Cf. also Y. 46.12d in which Ahura Mazdā unites (*həm. aibī. mit-*) the descendants of Friyana the Turanian with Good Thought. This figure is also in contrast to the one in Y. 46.11, as is rightly pointed out by Insler, p. 272.
11. S. Insler, p. 174.
12. See Insler's introduction to Y. 30 (pp. 159-161).
13. I am translating this according to Insler's suggestions, p. 173 by whom *haθrā. manā* is translated as "completely minded", that is, "(entirely) convinced"; however the Vedic parallel of Humbach (*Die Gāthās d. Zarathustra*, II, p. 23) *satrā́cā mánasā* "with a unanimous heart, with a concentrated soul" used in ṚV 7.100.1, 8.2.37 and 9.77.4 with the verb *yaj-* "to sacrifice" remains useful in my view: it indeed corresponds to the intentions in Zarathustra's prayer.
14. On expressions from the verb *zaz-* "to surpass, to win": K. Hoffmann, *The Avesta Fragment Fr D. 3* in *Aufsätze zur Indoiranistik*, I, Wiesbaden, 1975, pp. 222-224.
15. B. Schlerath, *Awesta-Wörterbuch*, II, p. 159.
16. See M. Durante, *Epea pteroenta*, pp. 257-158, whose attempt seems to me insufficient. His interpretation goes back to that of H. Lommel, *Die Gāthās des Zarathustra*, 1935, p. 153 and leads one to believe that Y. 50.7 follows the concept of the steeds moved by the prayer and harnessed like the cars, that lead the gods to the men. But Chr. Bartholomae has already compared Y. 50.7 to ṚV 1.82.1 in which Indra is incited to lend his ears to the songs that the poet harnesses like chestnut horses (*úpo ṣú śṛṇuhī́ gíro mághavan. . . yójā nv indra te hárī; yójā* is more likely to be the 1st person singular subj., as

Geldner had already suggested (But Renou, *Études védiques et pāṇinéennes*, XVII, p. 30 feels it is the 2nd. person). Bartholomae's observations are repeated by H. Humbach, *Die Gāthās des Zarathustra*, II, p. 83.

17. See another series of arguments in favour of this symbolic transfer in *Annuaire de l'École Pratique des Hautes Études, Sciences Religieuses*, t. LXXXIX, 1980-81, pp. 274 and 276.
18. S. Insler, p. 101, but see a quite different translation by P. Thieme in *Vorzarathustrisches bei den Zarathustriern u. bei Zarathustra* in R. Schmitt, *Indogermanische Dichtersprache*, p. 237.
19. See J. Duchesne-Guillemin, *Zoroastre*, Paris, 1948, p. 169: "the steeds of praise" who mount the call of the prophet.
20. On the cosmogonic significance of the killing of Śuṣṇa, a variant of resistance most often given the name of the enemy of Indra Vṛtra, a significance that is translated by the creation of the space between the earth and the sky, see B. Oguibénine, *Structure d'un mythe védique. Le mythe cosmogonique dans le Ṛgveda*, Paris-La Haye, 1973, pp. 81-84.
21. Indeed H. Humbach has already shown the Vedic parallel in ṚV 2.17.5 *ádhārayat pṛthivī́m. . . ástabhnān. . . dyā́m avasrásaḥ* "(Indra) carried the earth. . . and held up the sky to prevent it from falling" *(Die Gāthās d. Zarathustra*, II, p. 54).
22. All things considered, it is towards a quest for the common intellectual Indo-Iranian schemas that the remarks of E. Benveniste are directed in *Phraséologie poétique de l'indo-iranien* in *Mélanges Renou*, Paris, 1968, p. 73.
23. I. Gershevitch, *The Avestan Hymn to Mithra*, Cambridge, 1959, pp. 91, 113, 127.
24. Thieme suggested that *yaoxšti* could be explained as "aptitude for something", "alertness, literally: state of being harnessed (*yuxta*)", see P. Thieme, *Mitra and Aryaman*, New Haven, 1957, p. 31, n. 17.
25. By lighting the sacrificial fire, the inspired poets harness themselves to the *ṛtá* (ṚV 3.27.11 *agním. . . ṛtásya yóge. . . víprā. . . sám indhate*); it is only if they are harnessed to the *ṛtá* that the sacrificers can ask the waters to be favourable to them (ṚV 10.30.11 *ṛtásya yóge. . . śruṣṭīvárīr bhūtanāsmábhyam āpaḥ*); the officiant poets who utter the *ṛtá* (the true Word, no doubt) harness themselves to the *ṛtá* (ṚV 10.61.10 *návagvā ṛtáṃ vadanta ṛtáyuktim agman*), etc. Cf. Lüders'reservations in *Varuṇa*, II, p. 460: Should 'harness' be considered in the literal sense, or perceptibly decoloured? ("ob die Bedeutung von *yóga* schon so verblasst war wie etwa die "Anspannung", wenn wir dieses Wort im uneigentlichen Sinne verwenden?").
26. L. Renou, *Terminologie grammaticale du sanskrit*, III, Paris, 1942, p. 123.

27. The text and translation are extracts from M. Biardeau, *Théorie de la connaissance et philosophie de la parole dans le brahmanisme classique*, Paris-La Haye, 1964, pp. 444-445.
28. O.N. Trubačev (et alii), *Etimologičeskij slovar' slavjanskix jazykov, Praslavjanskij leksičeskij fond*, vyp. 8, Moskva, 1981, p. 207. According to the authors, Lit. *jùngas* "yoke" would be a deverbative formation of the Lit. *jùngti* for, with respect to Slavic **jĭgo*, it is distinguished by its vocalism and the nasal infix. For *junŭ*, "young" based on I.E. **i̯eu̯-*, "to stir, press, crush", cf. Lit. *jáuti, jauti*, "mix, mix together" compared with Slavic **moldŭ* "young, tender" and Old Indian *mr̥dú*, Lat. *mollis* "soft, gentle" on the semantic plane, see pp. 195-197; for *jutiti(se)* "to be in a reduced space", p. 199: the two common Slavic words would be a continuation of I.E. **ieu*. This will bring to mind Jacobsohn's old opinion (*Deutsch Literaturzeitung*, 1912, p. 2786) quoted by Wackernagel-Debrunner, *Altind. Gr.* II, 2, p. 76, according to which I.E. *iugóm* is a neuter that developed from the collective plural *i̯ugā* "yoke and accessories", itself preceded by the masculine **i̯éugos*. This is one more indication, provided the formal evolution is supposed to take place from the noun to the verbs, that these verbs have acquired their meaning from the noun.
29. E. Benveniste, *Hittite et indo-européen*, Paris, 1962, pp. 78-80. The Hittite word, an adjective turned into a substantive, is interpreted in the light of the Sanskrit substantive *yugá* "age, generation, era" (see further on).
30. Translation of *ša-a-ú-i-te-eš-za* by J. Friedrich, *Zum hethitischen Lexicon* in *Journal of Cuneiform Studies*, vol. 1, n. 4, 1947, pp. 291-292. Although there is no doubt that the word means "Säugling, young suckling animal" (J. Friedrich, *Hethitisches Wörterbuch*, Heidelberg, 1952, p. 189), the I.E. **sm̥u̯et* "1 year" can be seen in it (V. Shevoroshkin's letter dated 27.2.83). It is also worthwhile to mention Homer's evocation of the passage of time under the yoke in relation to the age of young animals. See Od. 3.382-383: "I shall offer thee as sacrifice a one-year old cow, an untamed (beast) whose broad brow has not yet been placed under the yoke." This reference does not quite cover the notion studied here, since it contradicts the Hittite reference in which a year under the yoke determines the age of the foal; nevertheless, the association of ideas is almost the same. Can we think that Homer once again referred to the old association between the age of an animal and the time it spent under the yoke (here, reduced to nil) without paying attention to coherence? This is perhaps a proof of the extremely antique nature of the association.
31. W.M. Austin, H.L. Smith, *The Etymology of Hittite* yukas, *Language*, 13, 1937, pp. 104-106.

32. V.V. Ivanov had already drawn attention to this when comparing Hittite and Slavic facts that are equally archaic if not even more ancient (Slavic themes in- **es*: Slovene *igô*, Gen. *izéⁿsa* "yoke"): V.V. Ivanov, *O značenii xetttskogo jazyka deja svranitel'noistoričeskogo issledovanija slavjanskix jazykov* in *Voprosy slavjanskogo jazykoznanija*, 2, 1957, p. 18.
33. E. Benveniste, *Hittite et indo-européen*, p. 79; K. Brugmann, *Setzung u. Nichtsetzung des Zahlwortes* Eins *zu Quantitätssubstantiva in den idg. Sprachen* in *Zeitschrift für die vergl. Sprachforsch. auf dem Gebiete d. idg. Sprachen*, Bd. 21, 1907, pp. 1-13.
34. While posing the inherited character of the two words, it must be asked whether the temporal value of the Hittite *iuga* is not based on a semantic model foreign to the Hittite, insofar as arguments have not been found to explain the semantic change from "yoke", to "time lapse"within Hittite itself. (J. Tischler, *Hethitisches etymologisches Glossar*, Lief. 3, Innsbruck, 1980, pp. 448-449). To this judicious question by Tischler the reply can be that by recognising in the Hittite word the value of "yoking", the problem obviously remains identical, but given the improper nature of the correspondence between Old Indian *yugá* and Hittite *iuga* having a temporal value, the problem is posed in a quite different way. It must be remembered that in an old study A. Götze read KUB VII.8, II.8 as er wird GIŠ *i-ú-ga-an* werden (= "er wird zum Joche werden)", in the context of a sexual union). Moreover, he felt that the Hittite term was borrowed from Old Indian and that the etymological relation between *iugan* "yoke" (the theme in *-n!*) and the adjective *iuga* "aged (one) year" was far from being sure. (A. Götze, *Hethitisch* jugan *"Joch"* in *Indogermanische Forschungen*, 42, 1924, pp. 327-328).

    Two years after I wrote this essay, I was able to consult J. Puhvel, *Hittite Etymological Dictionary*, Berlin-New York-Amsterdam, 1984, pp. 495-499. Puhvel's observations tally with my analysis. First, he dissociates *iuga* "yearling" and *iuka* "yoke" (pp. 495-496); then according to him, *tāiuga* means "of second yoking", "i.e., embarking on the second season of useful working life" (p. 498); Hitt. *iuga* is reconstructed as **yewgo* "yoking", its Sanskrit parallel is *yoga* while *iuka* "yoke" has Sanskrit *yugám* as pendant (p. 498). Finally, "the very fact that Hitt. *iuga* refers specifically to draft animals makes it likely that only inner Hittite references to yoking are involved, rather than any more general time-designation" (p. 499).
35. J. Duchesne-Guillemin, *Old Persian* yāumaniš in *W.B. Henning Memorial Volume*, London, 1970, pp. 140-142 and *Encore vieux-perse* yāumaniš in *Mélanges linguistiques offertes á Émile Benveniste*, Paris, 1975, pp. 137-140.

36. See the discussion in J. Duchesne-Guillemin's articles quoted here, especially the references to the objections of K. Hoffmann, R. Schmitt and W. Hinz.
37. In connection with this cf. Geldner's translation of ṚV 6.47.14 *áva tvé. . . niyúto dhavante* "Zu dir eilen. . . die Gaben".
38. L. Renou, *Grammaire de la langue védique*, p. 146.
39. Translated according to Renou's suggestions in *Études védiques et pāṇinéennes*, XV, p. 141. For *makháḥ* designating the generous patron of the sacrifice, who is also a warrior, see H.W. Bailey, *Atharva-Veda* mákaka in *India Maior (Congratulatory Volume Presented to J. Gonda)*, Leiden, 1972, pp. 41-45.
40. For the meaning of the Vedic *yu-* see again L. Renou, *L'acception première du mot sanskrit* yóni in *Bull. de la Société de Ling.*, 40, 2, 1939, pp. 18-24. For the Indo-European, it is interesting that Tokh. A *yu* if reflecting I.E. **i̯eu̯–* signifies "to incline, to tender to", thus indirectly confirming the contextual nuances of the Vedic verb (see, on the Tokharian verb, J. Duchesne-Guillemin, *Tocharica* in *Bull. de la Société de Ling.*, 40, 2, p. 149).
41. See G. Dumézil, *Mariages indo-européens* followed by *Quinze questions romaines*, Paris, 1979, pp. 280-293. Cf. on ṚV 10.102, R. Ambrosini, *Dal X libro del Ṛg-Veda*, Pisa, 1981, p. 102-106.
42. The *stercus* thus dropped probably signifies taking possession of the area in both cases. A bad omen for the augurs who see in it a manifestation against them by the driver of the team, their rival. A bad omen also for the rivals of Mudgala. Here lies the justification for the confrontation of the two situations.
43. In this connection, see W. Dressler's remarks in *Methodische Vorfragen bei der Bestimmung der 'Urheimat'* in *Die Sprache*, 11, 1965, p. 51 and 53 (The inherited nature of the family of derivatives of **i̯eug* denoting only "yoking" and the nature of Indo-Greek correspondences concerning the image of the poet-charioteer with references to the works of M. Durante of which we have already seen the merits and the lacunae).

Index Locorum

Pindar. Odes

Ṛgveda

1